The Expibasketics and Intrigues of Love

Peter Ateh-Afac Fossungu

Langaa Research & Publishing CIG
Mankon, Bamenda

Publisher:
Langaa RPCIG
Langaa Research & Publishing Common Initiative Group
P.O. Box 902 Mankon
Bamenda
North West Region
Cameroon
Langaagrp@gmail.com
www.langaa-rpcig.net

Distributed in and outside N. America by African Books Collective
orders@africanbookscollective.com
www.africanbookscollective.com

ISBN: *9956-763-30-6*

© Peter Ateh-Afac Fossungu 2016

All rights reserved.
No part of this book may be reproduced or transmitted in any form or by any means, mechanical or electronic, including photocopying and recording, or be stored in any information storage or retrieval system, without written permission from the publisher

Dedicated To All The Victims Of Moneyintriguism
&
Dragdownism And To All The Women I Ever Loved
&
Still Love, Including Those That Never Loved Me Back
At All

Table of Contents

List of Tables.. **vii**
Synopsis.. **ix**
Introduction... **xi**

Chapter 1
Moneyintriguing from Lecturer-In-Law
To Lecturer-In-Love..**1**
Learning from the *Scholeugenizing* April-Fool
Conspiracy against Children................................... 2
Asahchopination: An Intriguing Family of
Scheming Pretenders?.. 10
The Solomon-Violet Lectures on the
Atlantic Crossing.. 10
Loving Marriage or Scheming Marriage?................ 24

Chapter 2
Barthelizing or Blending Marriage,
Love, And Academic Excellence..........................**35**
Love Exchanges on Cameroon's
Quagmatickism and Professional Changes............. 36
Solomonizing the *Scholacademician*'s Intriguing
Communications... 38
Unemployed Qualified Entomologists in an
Agricultural Nation!... 47
Living in a Cobwebbing Trancing Limbo............... 51
Long-Distancing the Wonders of the
Scholastica Question.. 63
The Wonders of Family Instabilities and Academics............ 74
God's Positive Use of the Devil or Anything
like a Good Satan?... 82

Chapter 3
Intriguing Family Deaths and Poverty
Eradication Projects   **87**
"Operation End-of-Poverty" from the

Willing of the Gift?..103
In the Wilderness Crying for Love and
Understanding Dialogue...111
Queentalizing and *Forbehndializing* the Dieudonné
Irresponsible File..115

Chapter 4
Getting Into the Heads and Logic Of
Moneyintriguists with Confusion On
African Tradition.. 137
What/Who is Stalling the *Fossungunization*
of Canada?... 137
The Lying Machine of Momany's Financial
Efforts?..146
The Royal Ultimatum and the Confusion on
African Tradition..154
The *Asahndeming* Lecture on African tradition................ 156
The Yaoundé Lecture on the Elephant Money Fight........... 159

Chapter 5
Problematizing Love, Marriage and Sex:
Is Home Where Love Is?..175
Frantalkism Means Love, Love, Love and
Nothing But Love?... 176
Love Silencing What Happened on Earth?....................... 180
Love Is Knowing and Knowing Is Love......................... 188
The *Janeckinology* of Love and the Puzzles of
Flowers... 191
Rethinking the Marriage, Happiness and Sex
Nexus..195
The Corrupting Power of Roses:
Rosy Love or All-Weather Love?....................................204

Conclusion.. 215
References..221
Appendix of Photos....................................225

List of Tables

Table 1: Western Union Money Transfer
to (and for) Scholastica Achankeng Asahchop...................16

Table 2: Peter's Book Showing
"Money Which I [Scholastica Achankeng Asahchop]
Have Been Collecting From Mr. Elias Akendung"............... 20

Table 3: Western Union Money Transfer
to Queenta Ngum Afanwi... 124

Table 4: Money Transfer to the
Nkemanangs - Calistus & Manifuet Fossungu................... 128

Table 5: Western Union Money Transfer
to Dieudonné Asongu Fossungu................................ 131

Table 6: Western Union Money Transfer
to Njukang Paul Morfaw... 133

Table 7: Some Recent Deaths in the
Fossungu Royal Family... 135

Table 8: Samples of Travellers' Cheques
Sent to Scholastica Achankeng Asahchop....................... 149

Table 9: Contributions and Loans That Helped
Momany to Attend Burial of Father............................ 163

Synopsis

This book equips you with an enhanced understanding of the difficulties of blending love, marriage/family, sex, intrigues and academics. It is generally believed that Africans are shy when it comes to sex education or talking sex matters. That may be true as it may be false. If the first, then this book comes to alter it; if the second, it comes to disprove it. Whatever it is though, what the matter could be in reality is that the proponents of such a theory just expect Africans to handle issues of love, sex, marriage and family, and academics through their (non-Africans') lens. This book has dared to 'untraditionally' view the issues, using thorough real-life or *expibasketical* findings to both expand and delineate the frontiers of love (and, therefore, of marriage and family); showing the long-term negative impact that intrigues – taking the forms of *moneyintriguism* and *dragdownism* – do have on these institutions that are supposed to be built on love and understanding. Although many would find it outrageous, the ethnographic findings show, as one of the wonders of love, that most successful marriages also thrive largely on extra-marital love relationships. Not necessarily what some would jump to call adultery: unless love is narrowly defined just as having sexual intercourse. Are we here talking Lust or Love? The meaning of love goes beyond that. The book has already been written *inside* and I would be writing it all over again *outside* if you really want me to completely define love to you right now. Go inside then and get it!

Introduction

Classify this book as an autobiography, if you will, but it is not just that since it can wear many dresses. While the book is expanding the frontiers of love, it principally highlights and demonstrates the difficulty of blending love, marriage and academics. The difficulty becomes enormously magnified when we are poised to doing so "at long-distance". One of the main protagonists of the book, Momany's wife, is a very loving and good person. But her deplorable and bizarre comportment after she joins her husband abroad after four years of separation due to academics raises many questions of love and marriage that the book is seeking to understand. It is shown that it is *Quagmatickism* or the worrisome politico-socio-economic atmosphere that was (and still is) prevailing in the country that sent Momany abroad for the second time. This situation forced the newly married man to seek academic excellence abroad rather than continue lecturing in the university in Cameroon where even the university environment is not conducive to knowledge acquisition and imparting. Indeed, it is what moved the lecturer-in-law to be now lecturing love.

All the other strange and alarming love, marriage and family situations that you would be reading about are just fallouts of the attempt to audaciously blend love, marriage and academics 'at long-distance'. This is a problem that is aggravated by the existence of in-laws and other (extended) family members who see nothing in life than the money intrigues – *Moneyintriguism*. *Quagmatickism* and *Moneyintriguism* are versions of *Dragdownism* (the act of dragging someone down). While it is *Quagmatickism* that directly sent the lecture-in-law out of the country, it is *Moneyintriguism* that has imprisoned him abroad. Imprisoned because it was never Momany's intention to escape permanently from the country (like most of the cases catalogued in the book); but just to research on the means of redressing the prevailing painful conditions at home and then return to implement those solutions. The book is very rich in postulations for the love/marriage/family specialists and other experts to grapple with, as well as cautionary advice to both prospective couples and those living abroad like 'bush-fallers' or *mbenguists*.

In attempting to understand love, the book would be trying (with Momany's *expibasketical* aid) to do a few things, in a similar fashion as was done to 'Confusion' in Fossungu (2013b: xvi). That is to say that it would perceive the intended meaning of love; striving to perceive the significance, explanation, or cause of love. It will also strive to be sympathetically or knowledgeably aware of the character or nature of love; and interpret or view love in a particular way – a way that not many, if any at all, have so far interpreted or seen this phenomenon. When some people like Momany stay keen on maintaining contact with their *former* lovers and ex-spouses, many of us have this penchant for rushing to the idea that they do so solely because they want to continue having sexual contact with said loved persons. There is no doubt that this is often the case with a lot of people. We must, however, not forget, first, that general rules always have their exceptions. And above all that we have been adequately advised to know that this man called "Momany is exceptional in the domain and thus valuably learn something from his moving love and understanding experiences" (Fossungu, 2014: 119). Why wouldn't his intriguing experiences motivate the writing of another book like the present? Quite an intriguing understanding of intrigues awaits you (I can go to the insurer for that) in the intriguing secret letters that you are about to be privileged to publicly peruse in the chapters that follow. The idea of making sex the centrepiece of love's definition is highly questioned in this book.

Chapter 1 examines the process through which a well-known lecturer-in-law became an aspiring lecturer-in-love, a development that would justify the teacher's competence for mounting the podium before us. It shows how, going by the maxim that we learn more from failure than from success, the said aspirant becomes a qualified candidate since *moneyintriguism* and *dragdownisn* (defined there) have made the candidate to be well known in the Marriage Failures Hall of Fame; thus validating his qualifications. In Chapter 2, the worrisome politico-economic situation in Cameroon is also shown to be an exquisite example of *dragdownism*. This is because, without the said situation then (and still) prevailing in the country, Momany shouldn't have left Cameroon for the second time. This chapter thus examines how to blend love, marriage and academic excellence, showing the accentuation of the herculean task by both distance and *wayo* or *moneyintriguist* in-laws. At the same time, the chapter furnishes some strategies for judging the lovers' family relations who have some secret agenda regarding their (lovers') marital/love unions or relationships. The strategies of the *dragdownists* and *moneyintriguists* are then very elaborately studied in chapters 3 and 4. Chapter 3 scrutinizes the wrong questions being raised within Momany's extended family, showing how poverty can and would need to be eliminated in the family, an exercise that then aids us to smoothly go inside their heads to understand the money-getting logic of moneyintriguists in chapter 4. Chapter 5 examines the place of *Frantalkism* in love, marriage and family relationships (using *Odilimanyism, Momanijanism, Momalizalism* and others, all of them properly circumscribed in the chapters). The chapter moves toward the expansion of the frontiers of love by digging into the reasons why some lovers stay on even after marrying to third-parties. Is it due to their ability to combine the trio of love, *frantalkism* (properly defined there), and the rare ability to 'let-go' of ex-loves? The chapter continues digging into the puzzle by problematizing the wonders of love, marriage and sex. The suggestion that the durability of love even after marriage could be based on the fact that the woman's virginity was taken by the man in question is critically explored, with alternative explanations offered. There is a conclusion.

Chapter 1

Moneyintriguing from Lecturer-In-Law to Lecturer-In-Love

To proffer a word or two on the new terminologies, begin with love. Going to Google Search with 'loving' brings forth 388,000,000 results and one has, therefore, cautiously decided not to go there: except to indicate that its adjective indicates a "feeling or showing love or great care," with the noun being "the demonstration of love or great care" whereas the verb 'love' itself is said to mean to "feel a deep romantic or sexual attachment to (someone)." The noun 'love' then would obviously be the act of 'feeling a deep romantic or sexual attachment to (somebody).' Although this book would somewhat dispute this definition, let us not begin quarrelling about that here because there are more than intrigues involved for that from *Asahchopination*.

Asahchopination comes from an intriguing family (see below) that would justify the wonderful credentials of the Love-Poet or Lecturer-in-Love. *Moneyintriguism* derives from 'Money' and 'Intrigues,' leading to an *Intriguing Understanding of Intrigues*. Googling 'Intrigues' brings up about 11,200.000 results. As a verb, the term 'intrigue' means '(1) arouse the curiosity or interest of, fascinate, and/or (2) make secret plans to do something illicit or detrimental to someone.' The noun version refers to 'the secret planning of something illicit or detrimental to someone.' I think that would be the terminology's basic connotation(s) because, the colourful or *Mpakofrancizing* language notwithstanding, all the other meanings advanced do not divert from it. For instance, some others would say 'intrigue' is "to arouse the curiosity or interest of by unusual, new, or otherwise fascinating or compelling qualities; appeal strongly to; captivate: The plan intrigues me, but I wonder if it will work and (2) to achieve or earn by appealing to another's curiosity, fancy, or interest: to intrigue one's way into another's notice."[1]

---

[1] dictionary.reference.com/browse/**intrigue**.

Yet others take it to be "the activity of making secret plans";[2] "to interest someone a lot, especially by being strange, unusual, or mysterious"[3] and that "An intrigue is a secret plot. If you ever become the monarch of a small island kingdom, keep watch for signs of any intrigue against you. Intrigue comes from the Latin verb intricare, to entangle, and is related to intricate. It can be a noun, meaning underhanded plot, or a verb for the act of plotting."[4] How then does a non-believer understand believers? To be specific, how do you comprehend plotters when you are not one of them? I don't think I have the right answers to most of these things, being one famous hall-of-famer in marital flops. But wait a minute! Inversing the Paradox! Is that not it? Am I not mistaken in not thinking that we all are aware of the oft-forgotten adage that we usually learn more from our failures than from successes? This question seems to be so graphical to the whole raison d'être of this book (and this chapter particularly) that it has to be diligently handled. The first part of this chapter, therefore, examines this failure-learning idea, an important exercise that also makes good understanding of the expansion of the frontiers of love in the following chapters; chapters that we can get to only after having found out in the second half of this chapter if the idea of getting into marriage was a scheming tool or was marriage viewed as an institution to be entered into with love and understanding?

Learning from the *Scholeugenizing* April-Fool Conspiracy against Children

The conspiracy here is clearly against children (born and unborn); and not against Momany, as the conspirators might be shortsighted to think. What greatly amazes is the fact that this Momany can want all this *lovundelearing* (or love-understand-and-learn-from) rapport with *former* girlfriends (who may even be spouses of other people, for that matter[5]), but his former spouses (having children with him, in

---

[2] www.merriam-webster.com/dictionary/**intrigue**.
[3] dictionary.cambridge.org/dictionary/english/**intrigue**.
[4] https://www.vocabulary.com/dictionary/**intrigue**.
[5] The argument against disclosure of these relationships because of their marital status is handled shortly.

addition) would not even care about maintaining a frank learning relationship (or *frantalkism*) with him. Isn't that really mind-boggling? One is here talking about Scholastica Achankeng Asahchop (in Photo #1) and Henriette Flavie Bayiha (in Photo #2).

Odilia is a major and prominent character in this narrative; and because Odilia is not a very common name like the names of the other Momany sweethearts (for example, Anna, Elizabeth, Jane, Susan and others), Momany's initial concerns were that I should avoid as much as possible to identify Odilia's siblings because, through them, Odilia can be easily identified even by those who never knew of her pre-marital relationship with Momany. But then, I had wondered aloud to Momany, would the narrative then be as authentic (as the intention is that it be) if it can not call a spade a spade? The question here being directly drawn from the fact that this is an *expibasketical* study and it is well known that "one of the fundamentals of the *expibasketical* science is that *A Lie Is A Lie And Is Not Good And Bad Depending On Who Is Its Author*. Call that *The Lie Theory*, if you will" (Fossungu, 2015e: 78, original emphasis). Therefore, the lies that are always hiding behind the Dirty-Linen Theory (DLT) cannot become TRUTH and the DLT itself cannot fit into *Expibasketism*.

At that point, Momany then had to quickly agree with me that doing otherwise would also be unnecessarily depriving most of those concerned of the proper recognition for their enormous contributions to a better or enhanced understanding of love, sex, marriage/family and intrigues. It would as well not be aiding people to better value those they now have as spouses since knowing should normally usher in more understanding. Of course, that doesn't seem to be case though where scheming and naivety are on the table.[6] That is the truth and it is well known that "Those who cannot handle the truth are wont to hide behind the saying that we should not be exposing our dirty linen in public. Nay, I say; because if it is dirty it is dirty and hiding it from public view would not transform it into clean.

---

[6] Explaining perhaps why "For example, she had placed the problem of not conceiving on her husband, suggesting that perhaps his sperms were insufficient to fertilize her. She was obviously naively drawing on his past with women that he had laid bare before her in the hope of aiding her know exactly who she has as husband. Could this openness trait in Momany also be behind his wife debacle?" (Fossungu, 2014: 66).

The fact that it is dirty is even the more reason for it to be exposed *mafenly* (morning, afternoon, evening and night) so that steps can be taken to clean it up" (Fossungu, 2015e: 79-80). That may also warrant a one-sentence *frantalkist* take on the 'Momany' designate which I use in most of my writings mostly to distinguish me as the writer from me as the character and in order to let-go of one from the other without letting go.

That clarification sails us back to the attitude of Momany's ex-spouse; a comportment which can only lead one to inevitably ponder whether the said spouses separated from only Momany or/and the children (too)? How do we ever get close to rational responses without an *expibasketical* examination of love and intrigues? The significance of these questions is heightened by the following children-father abortive communication that has enormously given impetus to the writing of this autobiography and/or ethnographic book. On Tuesday, February 23, 2016 Momany wrote a letter to his son and daughter (in Photo #3). He sent it by registered mail to the address of the French-speaking school attended by his two children in London, Ontario. Until date of writing (last half of May 2016), the letter has not been returned for non-delivery. Yet, he has not as yet heard from the children, in spite of the earnest appeal in the letter:

My Dear Ngunyi and Nguajong:
I write this note to you with a heavy heart. I hope it finds you in perfect health. Please, I just don't know how else to reach you both other than through this medium. I have called 226-XXX-XXXX several times but have never heard from you: despite all the messages I left on the answering machine. I guess you are not aware of my phone calls. That is why I am now trying this other method of getting to you directly through your school address. Don't be surprised that I know where you school. I am your father and, despite that we are not physically with each other, I am always with you both, as well as with your three other siblings – Kelie in Douala (whose photo is enclosed) and Peter & Peteraf in Montreal, who you also see in the photo together. My recent photo is enclosed as well.

My Dear Ngunyi & Nguajong, you may not be growing up together with me and your other siblings, but that *alone* cannot change the fact that you are all *my* sons and daughters. Your senior sister,

Kelie, has never ceased sending her greetings and affection to the four of you. She has never stopped wanting to communicate with you directly. She has never stopped desiring to meet all of you in person. I know Peter and Peteraf are still too young to be able to independently communicate with the three of you. But the three of you are now mature enough to do so. Kelie [who you see in Photo #4] would have already contacted you but for the fact that I don't have your email addresses – the most appropriate means for that at the moment. Please, do let me have your email contact [if available] so that I can also reach you through it as well as pass it on to Kelie. Better still, you can also directly contact your sister by email: … [omitted email]. Kelie is French-speaking and will be enthralled to read from you. My own contact points are as indicated above and I would also love to read or hear from you soonest. We have a lot to catch up on.

I LOVE YOU!

Signed. Daddy.

Though sent as a single registered mail, inside it there are two different sealed envelopes, one each addressed to the two children. It is this same letter that you have read that is in each of the two envelopes. But the said sets of pictures in each letter are different. It is a package that, with the necessary modification, would also have been directed to the Montreal children (in Photo #5) but for reasons mentioned in the letter. They too are in the same soup since when their own mother high-handedly changed their day-care (as you probably already know from *Canadian Institutions and Children's Best Interests* (Fossungu, 2015d)) and is hiding them from their daddy, as this response to inquiries from former day-care provider can show. To Momany's observation (of Tuesday March 8, 2016 at 8.09 AM) to her that "I just do not know where and whether the boys are going to daycare/school," Filomena Pina Gonzalez (in Photo #6) responded on Wednesday, March 9, 2016 at 6.06 PM as follows: "Hello Peter: I have no idea where the kids are, last time she [Henriette Flavie Bayiha] spoke with me she sa[id] that, she w[ould] bring [take, that is, if I must not shy away from rectifying *normal* Canadian Chinglish] Peter to school near where she lives, and Peteraf to day care there at the same school there in Cote St-Luc. Thanks. Filomena."

Momany has (since May 2015) been calling just to talk to the children but Flavie's cellular phone would never be answered even as it always rang. On Thursday, 6, May 2016, he drove to Montreal to be able to see the children over the weekend. While in Montreal, on Friday, May 7, he called only to be told that the number was no longer in service. That number had been available a day or so before and he had left a message concerning his weekend trip. He then went to her apartment that evening at about 7 PM and rang the doorbell but there was no response till about 8.30 PM when he left. It was the same story on Saturday. Had they also moved? Momany returned on Sunday morning without being able to set eyes on the kids. So, tell me what is actually going on? How can we understand love and intrigues from all this? Is it not very clear that these women are actually feeding the children with a lot of lies relating to why they are growing without their father and are thus bent on not letting them get the other (authentic) side of the story? This book comes therefore to also provide a well-documented 'other side' of the absence of fatherly love screwed or intriguing narrative.

But I have also been motivated in undertaking the arduous job because of another more personal aim; that involves the setting of the record straight in regard of the extended family. Since Momany is not good at showing off what he does or has done in the field of ameliorating the lives of people generally, there is this unsettling trend within the Nwangong Royal Family which constitutes the case study here, to think and even gratuitously pass around that Momany has not done this and that to uplift the family from its current and persistent poverty-stricken level. This book therefore also comes to reset the mistaken records, the true documentation instead showing that it is largely the other members of the said family that have, in the major instances, frustrated the laudable efforts of Momany, either through the predominating *moneyintriguism* and/or their short-sightedness or *nonoselfism* or *Mamiteelization*. To put it in the smallest amount of words, there has generally been too much reprehensible absence of the self-help spirit; a spirit that is well appreciated in Scholastica Achankeng Asahchop, one of the mothers who conspire against their own children.

This conspiracy is better appreciated only in the context of *letterism* or the art of letter communication that has been aptly described in a popular African dictionary as *monologuing*. But for the issue of length, the second level of this book's title is "Lying Letters Don't Lie Until You Lovingly Read Them." I would thus lean very much toward giving you the full contents of such letters for a number of reasonable reasons. First, is the preference argument against *monologuing* over *dialoguing*, namely, that the first is not particularly good for love's rough times.[7] But it is the next idea that is the most cogent, and relates directly to the second level of this book's topic – lying letters not lying until lovingly or mistakenly read. The letter-writer's idea may be easily twisted to further the Lying Idea itself through calculated and selective citations of the person's letter. That is to say that – like what happened to Lapiro de Mbanga on CRTV as exposed by Boh (2014) and Vakunta (2014) – his/her argument can be aired without us getting the opportunity to know of the counter argument of the same letter, just like Western media does all the time.

Note must also be taken of the fact (flowing from the *monologuing* critiques) that we can better understand and assess a responding letter when we also know the important or critical contents of the one it is replying to. Therefore, in this book both versions would be presented, to the extent I possibly can. The qualification here is sanely justified, since I would surely be creating facts from nowhere in order to give you the exact contents of an *original unknown* letter to which the *handy* or available responding (secret) letter relates. Remember always that intrigues are *secret* plans! Conspiracies! Moreover, even those who keep record of letters they write can hardly have *all* of them in the album. By the way, we must not also completely forget that *Letterism* (as important as it is) is not an end

---

[7] "Letters are a kind of monologue that may be good when the ride is smooth but do not seem to aid matters when the road gets bumpy. For example, after a sentence, there is no possibility for the other party to interject or correct anything you have said or even slow down the anger; and, therefore, you just keep pouring everything out before sending to the other. And you will not be there either to listen to that other. Perhaps, with love and understanding problems like these people should rather talk one on one… than use letters?" (Fossungu, 2014: 44-45)

itself but solely as the *means* by which to reach understanding of love and intrigues.

These intrigues have caused the failure of many people but the real failure would be only to those who learn nothing from the flops. In the heated 2012 End-of-Year Party 'Food Shortage' narrative in the Cameroon Goodwill Association of Montreal (CGAM), Precelia Nkengasong Folefac, Head of the Food Sub-Committee, argued on December 25, 2012 that "We learn much more from failure than from success. I do not think it was a failure at all, just a pointer to our commitment. Goodwill's success is in the hands of a few, we all need to be committed. I cannot emphasize that it is [not] a membership association." In addition to other popular references that support of the 'Failure-Learning' thesis, we also get the maxim operating in Momany's April-Fool but eye-opening letter of April 1, 2002 to his parents-in-law detailing the sorrowful state of their marital union that took place in 1993 in Nwangong (see Photos #7a & #7b).

The April-Fool letter also mentions an important and urgent email; making it worthy to clarify right away that all email times in this book are those of Momany's Inbox. Cameroon and Canada's East Coast (where Momany is) have a six-hour time difference such that Momany's 2.00 PM would be 8.00 PM in Cameroon. That makes the 11.53 PM of said email to be 5.53 AM the next day in Cameroon: except during the 'time-saving period' that has caused several well-known unexpected and embarrassing job losses to unwary newcomers to North America. It has, of course, been a learning opportunity too for them. An intriguing family like the one Momany has as in-laws cannot but provide more than enough hindsight learning. That 'learning-from-error' April-Fool missive (that also exposes the travesty and hypocrisy in the father-in-law's letter of November 3, 2002 that is discussed at length in a later part of chapter 4's 'Elephant Money Fight') argued as follows:

My Dear Parents-in-Law,

I really do not know how to exactly say what I have to tell you in a letter. A letter, obviously, is a monologue and I strongly believe in dialoguing, especially when very sensitive issues are in question. That is why I had sent an email to Eugene [Lekeawung Asahchop] on the 11th of March 2002 at 11.53 PM which read as follows:

Hi Eugene, I really need to get into contact with your parents. I have been trying to contact you since last Saturday through Sylva's cell phone number (XXXXXXX) to no avail. I urgently need to talk to your parents, mum in particular, but I don't know how to get the message for them (or mum alone) to be in Dschang for this important talk. It concerns Schola who, as I write this note, is currently admitted to hospital. How serious her illness is, I don't know as I am still to find out.

Please, please, do try to get this message passed on to them as soon as you possibly can. Sincerely yours. PAF [paragraphing altered for this particular paragraph]

Not long ago, I have come to learn that you have never received the message because Schola warned Eugene and instructed him not to pass the message on to you. In that case then, I think I only have to write this note. It cannot sufficiently replace the dialogue I would have liked to have with you but it will let you know, at least, what kind of life Schola and I are leading here. It might also help you understand in a way why I seem to have become so silent.

On Thursday, 7 March 2002, Schola took upon herself to do away with the two-to-four-month pregnancy. She committed an abortion without caring about what anyone else, except herself, thought about it. Since she was trying to keep me in the dark about the abortion, she kept behaving as if everything was alright. I only discovered the truth, despite all her insistence that all was okay, on Saturday March 9, 2002 when the police got involved. In her attempts to go about as if nothing had happened, she developed complications from the operation and had to be admitted to hospital on 11 March 2002. I didn't even know she went to hospital that day until I was called at about 9.45 PM to be told she was admitted there. She was there for three days.

She is now doing fine. But our relationship keeps worsening at an alarming rate. I had wanted your advice to both of us, not only on the abortion issue but many others so that we can learn to move on with our lives. But it seems Schola does not want anything to do with it. I know I am not a perfect person. But I know that I like to learn from my mistakes and not allow them hinder my moving forward.

One major problem I find in Schola is her inability to know what her priorities in life are. Maybe she will tell you what exactly motivated her to do what she has done. But I don't think her saying that lack of money is the cause or reason is genuine enough.

Extend greetings to everyone.

Sincerely yours, Signed.

Asahchopination: An Intriguing Family of Scheming Pretenders?

The foregoing letter evokes a lot of love and family-marriage issues that cannot be confronted right away, but a few of which have to be circumscribed immediately, in regard of the Momany-Scholastica vows (seen in Photo #7b). There are already several known cases of this family's nosing traits but this particular question is posed here because of one of Odilia's letters that would also fortify the legitimate wondering as to why Momany never saw the clear writing on the wall. But such puzzlement may have to quickly clear out not only because Momany is not a schemer; but also so when more intimately linked to the knowledge that lying letters don't lie until you lovingly (or mistakenly) read them. Talking about lying letters that are lovingly read obviously necessitates exemplification. For that, we could commence by taking Odilia's 3-paragraph letter of June 26, 1996, in which she noted in the second paragraph how "I usually see your brother (Ben). They attend Alou (Lebialem) meeting in our house. Pat had her second child about 2 1/2 months ago. Denis too is doing fine with their baby. What about your wife? She came to our office a long time ago and introduced herself to me. You know I've never met her before." The brother in question is Bernard Mbancho Fosungu in Photo #8.

The Solomon-Violet Lectures on the Atlantic Crossing

The obvious questions that unavoidably crop up include these. Why was Scholastica taking upon herself to present herself to Odilia in the latter's office? Did someone (her "ears & eyes all over," as she is known to proudly put it) tell her that Momany and Odilia were having an ongoing affair? Was her act just a part of her intrigues passing for love and marriage? Hadn't Momany himself already told her of his relationship with Odilia, and that Odilia was the woman he had intended marrying before meeting her (Scholastica)? The questions are in place, especially when you consider the fact that Momany is not used to concealing his past; only having seen no "need to narrate all [of some of] these things to Schola because she had proven not to be learning anything positive from most of the things from his past that he had told her; instead drawing only negative and naive conclusions from them" (Fossungu, 2014: 66). Because he was so deeply in love (as he always is when he falls[8]) Momany would appear to have failed enormously to read the clear handwriting on the wall.

You get this sense even from Solomon Enoma Tatah (Photo #10), his bosom friend since their historical first meeting in Ngoa-Ekéllé (University of Yaounde - UNIYAO) that Photo #11 also captures. Solomon, in the second paragraph of his February 2, 1998 letter to Momany, made the point as follows: "Peter, I didn't feel comfortable to read that things are still rough with you out there. I thought your wish for Schola to join you was an indication of success recorded all round. In fact, Canada should be a difficult country for immigrants if hard people like you don't make it easily. Fortunately, Paul [Takha Ayah – Photo #12] is available to extend a hand to you. It will be all over with time." Anyone not lovingly reading would have

---

[8] Let some people who know them well school you a bit on what Scholastica meant to Momany. "Dear Power," Stephen Fomeche (Photo #9) wrote from Fontem in the 1st paragraph of his letter of June 19, 1996, "I got your letter on resumption from Easter break and thought wise to defer the spontaneous reply it called for until now that I can pretend to be free since I don't take early and cold bath to hurry to school. Man, I enjoyed your letter and felt much touched by your loneliness expressed, to wish that I was a Minister or anyone responsible for her reaching you. I pray that your target of December does not meet any impediment. It is only then that all the gold and silver placed at your disposal can make any genuine meaning to you." On his part, Solomon Tatah (Photo #10) in the 2nd paragraph of his November 2, 1995 letter declared: "Schola, your darling you want to read about before anything else has been calling to find out if you reached safely, unfortunately, it was impossible for you to call us. When I went to Kumba in early October, I passed and discovered where she was putting up with the sister. She said she had been sick just before I came but when I saw her, she was fine. The sister too was well. I saw the pedal lock you left for me but so far I cannot use it because Schola left the key in Douala. She said she will get it when next she visits Douala. I hope your first letter has also reached Schola by now."

gotten it right; meaning clearly that Momany should not have embarked on the trans-Atlantic affair until he was comfortably seated in Canada. Wouldn't that also signify that he shouldn't have married until he was already engaged by the Buea University? Did Momany correctly read Solomon's later when he still went ahead with the enterprise that culminated in Scholastica's 'miraculous, swift, and joy-bringing' arrival to Canada in April 1999?

Maylatelization

No one has captured those emotions and descriptions of Scholastica's arrival in Canada more beautifully than Violet Maylatey Fonenge (Photo #13) does in her letter of May 5, 1999 to Scholastica. Violet, who is cousin to both Momany and Scholastica,[9] also brings to the table significant insights on education, a lot of admired attributes of Scholastica (her cousin) who is supposed to be a role model and ideal spouse. Just listen attentively to Violet yourself as she *Maylatelizes* to Scholastica in her 6-page handwritten letter:

My beloved sister, I don't know how to express how jovial I was when I received your letter addressed and dated 24-04-99. I got the letter yesterday 17/05/99. In fact, it was unbelievable. I was jovial, proud and above all relieved. The content was well assimilated. Sister Schola, when I learned from Mamie about your sudden departure, a nostalgic feeling ran through my body. In fact, I was happy and sad. Happy because at last my only sister was going to meet her husband in another continent, sad because I will stay for a long period before I ever set eyes on my caring and loving sister, who was always advising and consoling me when things were not really moving.

As I returned from school that evening, I was on my way to fetch water down the road, when I met Mamie at the gate. In fact, I was the first to see her since I had dreamt about you the previous night, the first thing I asked was "Mamie, what about Sister Schola? Is she still in Yaoundé after a dream about her I had last night?" With happiness, Mamie revealed to me that "She has gone to Canada!" In

---

[9] Violet is the daughter of Chief Fonenge (aka Vincent Temenu Fossungu), Momany's uncle who you see in Photo #14. Violet's mother (Julie Fonenge in Photo #15) is the sister of Scholastica's mother in Photo 16. In this royal family, some use Fossungu while some (Forbehndia's household in particular) employ the *one-s* Fosungu. But it is the double *ss* one that the large majority would prefer.

fact, I was panic stricken with joy. I shouted and Joicy and Brenda came out. I revealed the news to them and we all rushed to the house and informed Aunty Justine. In fact I dreamt of nothing that night. I was just thinking of what my sister will be doing at the moment. I revealed the news to my friends the following day in school and they rejoiced with me. You can just imagine how I felt. Mamie explained everything to me and why you had to leave so abruptly. Well, we should praise the lord for that.

My dearest sister, we have just one month now to commence with the G.C.E. [General Certificate of Education] I am starting with mine on the 22nd of June, it is not that easy but I am doing my best. I cannot disappoint you in particular. I'm using all the precautions to see into it that I make my papers. I will make them with good grades don't be afraid. My only problem at this juncture is French. But I'm doing my best to polish everything up before the D-Day. I'm not going to leave any stone unturned. Our mock result was out last month and I had one paper with two compensatory grades. That was history. Well, I promise you that those subjects with compensatory grades will become A and B grades. I didn't have peace of mind during the mock as you best know. Presently there is no problem. I'm doing my best to see into it that I avoid anything that can upset me at this crucial moment of my life. I always pray for a peace of mind.

My only sister, thanks for the advice you gave me as far as boys are concerned. I will call upon you to be 100% sure of the fact that I do not misbehave. I have no time for that. I leave the house to school and back. There is no reason why I have to risk my life because of money; by the way, I'm not materialistic and I do not compare and compete with friends. In fact, these are some of the vices that can prompt most girls to be running after men since they want money. My elder sister, know as from today that you have a very respectful and well behaved junior sister. In school I'm known as a calm and gentle girl. I select my friends and know how I deal with them. You always made sure that you satisfied me, gave me dresses, shoes and whatsoever I asked from you, so why should I risk my life? I'm morally upright. No one can deceive me. I'm always contented and satisfied with what I have and there is no pleasure that one can derive from going out with men. If I do that I'm risking my life and above all I will tarnish my reputation.

Sister Schola, when you are writing next time, write in detail and tell me about that part of the world. I presume it is very different from Cameroon. Accept greetings from my friends, Geraldine, Caroline, Elizabeth and Gladys. They were very happy to receive their greetings. Geraldine was very happy and she has decided to write to you; and Caroline too [their letters are included[10]]. Do not forget to send the pictures you promised. I will be waiting anxiously. There is no news yet at the moment. The entire family is fine. Theodore wrote to me saying that when I finish the G.C.E., I should wait for him, that he will come and spend about two weeks here. I will be through with my exams on the 3rd of July and leave Bamenda by the 20th of July. So if you want to call on me as you said, you can do so before I go home. I will be very happy to talk with you once more. You can use this number – XX XX XX. It is that of our neighbour. Sister Quinta always phones with the number. So when you call tell the person who picks the phone to kindly call for me. Do not forget me in your prayers.

---

[10] Here is Caroline Kuoh's note to Scholastica on May 22, 1999:

Hello Sister Schola, How are you? I hope you are fine. Violet told me about your safe journey and we were so impressed after knowing the long struggle you have gone though. God has a plan for each and every one and he knows when to execute this. We praise His Mighty name.

Violet has been very nice to me. She is the most comprehending friend I have. We study together and by God's Grace we shall succeed. She introduced you to me as her elder sister and from all what she has told me I deduce you are a nice woman. It's unfortunate you forgot my name but it's no big deal. I am Caroline. Have a nice time and extend my greetings to your husband.

Thanks for reading, Caroline!

And Geraldine Nobi's letter to Scholastica on May 22, 1999 is as follows:

Dear Sister Schola: How are you and everybody in Canada? We got the good news of your safe arrival and we were so happy for you. I presume you know me already but I thought it wise to write to you and say hello.

Violet has been telling us so much about you and it is but normal that my closest friend's sister should be my sister too. Anyway, I just wish you the best, I cannot write so much now because I'm in haste. I will write more next time I'm opportune.

It's been nice knowing you. Bye. Geraldine.

What about Brother Peter? How is he doing at the moment? Extend my profound greetings to him. [Do l]ikewise to Sister Quinta[11]. How did she feel when she saw you? In fact, I can just imagine how contented both of you could have been. Two sisters meeting in a strange land where there is no family member I think it is really wonderful. Extend my profound greetings to her and the children. She never writes to someone. I have written over four letters to her plus my pictures but she has never replied [to] even one. Big sister, I wish that you should do me a favour not now but when you will be acquainted to the place. That is, I humbly plead that if there is a possibility you can look for a pen pal for me, she should be almost the same age as me or a bit older. I doubt if it will be possible. I will be very grateful.

I wish you the best in all your undertakings. Crave my indulgence to drop my pen at this juncture while taking into consideration that I have exhausted enough for the moment. I'm looking anxiously to hear from you. Do not also forget to extend greetings to Sister Marie-Claire and her children.[12]

With much love and concern, Your Junior, Maylatey [this paragraph altered].

P/S: Here is the address of Brother Godfred. He will be very grateful to read from you: ….. [omitted]. Our graduation is on the 9/07/99. I will do well to send you my pictures only after the graduation. I have no nice card at the moment.

---

[11] The mother of the Quinta here (note very well the different spelling with a prominent Queenta in this book from whom *Queetalization* derives) is also sister to both the mothers of Violet and of Scholastica. Quinta Asa'ah can be seen in Photo #17. You will be hearing a lot concerning this Quinta from Scholastica's (and other Asahchops') letters.

[12] Like with Momany, Violet is also cousin to Marie-Claire Efuelancha Fossungu (now Mrs. Afueh) who you find in Photo #18. Although she has a different biological father called Michael Akendung Fossungu (now of blessed memory), it is Chief Forbehndia (aka Emmanuel Nguajong Fosungu – Photo #19) who brought Marie-Claire up in the same household as Momany. You even get to grasp this better knowing that Chief Forbehndia's Will that was "Done in Yoke Village on July 29, 2002" talks of Marie-Claire in no terms different from his own birth children. That Will ordains in paragraph 2 that "The plot at Letia (Nwangong Village) should be used by the entire family including Afueh Marie-Claire and Fosungu Peter Ateafac to be crowned Nkem. The plot at Mile I – Limbe should be buil[t] and used by the whole family accordingly."

It must be indicated that, while all the jubilation and so forth were going on, it was Momany alone who was picking all the heat of creditors from whom he had acquired resources at short notice, some payments for services rendered in Cameroon still being on future basis. Going to references in earlier books may take much of your *moneyintriguing* time and they may not even be focused enough to acquaint you with the specific facts on the short-notice loans and debts that you can quickly obtain from Table 1 here.

Table 1: Western Union Money Transfer to (and for*) Scholastica Achankeng Asahchop				
Money Transfer Number	Amount (FCFA)	Equivalent Amount in $ (CAD)	Transaction Date	Agency
790-838-4146	210,000.00	646.38	October 2, 1998	612-Peel, operator 401
790-493-9404	105,000.00	338.35	Dec. 1, 1998	612-Peel
790-240-2813	202, 000.00	628.51	January 22, 1999	612-Peel, operator 401
790-827-5181	100,000.00	301.20	February 23, 1999	612-Peel, operator 120
790-858-3181	600,000.00	1595.13	March 16, 1999	612-Peel, operator 401
790-261-8752	900,000.00	2399.36	April 8, 1999	612-Peel, operator 401
790-542-5200*	700,000.00[13]	1819.64	May 11, 1999	612-Peel, operator 122
790-405-5810*	200,000.00[14]	494.13	10/02/2000	612-Peel, operator 163
TOTAL:	3,017,000.00	8225.70		

---

[13] This sum was being paid directly to Amingwa Henry Atem for settlement of debt still owing in connection with transactions leading to Scholastica's trip to the United States to attend the International Family Therapy Association (IFTA) Conference in Akron, USA.

[14] This amount was also paid directly to Edith-Rosa N. Khumba (Photo #20) for settlement of debt still owing with regard to transactions leading to Scholastica's trip to the United States to attend the IFTA Conference

Here Are Just A Few Cases of Money Being Sent by Scholastica to Her Parents & Siblings Rather than Helping to Pay Off Debts Contracted in Order to Speedily Bring Her to Canada				
790-629-2015, to Eugene Asahchop[15]	100,000.00	244.00	April 29, 2000	Doreen, 1:13 PM EDT
262-261-1355, to Bridget Asahchop	213,114.00	520.09	07/09/2003 @ 2:18	Pearson LaSalle, operator Comp.

Solomon Tatah can tell you a little bit of the hell Momany went through (before now) to eventually have her over here for you to better comprehend *moneyintriguist dragdowners*. In the 4th paragraph of his celebrated 4-page letter of February 2, 1998, Tatah disclosed:

Power, you know on my return from Holland, I met Schola in my house when she was making another attempt to obtain a visa. This time again as we all know it failed. And this was more painful because of the amount of money she had spent to fulfil the formalities. I'm going back to this story because I want to make the point that it was a blessing that she didn't have it. This is now permitting her to complete her course in UB for a very important degree in our modern world. When I saw her last week in Molyko, I was very impressed with her work and I'm confident she will make it this year. I've already promised her a party in Yaoundé together with Alice when she too graduates from ASMAC in September. But as soon as she is through with UB, we'll re-launch her visa application for her to join you. We know you miss yourselves very much. But a little more patience and everything will be fine.[16]

---

[15] It must be noted that all these hide-and-seek transactions would be going on not because Momany is a stumbling block to her helping these people, since the same Eugene Lekeawung Asahchop (Photo #21) had received from Momany the sum of 130,000.00 FCFA (CAD 341.34) sent on December 13, 1999: Western Union #7907196164 by 612-Peel's operator 135.

[16] Scholastica herself also made it known in her letter of December 1, 1996 to Momany that "If I am in Buea for two years, it will be needless for me to abandon it again as we wanted to do and I want to have my degree now. If God should help

Scholastica's arrival in Canada was to be that thing to make "everything fine." But No! She said because already in Canada, all those debts and other commitments (that the entire Asahchop family was well aware of[17]) just do not concern Scholastica Achankeng Asahchop whose only sole Canadian Enterprise is herself and her parents and siblings. You get the gist of the matter also from Eugene Lekeawung Asahchop's letter of November 7, 2000 sent to his "Dear sister," reminding her how "Before I left Fontem in October Dad never gave me enough money and I did not want to stress him up

---

us and I come and take in there, I come back and finish while expecting a baby. Don't you see that my idea is a good one?"

[17] Scholastica's mother (Photo #16) also made the point very clearly in the 4th paragraph of her letter of October 8, 1999 to her daughter:

>Dear daughter, we were very happy to read from you after a long time. I read from your letter God's blessings as concern your pregnancy. It was something that had worried me after your departure, but since God has given such blessings let's praise him and pray for success till the end of your pregnancy.
>
>For the past time I have been calling you through the phone at Dschang, but since you people changed your house and the address you have not given us your new phone number and for that reason it is difficult to phone again. So please when writing, include your new phone number. As concerns the post box we are trying to see how it can be opened. The situation of your sister's husband is becoming a problem to her and all of us in the house. So finally all we could do was to accept. But we told her that her life is in danger. So if it is successful then she is lucky and if it is not then all is left to her.
>
>John-Paul's name was on the waiting list for Seat of Wisdom College but finally he was admitted. We borrowed money from all sources to make sure he is in school.
>
>We understand that before you left your husband had a lot of debts but however since you already have a small job, you and your husband should struggle to build a small three-room house with mud blocks in your plot in the village. It would be advantageous for the burial of your mother-in-law when she is called by the almighty. Everybody is in good health including your mother-in-law. Extend greetings to your husband, to Quinta and her children.
>
>Thanks, Your mother Asahchop Elizabeth.

You will hear Chief Foletia (aka Vincent Agegndia Sixtus Fossungu in Photo #23) making the same house preparation point below in chapter 3 and Scholastica herself doing same in chapter 2 in her letter of September 25, 1997 (while she is still in Cameroon). What happens then when people have crossed the Atlantic Ocean? Prevent others (except their "family") from also doing so, of course. Love indeed and marriage!

because you had made that promise" of taking good care of all of them. You also get it from the first two paragraphs of her father's letter of June 3, 1999 to "Dear Mr./Mrs Fossungu Peter," which boldly (and inconsiderately?) stated that:

I had your letter on the safe arrival to Canada on 18/4/99. I was extremely happy to hear that she arrived safely.

I wonder if she had finished with her documents and if she is very free to move around. I also want to know your proposal either to attend school for now or to look for employment. I heard you were to defend by last March 1999 and later heard it was postponed to May 1999, and I wondered whether you defended as proposed.

If in the thinking of Peter Ngunyi Asahchop (Photo #22) Scholastica is Momany's wife indeed (and not just for the *moneyintriguing* thing[18]), why must he be so keen on asking these questions? And he is not alone as you will shortly hear his son (Eugene) doing the same thing. Wouldn't those be issues for the couple (if they are such) to decide together on their own? Note also that in the N.B. of this letter of Peter Ngunyi Asahchop sent to both his daughter and son-in-law, is the talk of "of some negatives of pictures we took and intended to be enlarged by Mr. Peter." But all the thanks for making the enlargements will only be given to their daughter in her mother's secret letter to Scholastica. Dated December 10, 2000 (note well the year), Elizabeth Asahchop's letter to "Dear Scholastica" said:

How are you and the baby? I hope everybody is quite fine. With us here, we are all well.

I was very happy with the children's shoes and all what you sent to us. The money you sent to us really helped me on certain things that I did not know how I was to solve them.

I was very happy when I heard that Peter defended his Ph.D. I saw Ngunyi's photo and was really glad how she is fast growing.

We were surprised to read from the letter that you sent through the bearer of the children's shoes that the shoes were also with dresses but we could not see the dresses. When we investigated he

---

[18] It is now very clear that this man, who is brother to Odette Ateafac who you see in Photo #25, knew very well that the baby Odette was then carrying was Momany's but pressured Odette not "spoil" his own daughter's chances of grabbing the money-tree for him (see Fossungu, 2013c: chapter 5).

told us that when you were about sending the things he told you to put the dresses in his own bag but you refused.

I have sent you crayfish, *egussi*, *jansa*, and bitter leaf in small quantities because the bearer told me he would not take anything if it is large or heavy because it could inconvenience him. I wanted to send some other things in large quantities but he refused; something like meat of which he refused [saying] that he could not carry large or heavy bags. I was very grateful for those enlarged photos. Most of my enlarged photos were already bad.

Yours, mother Elizabeth Asahchop.

Thus, even the money that she herself was collecting from Elias Akendung (Photo #24) wouldn't mean anything to Scholastica now that she has finally crossed the Atlantic. Table 2 tells you the story better than anyone else can.

Table 2: Peter's Book Showing "Money Which I [Scholastica Achankeng Asahchop] Have Been Collecting From Mr. Elias Akendung"

Amounts (FCFA)	Dates	Reasons
10,000	Sept 1995	The money Power used in paying his airport tax
10,000	Sept 1995	The money I used in buying some of my books and some school needs
55,000	Oct 1995	The money which was used in paying Njangie money
5,000	Oct 1995	The money I used for transport when I attended the death celebration of Mr. Elias' mother in Douala
15,000	Nov 1995	The money I used in buying some of my personal needs, photocopies & part was used as pocket money
5,000	Dec 1995	The money used for transport during x-mas when I went to Douala

The Year 1996: 30,000	Jan 1996	The money I went for holiday with
13,000	March 1996	Pocket money & part used on photocopies
15,000	May 1996	Pocket money & part used in buying drugs when I was sick
110,000	Sept 1996	Money used in paying school fees, part for rentrée scolaire & part used as pocket money
15,000	Dec 1996	Part of the money used in making Power's documents & part for photocopies & transport from Douala to Buea
40,000	Dec 29th '96	I used part of the money for buying house equipments, part for treatment & part for pocket money
The Year 1997: 30,000	Jan 18, 1997	I used the money for transport (from Buea to Douala) (to and fro to collect my things)
10,000	Jan 21st 97	Transport to the village when my grand dad died.
35,000	Jan 30th 97	Part for fees, part for transport to Buea and the rest for pocket allowance
4,270		Part of Power's money which was collected from the family meeting (sinking fund balance)
3,000	Feb 28th 97	I went to collect money but there was no money, so 3000 francs was giv[en] to me for transport
20,000	March 25th 1997	Part was used for pocket money & the rest to buy tablets when I was sick
2,500	April 14, 1997	I went to collect money to renew my passport, but there was no money

		& 2,500 francs was given to me for my transport
70,000	April ending '97	The money I went to Yaoundé with, to apply for a visa
96,000	Still April 1997	The money I used for medical exams
15,000	April 1997	The money I came to Buea with
3,000	24th May 1997	The money I used in paying transport when I left the embassy and a visa was not given to me
15,000	17th June 97	The money I used in finishing my friend's money which I took to make my new passport
5,000	13th July '97	Transport money on coming to Buea from Yaounde
13,000	20th July '97	Pocket allowance during my field work placement
10,000	12th Sept 97	The money I took on my way back from the village, i.e. to come & do summer in Buea
70,000	Oct 1997	The money I took at the beginning of the school year
5,000	March 15, 1997	During the first semester break when I went to the hospital immediately after my brother's death and spent all the money I had.

N.B.: From Elias Akendung's own calculations, which is affixed below, the above sums totalled 713,000.00 FCFA, an amount that Momany settled in full using Western Union MTCN #790-895-4826 of July 25, 2003 (Agency Doreen, operator 001), the sum being equivalent of CAD $1892.04.

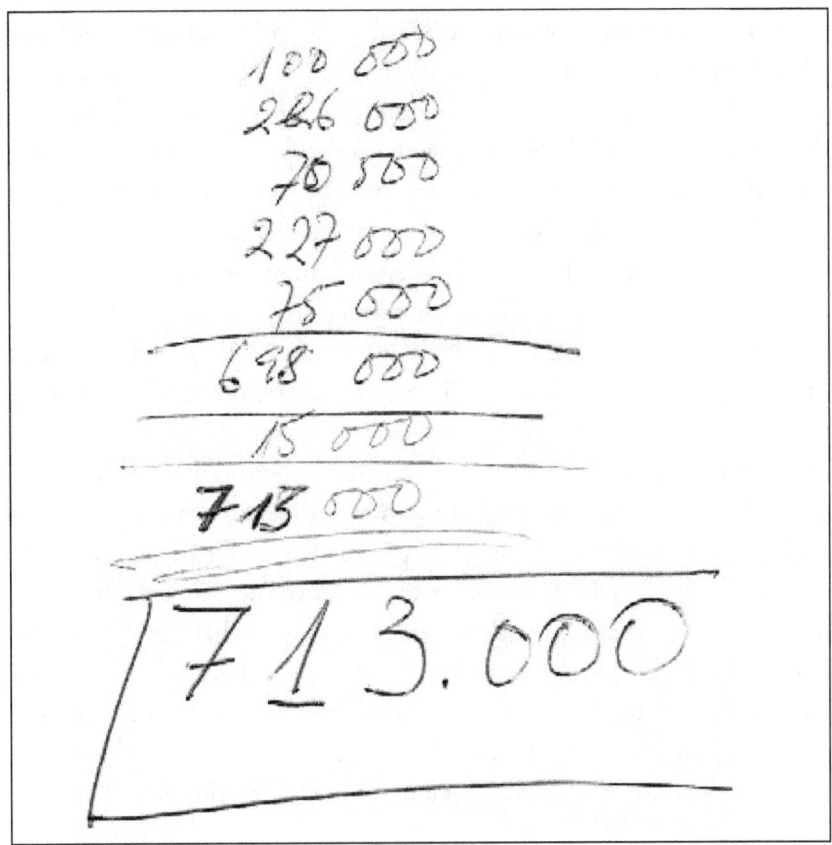

This affixed amount is the calculation in the man's own handwriting, just as the entire entry in *Peter's Book* (to which it is affixed) is in the handwriting of Scholastica Achankeng Asahchop herself. In her letter of July 31, 1997 to Momany, Scholastica stated that "Power, Mr. Timothy finally sent that money to me from the USA. It was a hundred dollars. When I changed it, it was 50,000 francs. I gave it all to Edith for her money I took and went to Yaoundé with. The money I used in protecting myself came from that money; that is why it was up to 65,000 francs. Anyway, I gave 15,000 francs when I collected that money from school." How much was that money? 'That money' here is referring to what the University of Buea entirely owed Momany for the one school year he taught there (1994-1995). Until this day Momany only knows that it was duly paid out to his wife but not what the amount paid out was. Would that even be a possibility with *money-centric* people? Is there also some contradiction here with the matters in Table 2?

It is also simply not clear if Scholastica had been repaying Elias Akendung's money or just showing her gratitude (or making a New Year gift) to Elias Akendung, their creditor who was peeving around the whole place with Momany's name, an act of riling that continued even after the entire debt had been settled by Momany. *Moneyintriguist!* This doubt is raised because there is evidence (left behind with some of the secret letters) of a 'secret' Western Union money transfer from Scholastica Asahchop to Elias Akendung on January 16, 2003 with MTCN #790-535-7422 (Agency #620, operator 256) in the amount of 120,000.00 FCFA (CAD $341.28). Of course, that could not be all there is to it; but only the two of them can actually know the exact number of financial transactions that have been going on between them. The question remains though whether she has been *secretly* paying a debt that has already been publicly cleared by Momany? If so, then is she also doing the same to the others (in Table 1) that were urgently contracted through the intermediary of her friend, Edith-Rosa Khumbah? That could not be the case because, as already indicated, all those debts don't concern her at all after the Atlantic crossing. But the evidence was all there before the marriage and the said crossing which Momany, as a man in love, could not still see?

Loving Marriage or Scheming Marriage?

To demonstrate the pre-Marriage writing on the wall query, let us take Scholastica's very early two letters to the man who had already talked marriage to her. The first, which was hand-written on December 7, 1993, entirely read:

Hello! How was your journey from Fontem to the village? I presume you arrived safely and dad didn't blame you.

We arranged that I was to come up and meet you in the village: I am not sound and am feeling very bad since they released our result. I didn't pass. It is really aching since all my friends in our study group passed. It is really ill luck and I don't just know what to do now.

Please, you should try and come down and let's discuss. Sorry for all the inconveniences. Please don't mind because it is not due to my own making. I even promised to come and spend some time in the village. For now, I don't have hopes to go to anywhere. I am really feeling bad for I thought I will make it this time.

You should not be discouraged please. If you were me, you could have been feeling the same. Say hi to all please. Hoping to see you soon! It's me. Schola.

Of course, it is only obvious that anyone not lovingly reading this letter would raise a hell of questions that would, on their part, be raising justifiable doubts about the two-sidedness of their love-marital relationship. For instance, Scholastica does not respect the village rendezvous because of the effects on her of failure in the G.C.E. Advanced Level, the results of which were published in August. First, was Momany totally unaware of these results at the time of fixing the appointment? Was that not even a better reason to rush to the one you love for comfort? Furthermore, if the appointment was near or before the publication of results, why were the excuses being tendered only in December? Is this not clearly reminiscent of 'The Golden Plus Three Gift' scenario, with Mr. "Officer LLE tak[ing] that long to fix the so-called mistake of Officer K?" (Fossungu, 2015d: 125). What would actually be the problems the *Asahchopination* was out to fix here with the marriage? And there is a lot more puzzles. But let's bring in one or two other members of this (in)famous family before getting to Scholastica's other early letter.

These further illustrations cannot have much sense if they begin with any other person but Scholastica's co-April-Fool conspirator, who might also actually be informing us in a very neat way of what their problem to be fixed through Momany would basically consist of.[19] I am referring to Eugene Lekeawung Asahchop's letter of

---

[19] Your grasp of the matter would certainly benefit from your having knowledge of the same guy's letter to Momany long before his sister ever crossed the Atlantic. On July 24, 1997, Eugene Lekeawung Asahchop wrote to Momany as follows:

Dear brother, I had your letter in April, but I couldn't reply because I was waiting for the admission requirement from the Sweden University which you proposed and wrote to them so that they could send the form. I and my sister (your wife) were very impressed about the proposal, the only problem in it is the fact that the people in the embassy are still making the visa problem difficult on her, since you said you can't do it [Sweden project] alone.

Well I had their letter of admission requirements in July (first week). I read the conditions and there was one problem which is that of the Swedish language. All students must have knowledge of the Swedish language before admission into any university in Sweden. The letter also said the Swedish language is written in the

October 1994 to her sister, who had just reached Momany's home in Douala in early 1994. Listen to him yourself and answer many of your own *moneyintriguing* questions. Undated but obviously written between October 10-17, 1994, Eugene Lekeawung Asahchop (Photo #21) stated to "Dear Schola":

How is your health? When Edith came here she told us that you were sick but I am sure you must have recovered. We were very happy with your results and the grade you hard [in the G.C.E. Advanced Level]. I saw the letter that you sent to papa telling him that I should not continue here [in Fontem[20]]. Well it was a good advice you gave him because I myself did not want to school here, but due to the hard times he is facing I was forced to do so. I even thought how Bridget went [back to school] because it came to a certain time when he said she will no more go but one Friday evening he told her to pack and go the following morning.

I started school last Monday (10/10/94) and we already have one teacher in Mathematics, one in Chemistry, two in Physics and two in Biology, but they are too lazy (those of Biology). My problem now is that of textbooks. None of them has been bought, the fees not paid, my uniform is now a very small one, my own one pair of shoes is going bad; my problems are many. So with all this type of problems at the start it would have been difficult to school outside [Fontem].

---

embassy of any country (Swedish embassy) in April each year. This is a copy of their letter enclosed.

In your last letter you mentioned that Nigeria is a very risky country, before I had your letter many students schooling there had mentioned it that strikes can stop school for over six months. So my father told me to forget about it and already it was out of mind. The P & T entrance I wrote in April was not successful.

At the moment, I am going to apply into Buea University and since I have devoted my mind in reading medicine, I will still try the entrance into the Faculty of Biomedical Sciences (CUSS) University of Yaoundé I. With these two, in September I will know where to belong.

Thanks. Eugene. Signed.

[20] Note that the scheming trend had long been in work even before the Canada Episode. Scholastica is at this moment completely dependent on Momany but is already giving such instructions (without the knowledgement of, let alone discussion with, Momany: who was to take care of Eugene's out-of-Fontem schooling? Foolish Question! Who did so while they were both in the University of Buea, to limit just to this?

Mamie has completed the new store in the market. She has started cooking food for sale such as *fufu* and *ero*, plantain and beans. She is asking if you had seen the letter she once wrote to you, if so why no reply? She says you should write and tell her where you are presently, either in Buea or Douala and doing (schooling or not), what!

We heard the Chancellor of Buea University calling your husband over the radio to come for interview, has he been admitted or not? We were very surprised that when they were reading the names of students who have been admitted in Buea yours was not there. Is it that you never registered or you are going to Yaoundé or you are not going to school this year? I heard you saying you will come here in December, please if you are coming help me bring a hand [wrisr?] watch, any type. I just want a watch or if you change your mind by not coming try and send it. I am in great need of a watch. Greet your husband for me.

Thanks. Yours lovely brother Eugene. Signed [this paragraph is altered].

Pretenders! Anyone can see that 'husband' is just a money thing. Like his father's inquisition about school and work, you see *moneyintriguism* all over it. Scholastica was being married out just for something else, not for marriage itself. Schemers! Extending greetings there in Cameroon but this same guy comes to Montreal (Canada) and prefers to perch for years in the house of his sister's friend (Lysly Ako Ayah who you see in Photo 59) whereas Momany (the same "your husband") is living in Montreal. Would Scholastica ever have been in love with Momany, to countenance such comportment from her brother? Love is real when it knows no season, weathering all conditions; not being only about sex. Eugene Lekeawung Asahchop's letter, together with those you already have from this famously notorious(?) family could have taken care of most of your intriguing queries. But if you are interested in one more, as already promised ('a promise is a debt,' it is said?), before the second letter of 'the newly acquired money-tree' that everyone is out to harvest from, then take that of Elizabeth Asahchop (Photo #16). Her letter is dated February 14, 1999. "My Dearest Scholastica," it opened,

How is your health and that of Peter? I hope everybody is fine. With me and your father there is improvement. I saw your two letters that you sent. I was very happy when the letter explained that you people were fine. The content of the letter was well understood and by the grace of God there will be no or little illness. I have taken treatment for 3 months while [treatment for] 3 months is left and there is improvement.

If you have been having little illness you should just be patient because that is how it does happen to everybody who is having same condition as you. The money you people sent to your mother-in-law was given to her and she was very happy. She is fine and one lady in the village came and took her to her own house because she did not have a little child who could help her carry water in her own house. The lady who took her to her house is by name called Lucia Njizi [Zinzi? She is seen in Photo #26] in Nweh-Ncheng. She is fine in terms of health; so this should not bring fear that your mother-in-law is not well.

We saw the money you sent and I was very happy but the fun there was that your father never wanted to tell me. But he told me and I understood, just that it was for quite a long time before he told me. Greet Peter for me and tell him success in exams.

Your mother Elizabeth.

Just hear her too pretending now to be extending greetings to Momany! She is not fit even as a grandmother! Most of you would find it hard to believe that it was only in Cameroon in 2014 (when he went to bury his mother who you see in Photo #27) that Momany learnt that Scholastica's mother has been living in Canada for years. I can now divine that this could even be why Momany's calls to London (Ontario) have since never been answered, making nonsense of Scholastica's letter of September 10, 2004 to Momany.[21] Some

---

[21] Here is Scholastica's letter of September 10, 2004 to Momany which clearly indicated that (it is the 3rd paragraph that is very important here):

    We hope you are doing quite fine. Well, I finally left Montreal and we arrived here very safely.

    Well, we have been together for ten years and thanks for all the help you have given me. I don't know precisely what I did to you that you treat me like this. Anyway, forgive me for whatever I did wrong.

    I wish you all the best in your endeavours and do pray and hope that you should be successful/happy.

hide their identity by calling *private* but Momany never calls *private*, having nothing to hide in doing that. Their reasoning must be that if Momany is talking to them, the children (since children don't usually know how to lie) would let him know that 'grandma' is there with them. Yes! Children don't lie! Who has not heard the story of the debtor, son, and creditor? The debtor hid himself in his bedroom and told the son to tell the creditor that he has gone out. On the creditor's inquiry of the father's whereabouts, the son said: "My father who is hiding in his bedroom told me to tell you that he has gone out." Hearing that, the father had no choice but to come out of his hiding place while creating other schemes to tell the creditor. Did someone not already tell you that schemers are always living in fear, thinking everyone else is scheming to do to them what they know they always do to others? Otherwise, what is it that these *Asahchopination* people are trying to hide? Even if she is in Canada illegally, is Momany an immigration officer or police officer or what?

You get the comportment of schemers even in Elizabeth Asahchop's secret letter, relating to the date which indicates that the letter was written *before* Scholastica had even touched down on Canadian soil in April 1999. Running so hard to empty the banks before anyone else can get there, indeed! Elizabeth Asahchop's letter (which must be kept close for the second part of chapter 4's 'Elephant Money Fight') is dated "14-02-1999" and I have racked my head, to no avail, trying to discover if there is a 14th month which could logically mean that Scholastica was already in Canada when the letter was written on the 2nd of that month! Either I have simply woefully failed to be intelligent enough to find that hidden calendar that has been secretly confiscated, direct from God, by the *Asahchopination;* or it merely explains the manner they think so much about harvesting the money (they never invested) that they get in

---

The children are going to miss you, and please do not hesitate to call them and talk to them. Do not stay away from them because they need you. You could pay them a visit.

I do hope you will be happy and get a job.

I hope you gave the keys to the Janitor. Our address and phone number are above.

Bye. Good luck. Scholastica.

advance of civilized existence, at all cost too, don't forget.²² Not to skip with you right away to chapter 4, let's just say "Keep to your promise!" Was *Onsilovundism* (one-sided love and understanding) clearly exposed in the Nwangong Marriage?

That brings us full circle back to the second early note of Scholastica, the person who is now hiding her mother in Canada and depriving the children of access to their father; also forcefully confirming the 'Children as Money-Making Tools' theory. One is here referring to Scholastica Achankeng Asahchop's second early note to her so-called husband-to-be. You would realize why 'so-called' is employed from Queenta Ngum Afanwi in Photo #28. She is the intelligent nurse of the Nwangong Health Centre that their "ears & eyes" chased out of Nwangong (see Fossungu, 2014: 127-129). Like many others, Queenta would be addressing Momany who has not yet even talked marriage to her as "Dear Husband," 'dear'…., and herself as: "Your wife". Not to leave the matter just vaguely hanging in air, Queenta Ngum Afanwi who had *temporarily* met Momany and fallen in love with him in June 2004 (with Scholastica still being at 'home' with the man), wrote a letter to Momany on June 5, 2005 which stated:

Dear Husband, It's a joy for me to pen you. How is life that way? Hope fine, especially your health which is the most essential thing in life.

With me, I am there. Health-wise I am fine. Please, know that tough times do not last but tough people do. So take time and do what you can. I kindly beg you, dear, don't be thinking too much because you can develop high blood pressure. You know how complicated it is. Pray that I should have a stand so that I will be able

---

²² In his letter of March 12, 1999, Solomon Tatah wrote in the 2nd paragraph that "Talking about mounting financial obligations, I want to mention the fact that it is always worse when you always have patients in your household. My dad was very sick for most of last year until he finally died on 02-11-99. My last daughter who is in Saker is today well tomorrow sick and vice versa." I am sure Solomon meant to write 02-11-98 because he certainly could not be talking about a future death in the past. You see what *Quagmatickism* can do to people's thought process? Could that also be the same thing with Elizabeth Asahchop's letter or could the two cases be properly distinguished? Could *Quagmatickism* be responsible for Momany's thinking process of leaving Buea for Canada without having consolidated his marriage first? More on the vexing issue is in the next chapter.

to be assisting you in taking care of mum. I also pray that God should take care in everything you are doing. Know that tough times do not last but tough people do. I am with you all the time. So don't feel that you are alone that way.

Extend my greetings to all your friends. Tell them that somebody all the way from Cameroon is greeting them. Permit me to end here. Stay fine, sweet dreams.

Your wife Queenta.

Is it not a mystery that Momany's acquaintances would all be showing great interest in his 'family' (nuclear particularly) but not those women that he has actually called 'wife'? Not to limit the examples to just Odilia and Jane, as to be seen in later chapters, listen again to Queenta who not only lost her job because of her daring to take care of Momany's mother as her own mum for a number of months, if not years (see them in Photo #29). She also would be referring to Momany's kids (that he has with Scholastica) as "our children" in her numerous letters, and especially this one of September 19, 2005.[23] Queenta too talks of documents sent to her and I think it is essential to note here that Momany is someone who helps anyone who needs helping whenever he can; and he does not

---

[23] Dear Husband, How are you? Hope fine. What about our children? Hope they are also well. With me, I am there with my problems. But thank God, he has really given me the courage and faith to withstand the problems. I know you have been calling and my line is not going through. Thieves had attacked me and taken away my phone when I was coming back from the hospital to see my aunt. She has been there for 1 month one week now. She has been diagnosed to be a T.B. patient. All this while, I am with her in the hospital. Before she started this cough, I had started working with the local Aids Control Office in Bafut. But because of her I could not continue again. Not forgetting, I have seen those documents that you sent. Dear, try and call me through this number xxxxxxxxx. Always call during the evening period. It is not my number, so when you call tell him that you are looking for Queenta. He will send message to me and in five minutes time I will be around. He is called Mohamed. There is no network around the hospital.

Dear. I will be very happy if I could hear your voice again. Permit me to end here. Bye-bye.

Your wife Queenta.

N.B.: I could not send you a letter because I was not around the Post Office. It is now that I have come to Bafut to look for food that I am able to write to you.

do some of these things you hear about in the numerous communications just to his lovers or family relations. You get this simple understanding in several letters to/from him as the next chapter voluminously shows. The important issue for now is the show of love, even in letters.

Furthering the theory still, is *Momalizalism* which has to do with Momany's relationship with his 'lost' fiancé called Elizabeth (Liza). Liza is one of Momany's many 'wives-to-be' that were transformed into 'wives-never-to be' by the 'outside' arm of *99-Sensism* (see Fossungu, 2014: chapter 2). Like Odilia and Queenta, Liza also shows great interest in Momany's extended family (parents, siblings, etc.) and even goes further (the reunion incident below in chapter 2 fortifying). You can see this working also in her interest in the man's friends that she even hardly knows very well. "Bonjour" is the title of an email of February 20, 2007 at 4.25 AM that Liza copied to Momany while sending to his friend that she had briefly met: "Good Morning Joseph! How are you doing these days? I got your address from Peter FOSSUNGU and I have decided to write a short note to you. I was very happy with the phone you gave to Peter after the terrible night he had in Bonaberi while returning from the village. You are a very fantastic Guy. Thanks again. Meanwhile, you can call me as more often as you wish but between 8h30-16h from Monday to Friday. Have a nice day. Elizabeth."

Comportment like this one would fail to endear the person only to a monster and Momany is no such beast as you can see in his "Love, Love, Love" email of January 17, 2005 at 6.26 AM in which he told "My Precious Love" (Liza) that "I have just gotten up this Monday morning and the first thing I see is your double greetings. I will have to go late to work today but that is okay with me because I cannot wait until this evening to write back to you. Just take good care of yourself and I hope to read from you today when I am back. I LOVE YOU." [24] Liza is married to someone else but still calls

---

[24] Liza's reply (titled "My Precious Love") was on January 19, indicating that "You are driving me crazy with all these lovely words (my precious love, my precious lady...). Oh my God! You're certainly pushing me toward divorcing my husband. Thanks for your new contact information. Love. Liza." *Original Text: Tu vas me rendre folle avec tous ces petits mots doux (my precious love, my precious lady...). Oh là la*

Momany 'husband-to-be,' and always seeking to know when their marriage would take place. Thus, in her "Happy New Year" email of January 9, 2007, Francophone Liza wrote to Momany: "Hello my Dear, Hereby, I wish you a happy New Year 2007. *Comment vas-tu? Depuis plusieurs jours je n'ai plus de tes nouvelles. Bien vouloir me faire signe de vie.* Your fiancée."

'Your wife,' 'Darling,' 'Dear,' 'Your fiancée,' they are all saying. But clearly not so at all with the wife-to-be (if not even already wife) proper called Scholastica Achankeng Asahchop. Written ten days after Scholastica's first letter above (that is, on December 17, 1993), this second one also un-lovingly declared:

Hello! A great pleasure to dispatch this note to you. Sure you have been questioning what is biting, what's biting me. Nothing! Just that I decided to write only after seeing my detailed results.

They sent my detailed results and I had history D, Literature Q. I don't know what happened with that Literature. I can't just understand! Literature is my subject and I thought I failed but in History.

I want to inquire something from you. My dad was asking if one can go to the university (Yaoundé) with two sittings. That is Literature and History. Please you write and tell me as soon as possible. You should also tell me your own opinion. I was telling my dad that you promised to help me through your friends in case I go to Yaoundé.

How is life? I am sure you are feeling quite fine and longing to see me. Same to me. I feel that [it] is the highest time for us to be together so that we know each other. How can that be possible? Suggest and tell me what you feel.

They have told me that this boy is coming to Douala just now. Please don't care about my mistakes because I am really in haste. I shall write better next time. I am still to write because I doubt if you will see this letter.

Say hello to all whom you know deserve my greetings.

I care. Schola

!!!!!!!! Tu risque me faire divorcer (rires....). Merci de m'avoir communiqué tes nouvelles coordonnées. Je t'embrasse très fort et bisous sur tout ton corps. Liza

NB: Care not about my writing paper please. It is not possible for me to get one now. There are no nice Christmas cards here also. I wish you the best.

Of course, it is clear that Momany would never have heard from her if her results were good enough for her to sail to Yaoundé or Buea. The above *Asahchopinationist* letters (to talk less of those that may still be coming) appear to speak for themselves and I have nothing more to say except to theorize, with some degree of certainty, that these secret-letters demonstrations have been pellucid in showing that, going by the failure-learning axiom, Momany undoubtedly stands in an appropriate position to give us this important failure-learning lecture since he is now well known to the Marriage Failures Hall of Fame. The essential puzzle becomes that of knowing why he even had to change profession?

Chapter 2

Barthelizing or Blending Marriage, Love, and Academic Excellence

The concept of *Barthélization* derives its meaning from the Momany-Barthelemy (Barthé in Photo #30) exchanges generally that are not only academically focused but also very vital in the domain of the reunion of ex-loves (*exloverexism*) and also to the question of whether home is really where love is. This question, an integral part of this book's mission, is especially important if you also carefully go through the *Momalizalist* exchanges, not leaving out the contacts of family members as well as their own role in the reunions too. What do these active and fruitful communications between Momany and his ex-loves, as well as with family members of his *ex-lovers* signify and bring to mind? If nothing else comes to mind, the fact remains that those families whose members actively and continually facilitate reunions had no ulterior (or *Scholaparentist*) motives for the marriage or no-marriage and breakdown. Those that had or have secret plans are not cooperative and are most often even very hostile to the idea.

You could see this theory being propped up by the mere fact that not only are Momany's ex-wives' relations completely out of touch with him. But also the said wives have effectively 'ostracized' the children from the essential father-children link, without in the least considering what that means to said children's emotional and mental health. To children like these, is home just where they physically live or also where the heart is? Always with the aim of discovering if home is where the love is, this chapter will handle the reconnection question that also significantly exposes the importance of open-mindedness. I have already given more than enough lectures (in some of my earlier works) on the significance of maintaining an open mind in ones dealings with others, what is often referred to as looking at the larger picture. Here, I will merely be demonstrating how that perspective is instrumental in Momany's reconnections with many of his *ex-loves* but especially Elizabeth (Liza) who shares the Pregnancy Story with Scholastica (for Canada). Liza is Manjo's well known Cameroon's Pregnancy Users' and the Rebellious Girl' of 'The

Strange REC (Rita-Elizabeth-Christine) Connexion' (see Fossungu, 2014: 85-91 &102-105).

If you are obviously pondering on why Liza is always involved in bizarre connections, then wait until you have seen how the three concepts of *Odilimanyism*, *Annamanyism* and *Momanijanism* are connected in this subject of ex-loves reunion. Their bridge is PAB (respectively the trio of Pat, Anthony and Barthelemy). As such, we will be *Barthelizing* marriage, love and academic excellence, in the course of which ex-love reunions will have an accentuation on the *Anthonization* of Love and unfriendly friendliness. In this chapters' Knowledge-gaining Enterprise, Momany has decided to fall back squarely on what he has valuably obtained especially from *Odilimanyism* (Odilia-Momany relationship). Odilia is the woman whose 'senior-sibling-fearing' attitude (better known as *Janodilism*) appears to have played Momany easily into the hands of *moneyintriguists* (see Fossungu, 2014: 56-57). While these schemers' ways would be examined in the next chapter, the first part of this chapter will study *quagmatickism* and professional alterations through some love exchanges while the second will elaborate on the wonders of family instabilities and academics.

Love Exchanges on Cameroon's *Quagmatickism* and Professional Changes

The concept of *Quagmatickism* comes from Fossungu (2016c) who declares that "Cameroon must be freed from *Quagmatickism*." Like *Odilimanyism*, *Momanijanism* also touches on Momany's relationship with his Jane. But what is different between the two similar Anglophones? This takes us back to squarely focus on (and draw some consequences from) the Momany-Odilia exchanges: with a lot of push from those of another Sakerite, Jane, who has an identical love philosophy called *Janeckinology*. These love monologues (letters, if you will) would aid a better grasp of Cameroon's *Quagmatickism*, a version of *dragdownism*. That is, in fact, what dragged down Momany, not so much the marital woes that are mere by-products of *Quagmatickism*. Let his lovers tell the story to you.

On Wednesday, January 26, 2006 at 9.40 PM Momany wrote to 'Hello Odilia' in an email message titled 'Greetings,' stating that "I just want to make sure that you and your family are doing fine. We are alright here. Extend greetings to Pat and other brothers and sisters of yours. Take care and bye now." It is not like this is the first time they were getting in touch since marrying. Odilia's 3-paragraph letter of June 26, 1996 to "Dear" Momany also noted in the opening paragraph that "I received your card a few days ago and I am happy to know that you are fine over there. Are you doing your PhD or working? For me things are not really moving as planned. I thought by now I would be doing my Master Degree in Europe but everything failed me [because] I went to Nigeria for my transcript but couldn't get it because universities were on strike." To this extent, Odilia was not as blessed as her 'synonym,' Jane, in strike-free France.

In her "Someone Like You" email of March 12, 2011 at 3.57 AM Jane told Momany the following which seems to be one of his best of all the *Janeckinology* lectures, it being clearly distinguished from *Odilickinology* (Odilia's love philosophy) by just the 'I know that feeling': "Dear Peter, How are you today? How is the little boy doing? He must be such fun to be with at this stage. I finished my training a little while ago, with honours and the company I did my practical training with offered me a job in business development and export sales administration. It has been a very hectic period and still is but I haven't forgotten my beloved friends. I have been to India and will be travelling to Brazil this weekend for a week. Just to share with you this feeling that hasn't left me years ago, but which I think is better this way as we have moved on and are happy in our lives. PLEASE CLICK ON THE LINK BELOW. Have a very nice day and please enjoy every moment with your kids and your partner. Life is good and I am very happy with my life here in France and some days I listen to some tracks played from the 80s, like Michael Bolton or Rod Stewart and I am like, "I know that feeling" – good oldies! Love, Janet." Now, just seeing how someone (like Odilia) can be so easily frustrated in their relentless efforts to have a better life in Africa by things that are not supposed to stand in someone's way, why wouldn't there be this mad rush to rush away from the *quagmaticking* African show and into the so-called Western world? Why wouldn't anyone be right in saying we greatly contribute to, if not actually creating, our own problems?

For instance, what else would you give as explanation for Momany returning to Canada for the second time? And how connected to his marital woes that you have just tasted a bit of in the last chapter? It obviously precipitated his leaving the country without having consolidated his marriage; of course, all in the business of looking for something better 'out West,' as was the general trend? The issues evoked in Odilia's letter are not unique to Odilia and do reflect the general malaise of the continent, but Cameroon particularly (see Nyamnjoh, Gram & Konings, 2012). In the 3rd paragraph of his letter of June 19, 1996 Stephen Fomeche (listen attentively to him, he has a lot in store for you) took a comprehensive sweep at the issue with this:

If winning the National lottery had been the dream of many Cameroonians, today it is winning the U.S. visa lottery. We were fooled to spend much money to compile documents for this purpose which simply helped to swell the expected size of the garbage in front of one of Mr. Biya's sycophants. That does not in any way discourage me from pulling out from this country. Power, I am bent on leaving. I don't want to task your imagination into narrating a long procedure of what you did when you first left the country or before gaining your visa now. It may be after December, you will be quite settled and at peace to start directing me what to do, how and where to start. If any application needs to be written which will need much time for one to get the reply, you can keep me informed to do so ahead of any other follow up.

This first part of the chapter will continue under two interlocking segments, with the first centring on the communications that contributed to academic excellence abroad and the second dealing with those on the horrible Cameroonian situation that prompted the idea of going back abroad.

Solomonizing the *Scholacademician*'s Intriguing Communications

The 'feeds' regarding the disheartening situation came from many acquaintances, former classmates, former students, and even hardly-known people. These many reports contributed enormously to sustaining Momany's decision to descend from the high-flying aimless Air and Space McGill Vessel and to focus on researching 'The Cameroon Question' at the Université de Montréal where he left a record, thanks to these feeds. But these communications are also more important in view of the earlier handwriting communications between the two 'in-laws' that touch directly on the priceless contribution Barthelemy Dongmo Jiomeneck (Photo #30) has made to Momany's academic undertakings. The distinguished members Jury of Momany's Defence Committee were gleefully shocked to learn that the research in the dissertation before them had been carried out without even a single trip to Cameroon. And yet it was as current and well documented as it was? Impossible! Some of them just could not even begin to think of trying to start believing that 'no-sense-making' nonsense. Luckily, the supervisor of the work (Professor André Tremblay) allied the fact that it was factual: since Momany (because of his desire to finish in record time and "be back home with a Golden Fleece"[25]), was meeting with this supervisor almost daily and there was just no way he (Momany) could have even sneaked his way out of Canada to Cameroon without him (supervisor) being aware. How did Momany achieve such feat then, you are asking? I hand that over to Barthelemy Dongmo Jiomeneck and Scholastica Achankeng Asahchop (Photo #1) who are both well placed to tell you through their endless communications to/with the *academicshatterer*.

As would be noted over and over, the great importance of constantly having news of what is happening at home while you are abroad cannot be overstated. None of Momany's acquaintances has been able to comprehend this and also be extremely *frantalkistic* about it (when there is a lapse) than the other 'Power' in Yaoundé called Solomom Enoma Tatah. Listen to him dishing out education to us on a lot of vital issues in his letter of March 12, 1999:

Dear Peter, It is with a very heavy hand that I am managing to write this letter. I feel guilty very much. This is because I have not written or called you for a long time now. If I don't do this, who do I expect to feed you with vital information from home, from the male

---

[25] That is from the 4th paragraph of Ngi-Nyam's April 18, 2006 letter to Momany: "And now Peter, how has it all been with you? Hope fine as proven from the fact that you now, by dint of hard work, hold a Ph.D. Congratulations from all of us as someday, you would be back home with a Golden Fleece."

perspective? This has been a poor show from me and I admit it. Please, I appeal that you forgive and receive me back. I know you've done so and I thank you.

[Missing paragraph 2, cited elsewhere]

On a happier note however, although also financially demanding, Alice finally successfully defended her Thesis in the Advanced School of Mass Communication (ASMAC), Yaoundé. She is now a professional journalist. No more a teacher. My daughter, Enoma Tatah, too had a double promotion last year from Class 6 to 7 and therefore gained admission into Our Lady of Lourdes Secondary School, Mankon, Bamenda. She is now a Form I girl, but still learning to adapt to boarding life.

Congratulations for Schola's success. Although, this has been obtained at the high cost of your separation, I believe it is the best prize we have won. The time has not been wasted. And as you did mention in your letter of April, 15 1998, "God works his miracles everyday. If we just look a bit harder, we see it everyday, everywhere, every time" – (Peter Fossungu, Montreal: 15-04-98). I think everything happening to you and Schola is ordained by the Almighty so let's just be patient and you'll be reunited when God finds it appropriate.

Now, how is your PhD programme going? The best news I want to hear is when you'll be terminating it so that we may hope to see you and rejoice over it.

As for your articles in The Herald, they are always published from time to time. Schola even showed me photocopies of some of them. Congrats, and continue to write more of such articles. They will fetch you/us dividends in future.

Power, let me have your reply and from there I will know how to shape afresh our communication relations. I need your details as regards socio-academic developments that have affected you in the past year that we've been out of touch.

Regards to all your dear ones and accept love and greetings from all of us. It's Solo.

The dear ones Solomon talks of must obviously include Scholaslica, on 'the female perspective'. Momany used to love receiving Scholastica's parcels that some of the names she mentions in her letters (to be shortly seen) used to help send by EMS (Express

Mail Service). And Momany has duly acknowledged that help in his Dissertation when he thanked "Claude Esundem and Romanus Ateafac, both of Douala, Cameroon [who] have always assisted enormously with the large number of documents that my wife has had to send to me here. Thank you both." He used to enjoy receiving Scholastica's huge parcels because these always kept him abreast of what was happening back there. Her numerous letters of those years could constitute a volume of their own. They just cannot fit into this book. But a few (in addition to those already seen above) can make the point. For instance, take her letter of July 31, 1997. As quite lengthy a letter that it is, it is so short: if you consider the barrage of topics it sweepingly covers:

Hello Dear, I have found that *Messager* paper. That our lecturer finally gave it to me although I paid some money for it. He gave me two of the papers. He told me that the June 20th paper is a follow-up of the first one. When I told him that the paper is for my husband who is doing his PhD, he said he likes those who are intellectuals and that I should explain to you that he will be ready to give you more for your Ph.D. He is a sociologist. He is even our head of department.

I saw your letter yesterday with your two cards. One of the cards was very nice and the other was not so nice. Power, do you strain so much over there? You were looking tired. Anyway, it may be it is the temperament you were in before snapping that picture.

I heard yesterday that my father is sick and is hospitalized. I felt so bad when I heard this because we keep praying every new day that he should live a bit long. Our Belinda is going to form one this year. If not of my father's ill health she could have gone to a boarding school. She is so small to attend grammar school Fontem but my parents cannot do otherwise.

I am almost through with my field placement research. The problem now is to write it out and type it in a computer. We are going to hand it to the school in September or when school resumes. This year is a very expensive year because we need to write out long essays also. I have not even gone out for data. I am writing about our village. My topic is "Multiple Roles of Women in Rural Areas: Case Study of Nwangong Village." I need money for all these things.

I shall go to the village by September when I have paid my school fees. You know classes have been starting effectively from

November or October. I shall go only when I have paid my fees. If I knew that a visa would not be granted to me, I could have applied to work in the G.C.E. Board secretariat because they pay those working there 50,000 to 60,000 francs [CFA] and that could have been of great help to me.

[Paragraph 6 is cited elsewhere]

I went to Muyuka last weekend and Pa showed me the letter you wrote to him. He complained that he got the letter very late. He got it three months after you sent it. He was worrying about your situation and said you shall attend all the universities in the world because of the economic situation in the country. Mamie Thecla was very sick again until she almost died. She was very lucky from the way they explained to me. She said I should tell you and also greet you when we next communicate. Your father also has many wounds on his legs and is gradually getting tired. I don't like to be going there so often.

I also visited your brother Dieudonné [in Photo #31] and he and wife were fine. Justine [in Photo #32] did very well in Bojongo. She passed in 12 subjects out of 13 subjects and took the 17th position out of 95 students. I mean, I was so happy with her results.

Edith [her friend in Photo #20] says I should greet you; that she will write to you next time. I spent a night with her. I am planning to go and give this letter to Claude to post it for me.

Power, Mr. Timothy told the wife that some of my things are still left with him. He said you took some of the things and left some. Edith's sister who is lodging him in the USA called and said the very thing – that they shall send my parcel from my husband. I think they said some of the things were shirts. Please, you should check what you collected from the parcel and tell me what is still left, what I shall take from them exactly. He sent things last week but said in his wife's letter that he shall send my parcel next time. He also explained that my letter got missing and my money, that the money they have given to me is his own personal money. I took my money because I needed that money to pay Edith's money. It is better to be poor than to be a debtor.

What of the Whistance-Smith family [in Photo #33]? I presume they are all doing fine. I shall try and write to them next time. My cousin Quinta [Asa'ah] wrote to me and I have not yet replied her letter. I shall do that next week.

Solo came back from Holland when I was in Yaoundé. He promised to come to South West together with the family but I have not yet seen him. He bought his car there before coming back.

Power, the name of that Bangwa man from Mmockgie working in the Cameroon embassy is Colonel Tiamoh. Please, please try to inquire and send those my dresses through him.

How are you preparing for your 37th birthday? I wish that we should spend the next one together. Please, Edith says I should wish you a happy birthday. My problem now is our kids. It is not nice to pass through a certain age without having kids.

Power, I presume you shall really take time in reading this my letter.

Greet all those who you know deserve my greetings.

Your wife, Schola.

P/S: Please, post Quinta's letter for me.

As you can see, in the information and research business Scholastica was unequalled in the whole family as we know that concept in Africa, making it no surprise that in Momany's Dissertation "A special word of thanks [also went] to my lovely and understanding wife, Scholastica, who not only encouraged me to go for it, but has also had to selflessly put up with the agony that flows from being separated from her husband from September 1995 to April 1999. Schola, you are simply the best. Thank you for making it all happen." As you have seen above, several non-family members gave "feeds." Scholastica's contribution to the enterprise is just so enormous but can be summarized and accentuated by her other letter of September 25, 1997 that is also very long but also graphical on the issues of this part of the book and other sections. She wrote:

Power! I got my birthday message immediately when I came back from the village as I told you when you called.

Presently, I am writing from Douala. I shall be going back tomorrow. One of my friends is getting married on Saturday and I shall attend the marriage.

My trip to the village was nice as I mentioned on the 22nd. I came back before the day I planned because I had to re-sit some courses. I wrote two of them and may still have problems because I didn't pass the continuous assessment well last semester. They are going to consider the continuous assessment. I may still fail because of that. I shall be very serious this academic year since there will be nothing to disturb me as last time.

I thought I shall change my room as I explained to you but things may not be possible. Elias has his own problems. I have not yet discussed with him but he is complaining a lot. He even asked me last night what you did say when you called me. I told him that you were only asking how my trip to the village was. He once told me that you promised to send some money to him. Anyway, I can't tell why he was very anxious to know what you said.

I have my fees with me but my problem is that house; the toilet is terrible now. I even feel ashamed when my friends come to my room. They always complain of our compound smelling and not only that. I don't also feel very free in that compound. We have told our caretaker to arrange so that they can come and drain the toilet but he keeps promising us. The difference with self-contained rooms is not also great. Most of them are between 12000 and 15000 francs but there are some for 10,000 francs. It is only that those for 10,000 francs are very scarce since students are always scrambling for them. I was following up one because I thought I shall have money by October but now if Elias [Akendung in Photo #24] is not able to help me, I shall give up and wait till November as you promised me. The only fear is that by November I may not see one for 10000 francs. God who has been helping us shall take care of everything.

Power, thank you very much for the travellers' cheques you sent to me. I saw the cheques, papa. I am very grateful. I went to the village for the first time as someone a bit responsible. I mean that I was able to buy a few things and take along. I am poor now but don't care because I used the money you gave me well.

You told me of your computer which got bad. It is very necessary because if you don't have it you can't do your work well. It is thus better that you buy it and I remain in that room till when you have money if Elias cannot solve my problem. At times I sit down and cry when I imagine how you are surviving that way on nothing. People in Cameroon do not know that, they think that it is like in Europe. Most people keep asking if you can send a vehicle to Cameroon. You know I must always cover you. I used to tell them that your programme is very expensive and you spend more than 7 million francs CFA on your fees alone, not forgetting of the yearly cost of living.

Every day I keep praying that God should help us to have a good start so that those people who always minimize us will be shocked. I am very optimistic about that. We shall one day be fine, we are struggling for that and God will help us one day.

Mamie (your mother) said it is not all that necessary for her to come and stay with me. She wrote a letter to you and explained it inside. I told her that in December I shall go to the village and collect her so that we go and spend Christmas together in Menji. My only obstacle can be money but it is very necessary because there is a certain celebration in Papa Khumbah's (Edith's) compound and they have invited me. You know Edith is so close to me and I can't miss such things. She really insisted and all her sisters and brothers in the USA are going to be in Cameroon.

A family meeting shall also be in the village for us. It is on my mother's side. They really pleaded that we shall struggle and come because many things will be discussed there. It is going to take place on the 21st of December. You should inform Quinta for me.

Tell Quinta Asaah that her grandmother (paternal) died two weeks ago. I doubt if she has heard it already. I shall write to her later. I have not even written to her mother. I hear her father is still in the village. Tell her to try that number and call me. I shall ask you to inform her immediately if I should change my room.

Power here are the birth certificates you asked me to send. I have also sent that American DV 98 Program. Let's be serious about it because God may help us this time. The address should either be care of you or Romanus because we don't know when the results will be out.

It would be nice for you to register the Canadian Nationality program as you told me but the problem now is how to get money, it is very expensive. Your staying in Canada while writing your thesis is better but now that there is no job for you I doubt how you shall survive. I shall put that in special prayers. If I am chanced to photocopy my crucifix prayers, I shall send one to you. It is very nice. It is very good for protection. I shall also send a spare copy of that

DV Programme signed, so that in case of any mistake, you fill and send for me.

Please, send this letter to the Whistance-Smith family for me. You can read the letter before sending it.

Power, I am sure I explained the idea of the plot to you. As I said, I told Fonenge that it was conditional because we are still students. I was so interested like that because of the site and also because of your mother. I am not praying that she should die but it can be a possibility. I said the plot was to be 230,000 francs though I was still bidding the price. Please, Power, don't be angry with me if you don't buy the idea. It is only a suggestion. In case you are viable, by December when I shall be going to the village, I shall go and tell the man when we can start paying the money.

Accept greetings from my junior ones, and almost everybody in the village.

Your wife, Acha.

P/S: Please, Power it is necessary to send a thank you card to Claude. He has really been helping me because last time he was saying you could help him and buy a tape recorder for him. I forgot to tell you. Even if you are not viable, it is nice to tell him that it would be difficult to send it. But if you are viable, it would be nice. He is very kind to us. My father has also written to you. The CUSS results are out and Eugene did not succeed. Are you the one who made correspondences for Edith in Belgium?

Scholastica's question tells you that Momany was not just relying on people while there but also was very dependable even to those he never personally knew. One of these messages that support the thesis was sent on October 5, 1999 by Fozao Dennis Shungse (at the time at National Advanced School of Public Works Annex in Buea) who told 'Dear' Momany that:

It is with pleasure I am writing to you these few words of greetings. I hope you are doing fine.

I will start by apologizing for not writing to you to acknowledge receipt of the application forms you sent to me. It was due to much work. Mrs. Scholastica, your wife, must have told you how occupied I am always here. I was very grateful for the assistance. I will send the forms any time from now. I am still working on my research topic; that is why I have not been able to send the forms.

Actually, we have never met before but your names were not strange to me when your wife mentioned them to me. I grew up with your senior brother [actually uncle], sub chief Fonenge, who used to be called Mr. Fossungu Vincent, father to Mr Fossungu Godfred. I spent three years with him when I was still in primary school.

When will you complete your PhD program? I hope things are moving successfully.

Extend greetings to your wife and friends.

Yours sincerely, Fozao Dennis Shungse. Signed [this paragraph altered].

Unemployed Qualified Entomologists in an Agricultural Nation!

If Fozao failed to follow up, it was not the case with most of the others. Notable among such cases is that of a Yaounde-based professional/student which exposes the enormous cases of well qualified entomologists remaining unemployed in an agricultural nation. This case is that of Barthelemy Dongmo Jiomeneck (Photo #30) who you have seen hotly competing with Scholastica in the domain of blending love, family and academics. What strikes me a lot with Barthelemy is what you yourself will be left to capture, 'choping Christmas with your own eyes' that is. A packet of newspaper articles came in for Momany with a letter dated October 15, 1998 in which Barthelemy, after greeting "My dear Peter" with "Good day!," told him to

Accept regards from the entire family. I am certain you are ready for your Ph.D. defence which should be coming up soon. May the grace of God be with you now and during your defence.

I am still in *Chomecam* but have learnt to support the situation. It is, however, quite difficult, more so when I find myself every time requesting for aid from dad. At times we disagree.

Well, I thought of finding out if you got my last letters and the outcome. Also you will be happy I am sure to get more of your newspaper articles. Here they are: [a listing of them]. So far these are the ones I have got. I will keep tract as the papers roll out of the printing press for more of your articles.

The people from Singapore (i.e. NUS) sent me a complete application kit for scholarship and admissions. I have so far filled and returned them to them. There has been no feedback from Greece. If you could again contact them I would be grateful. Neither also have I got response from the World Bank. I am keeping my fingers crossed and hoping God will see me through my sufferings.

Jeannette has been transferred to Ngaoundéré and we don't have contact for now. If you, however, write to SATOM, B.P 228, Douala, she will get the letter. May God guide you ever. Sincerely, DONGMO JIOMENECK BARTHELEMY [this paragraph altered].

Against this background to a background, therefore, you would better appreciate Momany's initial inquiries as to what was happening in Barthelemy's regard and even more so the former's re-response to the latter's response, both of which are coming but in the next few minutes, since an even better understanding comes, *en plus*, when you first have knowledge of his academic or professional background – an entomologist! I am gleaning this helpful information from "a copy of the letter I have sent to Prof. Stewart" that Barthelemy attached to the letter he sent to Momany, dated August 24, 1998. This 5-paragraph letter tells "My dear Peter" that:

Top of the day to you! It has really been great to receive the numerous letters and application forms you have sent to me. Not only I myself have been extremely happy, but the entire family for all what you are doing. May God bless your endeavours and that you defend your thesis with much success. That said, do accept all the regards of the family without distinction.

I am sending back to you the completed application forms for McGill which I plead you help me deposit. Also enclosed is a copy of a letter I have written to Prof. Stewart that I want you to know about. Dear brother, suffice to mention that at this present moment papa and mama are in the village only to come back in the first week of September, the reason why I have not included the $60.00 application fee. I beg that you exercise your spirit of good brotherliness I have always known to pay for me. I could neither reach Jane in Douala which I am sure would have been of help.

Do endeavour to reply soon so as to let me know my fate. On the front page of this application form there is a caption 'fellowships' under Financial Aid. Please try and send me information as well as application forms relative to that so that I may apply.

Suffice to mention here that the letter containing research you want me to do on your behalf with the HERALD and the Focus have not yet reached me. If I do receive them I will not hesitate to do so and send them to you. However, when replying to this letter, still include the said information, that is, what I am to sort out for you from these pages so that I may do so. Lest I forget, Dad's card you mentioned has also not yet arrived.

Well brother, so far it will also be good news that Simon has just passed his O' Levels in four subjects. The general results were catastrophic so we had to be glad that at least he passed. Didier has been at ASTI since November 1997 and presently is in Yaoundé for a *stage* [training] with National Assembly.

Accept once more our sincere regards and may God bless your endeavours ever. Help me with my application fees.

Yours faithfully, Barthé

NB: I have enclosed the following: 2 reference letters and 2 transcripts (post graduate & undergraduate). The only thing lacking is the $60 application fee. God bless you.

How would any right-thinking and progress-loving person not dive to the assistance of people like this? But here is what relates to the letter of the same date addressed to the professor of the Department of Natural Resource Sciences of the Macdolnald Campus of McGill University. Barthelemy indicated to Momany that he had been advised to write that letter by "Dr. Mrs. Arogi who studied for her PhD in Canada," and therefore requesting for Momany to "get me application forms and other information from McGill relative to that. I have been to the Japanese embassy and got forms but they are not encouraging. I am going to the Greek today." With subject being "Re: PhD Supervision," the Entomologist's letter to "My Dear Prof. Stewart" stated:

I have applied for PhD admission into your department and your area of specialization is of particular interest to me.

I am a Cameroonian and holder of an M.Sc. in Agricultural Entomology with reference to host-plant resistance. I wish to continue for a PhD in Entomology with continuous focus on host-plant resistance.

I would be grateful if you will consider me as your PhD student, the reason why I am sending this letter to you. I will be glad if you assist me in developing a research project in a subject that will be of mutual benefit. I will be ready to work on any research project you are involved in.

If there is any additional information you may require from me regarding this matter, do not hesitate to contact me.

Yours sincerely,

Dongmo Jiomeneck Barthelemy.

Oh how Africa wastes its talents! An agricultural nation like Cameroon for that matter! Wouldn't the West just be so happy that they no longer have to come and drag us along in ships by themselves? Is this the idea behind 'voluntary slavery' that is now called 'brain drain'? Stephen Fomeche made this point exceedingly clearly in the 4th paragraph of his letter of March 4, 1997: "You were equally interested to know what I intend to study in Malta or elsewhere. You know I did English (language and literature) and specialized in English. Besides, I studied in the School of Education (E.N.S.) and did secondary Education as minor. So I will like to pursue postgraduate course in Education (Master's or PhD) or in Commonwealth Literature (or any branch of studies in English). The essential thing is to have the means of leaving this country before it is too late. I'm sure one can just hear afterwards that this and that has happened." Leaving the hotly unpleasant hole is what everyone wants to do, including our entomologists who should be aiding us toward food-self-sufficiency, as the sing-song goes. But the Wonders of Home increase when we would bring in so-called experts from non-tropical lands to do the job? Do they even do the job commensurate to/with their overweight pay cheques? Is home actually home to *Homers* here? Who wants to gladly call a cobwebbing trancing Limbo home?

Living in a Cobwebbing Trancing Limbo

Florencemartinization of Postal Service: The beginning of this second section has to do with Florence Martin who many *Ngoa-Ékelleans* mistook for Momany's girlfriend (sexually) in the Yaoundé University, especially after the Joan fiasco. Joan was Momany's lover who surprisingly left him for another guy who had just passed into ENAM (the National School of Administration and Magistracy) to become one of those officials giving headaches to people like Solomon.[26] But Florence was not another Joan or her replacement. That rushing mentality is itself a major issue to the issues of this book. A lot of people just cannot come to think of a male-female friendship without the *mbombo-mblacaus* idea being the end. Jane would not agree with that and, if permission is accorded, we would shift gears a bit to the neutral position and give room for Jane's little input before entering the drive position again with Florence. Momany hates silence even as he often falls into it as well (just natural, eh?). Feeling like he was not getting the feeling anymore from the other half of him across the miles, on Sunday, November 9, 2014 the Love-Poet wrote to Jane asking "My Dear Jane: Why can't I just simply forget about you as you seem to have done about me? I am sure you are having a real good time there in France. That just makes my day too, knowing. PAF." Jane's reply came in the next day, on November 10, 2014 at 3.54 PM, telling him: "Hey there my Dear Peter, Never will I stop loving you. But Life has its mysterious ways. I do hope that you are happy and that we can make with what we are today. I have had my bumps along the drive way like you too. It is not just easy cruising all the time but as usual there are days with and days without. OUT OF SIGHT BUT NOT OUT OF MIND... What about that for our next movie? Big hugs and kisses. Yours Jane." Can people like this ever do the *dragdowning* thing even for a second?

---

[26] In the 5th paragraph of his letter of February 2, 1998 Solomon Tatah recounted to Momany his ordeal with the other rogues at the Douala Port called custom officers, stating that "As for your man, last year was quite a rough one for me financially and even up to now. It all started after my return from Holland in July. Two weeks after I returned, my television set and video deck were stolen by thieves who broke into my house while we slept peacefully. After this, my car which was supposed to be shipped in early July was eventually delayed until August and it only arrived in Douala in September. By this time, the little money I had brought to help me pay the custom duty was already consumed by family obligations. I therefore had to borrow at an interest rate per month to get the car out of the port. With the meagre salaries we earn, you can imagine how long it will take me to repay the loan. At the same time I cannot afford a TV for my house. This keeps the children on my nerves every day. And this is not all. Due to the delay in taking my car out of the port, most of my personal effects were stolen. In fact, your man has never had it as rough as what I'm going through now."

As you can see from her answer, love and friendship are not all about sex as most of those Yaoundé students were thinking in regard of Florence. Out of sight but not out of mind. Sex-driven friendship would have it as 'out of sex (sight), out of mind.' *Odilikinology* and others will confirm that soon. But not before Florence drives us there. Her letter (which would not even have been coming, if she is in the 'out of sex' category) was dated September 25, 1996 and told Momany that:

You must be wondering whether we got your letter to us. It did arrive here after two months. It was really wonderful reading from you. We are really happy for you. I'm sure you made up your mind for the better, for the situation in Cameroon has not changed.

How is life with you there? Has your wife joined you? If so, extend our best wishes to her. We are very fine. I'm still jobless. I'm trying to do a few things on my own. I am hoping that by next year I'll pick up a job anywhere.

The kids are fine. There are three of them now. I had a girl last year. Now I can go job hunting and forget about having more babies.

Peter, you know I have never been too ambitious. I did not expect things to get this bad. If I knew, I should have gone to Nigeria for a master's program. Now things are so difficult and with kids around, it's not easy to leave them and go back to school. I just don't know what else to do. I keep praying that God will show me the way someday.

My sister from Nigeria has also graduated and, of course, is jobless. In fact, she is trying to get a scholarship to study abroad. I don't know if you can give me some information for a master's program in fields like: WILDLIFE MANAGEMENT; NATURAL RESOURCE CONSERVATION; and ENVIRONMENTAL MANAGEMENT. She has already applied to a few schools in Canada and they sent her some information. Please just try and get some information on that for me.

I will be hoping to read from you very soon. My phone number is XX XX XX. This is the home number. At any time you can call there will be somebody at home to answer if I am not there. I will be glad to talk to you people. I would have called from Abdou's office but their phone has a problem. So we cannot even "steal" and make a call at night. I will be very happy if you can call at home.

I'll give your phone number to a family friend of ours who is attending a conference there, so that he can chat with you. His name is Dr Maurice YEWAH, lecturer in University of Yaoundé. He is Abdou's boss.

Accept greetings from everybody at home. Take care of yourself.
Sincerely, Florence Martin.

A little question to ask is: Do we actually have a 'Posts and Telecommunication' or 'Picking and *Thiefing*' (like their comrades of the Douala Port) that letters take that long to get to destination? The question is not trivial because experience has shown that we sometimes just accuse the system for no good reason other than as a means to hide our personal deficiency. Stephen Fomeche, again, provides a hint in the first paragraph of his Letter of March 4, 1997 by *frantalkistly* making known that: "Dear Power, Happy New Year in arrears! I hope there is everything of great wish as desired and health is equally okay. Back here we are just sound now. I am sorry to have stayed for long without writing, and the least I can say is that I have been very busy over nothing – vain pursuit of shadows." The *Maylatelization* letter in the last chapter praising Scholastica's triumphant arrival to Canada shows that the letter from Canada reached her in Bamenda within 25 (twenty-five) days of its writing. Also, check Ngi-Nyam's from Boston, USA, which took about thirty-five days to get to him in the village. All these are then followed at the heels by Solomon Tatah's first paragraph of his own letter of November 2, 1995 that shows letters from Montreal to the same Yaoundé destination (where Florence is based) arriving within two weeks. "Dear Peter, I got yours of October 19th 1995 on the 30th. Thank God I got the evidence we've been waiting for of your safe arrival in Quebec, even if it means perching in someone's wing for 10 months, no problem. The most important issue has been settled: your reaching there safely and in time to catch up with your program of study. I hope you did so and everything academic is just going on smoothly now."

But that would not in any way be implying that Florence (like Anthony to be seen shortly) was lying because Eugene Lekeawung Asahchop also expressed the same surprise at the postal issue in his letter of December 23, 1998 to Momany. His letter also touches on very sensitive issues of the country's educational institutions, professional changes and other calculations consequent on the *Quagmatickism*'s trancing-limbo-home. Let us thus listen to Eugene who narrates as follows:

Dear brother: How is health and conditions of living in Canada at the moment? I hope everything is moving smoothly. How about your PhD program? Are you through or you are still to? If not, I hope very soon you will be through.

I saw your last letter, but it took a lot of time on the way. I had it in November. You can imagine how long it took for me to see it. However the content of your letter was understood. I was very happy because your letter to me implies you have me in mind. Unfortunately, the visa program for your wife (my sister) was again impossible. However, her graduation was successful.

As concern my own program of studies, I have changed both my department and faculty. The new faculty in U of B started last two years. Admission into the faculty is through a competitive entrance which the candidate must pass. The faculty is made up of two departments: Medical Laboratory Science, and Nursing. Students graduating in the departments have a B.Sc. in the above mentioned departments. The program for studies here is four years.

My own department is Medical Laboratory Science (MLS). I made the decision to change the faculty and department because already it is a profession on its own. The program is for four years and I started from the first year. After these four years, if it is impossible for me to continue studies, I can occupy myself in a private clinic. The only problem students are facing in this faculty is that of textbooks, because the school hasn't got books for students to borrow and read.

Thanks. Eugene Signed.

The Anthonization of Love and Unfriendly Friendliness

If there are doubts that could be validly cast about the postal services, none appears to be able to defend itself about Anthony's lovers' reunion obstructing comportment. As noted above, the concept of *Barthélization* derives its definition from the Momany-Barthelemy exchanges generally but particularly a letter that Momany sent to Jane's brother on Sunday, October 9, 2005 at 5.47 PM. titled

"Are You There?" But, before we get to discovering if Barthelemy is still there (as he has always been since his sister first introduced Momany to them), it is important that we first read again the translation of his father's famous letter in chapter 3 that greatly helps us in chapter 4 in getting into the heads and logic of *moneyintriguists*. Barthelemy himself would completely concord with the ex-loves reunion thesis while also sustaining his own father's *"reconnaissant en vers ma famille"* theory and, above all, the other central issue of reconnection (or reconciliation) with *ex-lovers* through understanding family members. As said and emphasized later, there is truly what is called love in this Jiomeneck family. I mean people who understand that life is not to be based on intrigues and scheming but on the larger picture of things, requiring reciprocal give and take.

In his letter of August 27, 1998 Barthelemy Dongmo Jiomeneck wished "My dear Peter, Good day!" and continued to inform him that:

Just as I had returned home after posting the application forms to you, someone from IRAD came in with two more letters from Montreal; one destined for me and the other containing papa's card. Thank you on his behalf as I am sure he will be very glad when he returns from the village.

The next day I didn't waste any time in pursuing my search for your articles as prescribed in your letter. The university of Yaoundé and related higher institutions are a mess for one should never hope to get such information from them. I did however get something for you from the Herald. Here enclosed is a compilation of your articles from September 1997 till date, including the most recent you will have pleasure in reading. I will keep track of your articles in order to send to you further copies when they are published.

The editor-in-chief, Dr. Forbin, stressed to me that I should let you know that, henceforth, letters concerning your articles should be addressed to the editor for they/he will no longer allow anybody to do research on your behalf. He said it was out of goodwill that he was allowing me search for your articles. I am nevertheless certain that you will be quite comfortable with these listed.

May I also still plead here that you help me pay $60 for application fees into McGill and also get me application forms for scholarships. Suffice to state here that I have been to the Greek embassy in Yaoundé and the lady there claimed ignorance of the State Scholarship Foundation. She told me no forms were available but I have written directly to the authorities in Athens. I hope they will reply.

Jeannette wrote to me stating that you called her and that she was very happy. She says she has been posted to Ngoundéré – Bellel where they have a project to undertake for the pipeline. If you wish to write you can post it through SATOM, B.P. 228 Douala. She told me in her letter that she had written to you. I hope you have got it. Well, Pierre, permit me to stop here as I promise to write and send to you more of your articles when they are published.

May God bless you. Barthé

To repeat and emphasized, the Jiomenecks are clearly a family whose members understand what love is all about; that life should be defined by give-and-take, not take and take and take; that nosing around and scheming should not become a way of life. In short, that *frantalkism* is what should be the rule. In view of all this, Momany must surely have cried himself to death at one point for thinking that he might have overreacted in the *Douala-Tripping Affair* that caused the breach between Jane and him. As well as the 1991 send-off palaver, when Jane failed to show up most probably because of the fear of her "senior college" students that were to be present, whereas Momany wanted to make the big marriage announcement then. I say all this because you will find families of the other ladies not only working against the love between their daughter/sister and Momany; they would also actively prevent his ever getting into contact with said separated lovers. But you quickly notice a slight change in attitude as soon as they think they can reap where they never sowed. This scenario is well exemplified by no other case than that of Anna Ngomateka Bilong (Photo #34) – Momany's very first wife-to-be. You will certainly not be hearing a lot of analyses about Anna but suffice to note that, as far as the issues of this book would go, she imposingly stands as a measuring rod to all the other ladies being discussed.

The fatal forced separation from her took place in 1983 and Momany left Cameroon to Canada for the first time in 1991. It is futile to try enumerating the countless times the man had tried between those dates to get an idea from Anna's senior brother how to re-establish even 'blind' contact (let alone see her). It was all in vain. 'Let alone see her' is explained in the sense that Momany would even write no-address notes, put in unsealed envelopes and request that they be handed to Anna by his brother. All that because he well understood what it meant for the poor girl's state of mind just knowing that Momany has never stopped loving her in spite of all what happened. You have just heard from her own brother how Jane would be doing everything to reconnect and how happy she was just because of Momany's calls. That is the proof of real love that even needs no proving, as Jane herself has said.[27] That was just all that Momany also wanted for Anna, another virgin of his. But the brother, who was also very instrumental in the forced marriage, took that to be like Momany wanted to get Anna out of the bondage they had put her into (anything even wrong with that?). And he was somewhat right because, even with all the intrigues and force employed, I think all what Anna needed to better free herself, was the mere knowledge that his first love was still there for her. I say this because Momany was in Cameroon last December (2015) and realized that Anna was no longer in the man's house and was staying on her own. As Anna put it herself, she has been reborn after having died for thirty-something years. All that happened because of the May 2014 historic face-to-face meeting with the love of her life.

As previously stated, some of these people only have a lukewarm alteration of positions with the idea of taken advantage in mind. Otherwise, it is very hard to elucidate Anthony's attitude when Momany is out of the country. Note that this is the only time he will really entertain any vague talking about Anna to Momany. Even out of the country for the second time, Momany never stopped trying to reconnect as well as never carrying any grudges around with him for Anna's brother (or any other family members), always staying in touch with him as a friend as even Anthony's own letters to Momany

---

[27] In her "Re: HAPPY NEW YEAR 2016" of January 7, 2016 at 6.47 AM Jane wrote: "Dear Peter, As you know, we understand each other so well that words don't need speaking. I am okay so long as you are okay too and I do sincerely hope so, dear. It is difficult to catch Barthé as he is based in Nigeria for work and comes home every 3 months for 2 weeks and runs around as much. My parents' contact: Dad is XXXXXXXXX and Mum is XXXXXXXXX. Just hoping you are having a great time in Cameroun!! Lots of love. Xoxo. Yours Jane."

(now in Canada) can show. Take first the one he wrote on October 31, 1997 in reply to Momany's first letter to him from abroad:

DEAR PETER,

I received your letter on October 29-1997 in good health like other members of the family. I was happy to receive it though late as you have rightly mentioned.

I knew, however, that your doctorate program was the cause of the delay. From your letter, I have been made to learn that you have little or no time to spend on leisure. Please, just have courage because it will soon be over.

Back home, everybody is fine except my Dad who is sick in the heart. Anna is with her husband in Douala where they share the joy of living in a family of five children (four boys and a girl). She still looks young and agile. Cecilia, her daughter (Mary-Bernadette), Joseph (my junior brother) and I myself are in Yoke.

In order to keep body and soul together, I am now operating a small matango bar attached to a small provision store. I have tried, in vain, to get a job here, you know? I have enclosed in this envelope a photocopy of my birth and Ordinary level certificates and Advanced level certified slip. As regard my future profession, it has long been my wish to be a pharmacist, a wish I still very much desire.

So long, I have not heard from Sabum. I do not really know where exactly he is stationed. It is worth mentioning here that Sabum lost his maternal mother and later his step-mother (Mamie Ndedi).

I have extended your greeting to many old friends who received it with much delight (Foncha, Godwin Ndango) to name a few. I also spoke to your father about your letter, and how busy you are in pursuing your course. He was very anxious and hoped it will soon come to an end. He asked me to greet you just like my dad and all the members of the family.

Hello Pierre, it was only after reading the note below that I realized your machine was running out of ink. I read through the letter with no problem. In addition, I very much admired the printing, the texture of the paper and envelope.

For now, my address remains C/O Catholic Mission Muyuka on which I rely. Do not forget to extend my greetings to all your friends.

While waiting for your letter, I remain yours sincere BILONG MBABE ANTHONY.

As you have noticed and will continue to do so, Momany has been able to reconnect with Jane not on account of *always* asking. Most of the times, her brother has furnished the information on his own volition or because Jane herself has been asking him about the man. What is not understood is why some other brothers (or sisters) would be so interested in ruining their sibling's life by preventing them from being happy through being with the person they love. I come back here to Anna's case, for that is a classic in this matter and one that puzzles a lot. Momany was in Cameroon in July 2014 for the burial and funeral of his mother. The programme had, of course, circulated and having a lot of family members in Yoke, Anna's brother (Anthony in Photo #35) was current with it. He is even the one who informed his sister about it. So, Momany was not only surprised to see Anna at the mortuary but also that she came prepared to accompany the man and corpse right up to the village. But that is not any matter of amazement even, because it is not something strange with Anna.[28]

What beats the mind relates to how Anthony was so confused by the way the love between Anna and her lover has not changed one bit. Again, he was taken aback realizing that, despite all the efforts at protecting the separation, the meeting at the mortuary which he was assuming to be the first in thirty years was actually not. What he just did not know was that in May same year Momany had been there and that was the first time ever he met Anna in person after all those years. It was a historic reunion. What any right-thinking person (in view of all the talk in his letters until then) would be expecting from Anthony at that unique mortuary meeting of all three of them, was a heartfelt apology to both lovers (or at least to the sister) and *frantalkism* thereafter. That was not what a perpetual schemer would ever be able to do at all; always searching instead more ways to

---

[28] Because "As usual, Anna was more than a 100% in the combat as she told me: 'Piero, with you and me together, nothing can stop us. I know it is not going to be easy when you are out there alone; but I also know you know I am always there with you. And this knowledge by itself is both our shield and sword for the victory.' What better wife than this would any man ask for?" (Fossungu, 2013c: 74).

advance plots to obtain what lies behind the head. Not then even realizing that with this face-to-face meeting of both lovers the truth of his machinations was to be openly known.

I have just talked of all attempts at protecting and prolonging separation and it is important to throw light on it. And that can be easily done using Anthony's other letter in which he would be claiming having passed on Anna's letters and how she has been the one delaying in having her reply reach him (Anthony). In person, Anna was completely surprised and extremely angry that she never got said letters. How just reading anything, no matter the length, from Momany would have done so much inestimable good to her! Listen to the brother's mail of December 29, 1998 to "Dear Peter":

Your reply to my last letter reached me intact. I am sorry for the delay of this reply. Really, I wanted to post Anna's reply with this at once. So far Anna was happy to receive your letter. She is always very busy and has not been able to write though she promised to.

Back here (Yoke) so many people you may know are now of blessed memory. My junior sister (Cecilia) died on 24-12-97. Certainly, you must have heard of the death of one of your cousins (Valentine). At home, there is no strange news, except that I have got a baby girl with a girl of your tribe. The baby's name is Ngombabi Sylvie.

Mondialman Matango bar, as it is popularly known, is the life cable behind all my financial achievement. I work hard with the little means at my disposal to update the bar, nevertheless, much still remains to be done. So far, I have attached to the bar a small provision store.

My dear friend, Pierre, I have you in my mind every day, every night, in all my prayers. Distance has never separated us; you have always contacted me even when you are so far away. My GOOD FRIEND, MAY THE ALMIGHTY GOD BLESS ALL YOUR UNDERTAKINGS.

I am your friend,

Bilong Mbabe Anthony. Signed. Any suggestions are welcomed. Bye.

An essential point to note here is that Anna is not a kid and would not really need to rely on Anthony to post a letter to Momany when (this time) there is an address to which the letter has to be sent. As you will see shortly, Elizabeth never asked Pat to post hers for her; Pat instead insisted on doing so for her, with Pat's insistence on doing so being right too, because she was not about to play stupid. You will better understand it when you have the whole story. From the day Francophone Elizabeth fell in love with Momany, she instantly became Anglophone; having this unrivalled pull for anything or anyone English-speaking. As you will see and have seen already, she writes most of the time in English. It is her Anglophone-pull that is responsible for her reunion with Momany. Pat (Odilia's sister) was at the hospital in Douala where Liza works. Just hearing Pat talking in English played the game on her as she quickly approached Pat and began asking if Pat might know a certain Anglophone, giving Momany's full name. BINGO! Wasn't she just as lucky? Because Momany has never also lost contact with Odilia's family, Liza was cut in the *cobwebbing* UB-timetable, as Pat had every detail regarding Momany's contact and it was current to the minute. Asked to give it to her, Pat instead suggested that Elizabeth could write her message and hand over for her (Pat) then to send to Momany in her own letter, which is exactly what both of them did. When Momany got Pat's letter and the enclosed note from Liza, he then called Liza! Now, would you say Pat's action validates Anthony's? The latter's manner of handling the issue just makes no sense, except in making sense in the sense that he is a liar.

What the point is here concerns the sincerity of Anna's brother's behaviour. Just go through this other letter from someone claiming things that are all showing a completely different face. I am referring to Anthony's letter of February 26, 2003 which talks of Momany being already a member of the family and brother and the like. Do note that it was written after Momany's trip there in 2002 to bury his father, a man who would still be alive today but for the 1983 conspiracy against Momany's *in-lawship* to which Anthony was an active party. His letter stated:

Dear Dr. Nkemtale'eh P.A. Fossungu, I received your letter on the 26-02-03 and we were very glad to hear that you arrived safely. In fact, we have been anxious to know if you had arrived safely. We were also happy to know that you met your family in sound health condition. THANKS BE TO GOD.

Thank you for appreciating me as a result of the little progress I have struggled to achieve so far in life. Really, I am ready to work even harder because it remains the only way out if my family and I have to survive. I know how much concern you have about my wellbeing. What else should one expect from a good friend? For my part, I will continue to do my best to keep the flame alight.

The entire family was delighted when we saw the enclosed photograph. You should know that, this family already considers you a member. In fact, if wishes were horses, the reception would have been far better notwithstanding your tight schedule. We are now engaged in preparation for papa's *cry die* [funeral] ceremony which will take place on March 29-2003. Ndango Christian was in town and promised to come down during the occasion. He was happy to hear from you. I regret your absence. However, we shall have time for everything when next you come.

Extend our warmest greetings to your family and friends over there.

From your Friend/brother. Bilong M. Anthony. Signed.

This is very different from the Jiomeneck scenario where, having lost contact for a while due to the *Asahchopinationist* family issues you already know of, Momany had to find a way to re-establish through the famous "Are You There?" email above that began this *Anthonization* discussion. In it Momany wrote: "Hello Barthelemy, I hope my several days of digging into the archives have not been for nothing. By which I mean that when I eventually click the Send button this message would not come back to me undelivered. Please, get back to me as soon as you read this. Peter." His reply to "Dear Peter" came in and made it known that it was "Nice to read from you after a very long spell. Hope you are doing fine for the moment. By the way, where are you and what are you doing? I am in Yaounde with family and they are all doing fine for the moment. I can be reached through: XXX.XX.XX Cheers, Barthelemy." There were obviously promising signs of progress and in "Re: Are You There?" of Sunday, October 16, 2005 at 2.39 PM Momany again wrote: "Hi Barthelemy, I am glad the e-mail contact address is still good. Really, it's been quite a long time and I am lucky that I don't usually destroy written materials. It has not been easy with me here for some time but I am alright now. I am still in Montreal, Canada, working as usual.

It is good to know that everyone at home is doing fine. Thanks for your phone number. I will only use it later since I don't have a calling card on me at moment. Are you doing anything at the moment? I mean with your academics? What about Jane? Peter."

Long-Distancing the Wonders of the Scholastica Question

You would better understand the last questions here from what is being said about the economic quagmire in Cameroon and the general hard life experiences there. In the 3rd paragraph of her well known June 26, 1996 letter to Momany, Odilia confirmed all what the previous speakers, including Florence and Stephen, have said: "Life in Cameroon is not the best. Things get worse every blessed day. I am sure somebody like you can always get a teaching job in one of the universities over there. It is needless coming back home so soon." Tell me for real if a person calling self your lover would be according you such advice if sex with you is actually all what he/she is interested in? Can you actually have long-distance sex that wouldn't abuse that concept, as Africans understand it? If so, then why would Richard Ngufor Fossungu (Photo #36), for instance, have been talking 'the nonsense' of *cold finishing* for Scholastica because of her having left the *Quagmaticking* hole called Cameroon to Canada? One is here talking about Richard Ngufor Fossungu's August 3, 1999 letter to Scholastica, which went like this:

Dear Schola, We were indeed happy to read from you despite the fact that you went without telling us. All the same, it is what we were all fighting for, so far as you succeeded the way and you're there thanks to god almighty. How joyful was Peter when he heard that you were in the U.S.? In fact he saw you as a dream. Well, all we need is a happy stay.

How do you find the climate there as compared to that of Buea where you were residing? I hope you are feeling extremely fine as you're besides him after a couple of years in cold; how far is he doing with his defence you told us about?

There's nothing strange in the village where everybody is well, except the sudden death of Nkengafac Elias Fonge through a bus accident travelling from Dschang to Bafoussam alongside his wife, but she had some bruises only. It was on the 6th of July. In my house, only Linda and his small brother, Nguajong Benson, who worry me with fever but at moment they are recovering.

Accept greetings from us to you and husband, not forgetting your well-wishers. Bye. Signed.

One would have expected that the "couple of years in cold" that had finished in Buea would greatly warm up Canada. But that seems to have been a big mistake because there appears to have been no cold in the first place. It is in the sense that Scholastica's sibling and parental bonding had never been displaced by the spousal one that usually generates that cold when the couple is separated. You could even read this too in Violet's statement above that would be talking of two sisters (Scholastica and Quinta) 'meeting in foreign land with no family members.' Momany has never been 'family' to her: as even her definition of 'family' excludes both spouse and children. The point is easily made with Stephen Fomeche's condemnation of the incessant and unbearable family separation due to academics. It is very important to a correct grasping of the Scholastica Question. Some people fall in love at first sight and it is for real. This book (just like the others before it) would be replete with cases: Queenta, Jane, Liza, Anna and Odilia. Others do not fall that quickly and may take a lot of time to actually love, even the person they are married to. Odilia has put this theory so well in chapter 5. Now, it is very obvious that Scholastica did not come into the union with such love (there was even no courting period as you have seen in chapter 1). But the potential to give her all in the love and marriage domain (like Anna) was not anything to be doubted about.

Quite apart from Violet's lectures in the last chapter that point in this direction, Ngi-Nyam's and Solomon's surprise at the turn of events in Canada would exemplify that so well as well. In "his [letter which] comes from a man hitherto forgotten – Ngi-Nyam; ESAMBE LOBWEDE, Lucas, the *Lion of Judah* and one of your close associates in Yaoundé," Ngi-Nyam's (Photo #37) interestingly sincere letter of April 18, 2006 which was type-written from his beautiful Elma House residence in Baseng (Tombel, Kupe-Maneguba Division of Debundschazone in Cameroon) stated in the 4th paragraph that the "next thing I would be interested in is how you are faring on with your wife and children, if any. In Solo's letter he mentioned that you and your wife and children live in different places which gave me a rude shock. However, if and when you do write, give me details of why you live apart. I may, as always, give advice as to how things could be resolved." Ngi-Nyam is very entitled to be shocked at the news of the Momany-Scholastica marriage breakdown just as Solomon himself understandably was,[29] if you merely consider what these same people did and witnessed in Yaoundé during the newly-wed couple's honeymoon. You could also pick up something relevant from some letters to Momany from those who know the couple well. The example is from no other than Stephen Fomeche (Photo #9), then teaching in Government Bilingual High School (GBHS) in Fontem, who, in the 6th paragraph of his letter of March 4, 1997 asked Momany "How far have you gone with your course? How much do you still have left? We pray for God's blessings especially in your efforts to get your wife across. Don't lose heart with the difficulties you faced last time, for overcoming them is POWER indeed. Accept the deepest love and prayers of Jacinta and Yeye."

The problem then could be that Scholastica never had that chance to build that potential love into her own marital relationship and home because of the separation, thus exposing in a unique way the Herculean difficulty of blending academics and love/family "at long-distance," making it more onerous than the Fomeches. In the second paragraph of his letter of January 7, 1999 Stephen again tells us that "Once again the family has to split. Jacinta got engaged with the Public Service and was posted to G.S.S. Buea Rural (some few kilometres inward from the Molyko stadium). She lives with the children at Molyko. I have once more resumed my bachelor life in Yaoundé. You can imagine me in the dense students' *quartier*. The beginning looked far-fetched and strange but after a year, I am already acclimatized. If all goes well, I would finish the course in August." Momany's understanding of Scholastica's trying situation could even be picked up from some passages in his own letters to colleagues back there in Cameroon that have been quoting back to him, such as is done by Solomon (above) and Stephen. In his

---

[29] In his "Re: How Was Your Trip Back Home?" Solomon pondered: "Power, I am really troubled by your reply to my last message. I never knew the matter with Schola is now a court case. What does she want? Take courage brother. You will weather the storm. Solo."

December 15, 1995 letter, Stephen Fomeche put it in the second paragraph thus:

We got details, fears and updates of your preparation, problems and courage towards your departure. Thank God all worked well and the surprise, whether pleasant or unpleasant to others, was to us received with great joy. For the short time we were together, we understood the importance and necessity of your return to Canada. From Schola's letter we received last month (shortly before yours) we understood that the good side of it notwithstanding is not without the feeling which we deeply share in the pleasure of being together. Do all in your power "to make the tedious less tedious for her," as stated in your letter, so that the obvious situation in which she finds herself will be sweet trouble. We will equally try to be in touch with her often.

The break from 'daddy's loyal daughter' to 'my husband's loyal partner' had simply not occurred by the time separation, due to academics, happened – both within Cameroon and across the Atlantic – explaining why that "loyal partner" bond just wasn't there when she landed in Canada. You can also read, for the support of the Long-Distance Theory, Scholastica's penchant for secretly dealing financially with Elias Akendung (sending him money) since she got to Canada, but never wanting to share in the debts with Momany who was actually shouldering everything financial in her regard. The 'within-Cameroon' split also had academics at the heart of it. They were separated almost immediately after their honeymoon in Yaoundé because her husband had enrolled her for studies toward obtaining her G.C.E. Advanced Level in a private school in Buea, whereas the matrimonial home was in Douala. (In some of her letters to the husband she reminiscences a lot about her Buea-G.C.E. preparation days 'when she lacked nothing and lived like a queen' compared to her later experiences of hard times in the Buea University that you read a lot of in the mails you have encountered and will be meeting further on.) As soon as she obtained that certificate, they were (like the Fomeches, internally) separating intercontinentally, still on academic grounds. But that is not all, because the 'out of sight' phenomenon provided the haven wherein her pre-marital 'father's loyal daughter' status got fortified. You can see then that Scholastica was married only in name as she was practically still daddy's daughter. Her father's claims of assisting Elias Akendung while her husband was away (seen in his letter in chapter 4) would only apply to the money transactions in Table 2 in chapter 1. Scholastica was not living with Elias and then only visiting the parents – the reverse instead being the rule. Why she could not have lived with Money's own parents during the 'academics' separation too only goes a long way to exposing the *moneyintriguism*, distrust and disunity that would exist in the Fossungu family that treats Momany (and other children) most of the time as an "outside" and some persons only to be exploited (see chapter 3 for more). Scholastica herself has clearly told you above how she didn't want to be going there often.

It may seem surprising; but it is the hard reality that Scholastica Achankeng Asahchop is a very sweet and loving person and is herself only a victim of the parents' *moneyintriguism*. And these parents easily succeeded in the enterprise because of the marital separation occurring at a time she had not even matured at all in acquiring the essential knowledge that, in the business of marriage, "the best principle of marriage is forgive and forget" (Peter Asahchop's letter of November 3, 2002 that is fully analysed in chapter 4). You evidently see this immaturity and confusion in Scholastica's communications too. The sibling and parental bonding had not been disturbed at all by the spousal one, which woefully failed (because of academic pursuits from both sides) to grow before the continental long separation. That could explain her attitude in relation to the debts and other provocation, including the abortion; because anything that appeared to stand between her and those persons she bonded so much with was just as good as dead. These surprising complications would be products of the hard reality of attempting to blend love, marriage and academics "at long-distance".

Newlyweds must then see the importance of consolidating the marriage before venturing into 'voluntary separation' for whatever reasons: if they dream of the Ngi-Nyam 'Golden Anniversary' type of marriage. In his letter of April 18, 2006 to Momany Ngi-Nyam stated in the 3rd paragraph that "Although you may have already had wind of our GOLDEN JUBILEE (50 YEARS) CELEBRATION here in Baseng on January 3, 2005, it is important for me to tell you about what happened. Yes, it was a fantastic show indeed, a celebration with pomp and pageantry ably organized by my married daughters under the leadership of my beloved son-in-law Solomon. It was a day we, as a couple, will never forget the rest of our life-time. The whole event was covered by cameras and video which will help rekindle the memory of what happened to future generations. Maybe someday you too will see these pictures and video." The man's son-in-law called Solomon Tatah must be a very good lecturer on this marriage-consolidation issue, judging from his part of the Solomon-Violet lectures on the Atlantic Crossing. Actions like Momany's (such as the much criticized trans-Atlantic crossing), taken solely because of the earnest desire to make things better for a whole lot of people, would present no problems though where the parents-in-law are like the Jiomenecks, one of whom shares the spotlight with Scholastica in the Montreal Project.

Notwithstanding the foregoing analysis, is it really worth putting Scholastica's show relating to this Canadian university project in the same basket with Barthelemy Dongmo Jiomeneck's? It is just as if Barthelemy had been employed and was working so hard like the G.C.E. Board workers; but very unlike them because the latter earned something in return: irregular, insufficient and brutalizing as it might be. That was not the case with Barthelemy Dongmo Jiomeneck (Photo #30). But he never for one moment complained about it, excitedly combing all the 'hooks and nooks' of Cameroon newspaper houses on a daily basis to obtain the latest issues and even back issues to send to Montreal, Canada. Tell me Scholastica did that too, and by express mail services a lot of the times. Yes indeed! I have noted that. You can then see why and how the reaction of Momany would be on hearing the Entomologist saying in his "Re: Are You There?" of October 25, 2005 at 3.42 AM to "Dear Peter" that it is "Nice to read from you again. I have been home since 2000 and was lucky just at my return to get a job with SATOM for the pipeline project. Since then I have been with the company. Presently I am working in Yaoundé along the Yaoundé-Soa road which we are constructing. Activities are scheduled to last for 2 years. Family wise all is OK. Jane is in France with the husband. They have two daughters for now. She will be at home sometime in January next year with her family. Things always are not easy but we have to keep fighting. Will get back to you. Cheers, Barthelemy."

A square peck in a round hole indeed! But at least he is out of *Chomecam*! Thus, in his 'Good News' email of Tuesday, October 25, 2005 at 5.21 PM, Momany wrote to "Dear Barthelemy," telling him how:

I am really happy to know that you're no longer in the trying *chomecam* situation. Just hold on well to what you have (while still looking around for something better, perhaps). I am also glad about the news regarding the rest of the family – a family that I hold very dearly to heart. I only wish I had long become part of this nice family (as I had sincerely hoped to, from the very first moment I was introduced to the household by your senior sister). Nevertheless I am still doubly contented that Jane is happily married and now a mum to two beautiful girls. Extend my greetings to her and family when they get there. Also do specially greet your mum and dad for me. In short, say hello to everyone: Rosa, Didier, ...(one or two names is/are escaping as I try to type it/them).

I am not sure if you're settled now or are still interested in overseas adventures.

Take care. Peter

In fact, Cameroon is Cameroon, as the regime prides itself by often saying to the suffering people as some sort of consolation. You would better comprehend why some Cameroon-loving academicians even had to join the exodus when beautiful and intelligent Odilia finishes her theory. Odilia went on in her mail to exemplify her thesis on the Cameroon disturbingly declining atmosphere with "A place like the G.C.E. Board" which many people had considered to be a "heaven" and which is gradually collapsing; how its workers have not received their salaries for a couple of months and "it seems more problems are ahead." The paradox of the situation, according to Odilia, being that the Board's workers put in so much, working their asses to death "for the past three months" and "working for at least 15 hours a day and it seems it is not being appreciated." What makes the case pathetic relates to the rudeness of the bosses who are well known for treating the workers "like school children. You know [that] nearly all of them were teachers. They work as if they are in the classroom with their students." Let in a real confused student for them to shout at then.

Talking about student treatment in Cameroon brings to mind "the so-called UB [University of Buea] authorities, who are champions in fighting for their stomachs rather tha[n] the welfare of the leaders of tomorrow" (Nyamnjoh, Gram & Konings, 2012: 203). For the one academic year spent there, Momany never succeeded in being able to see Vice-Chancellor Dorothy Njeuma. To see the woman was even more problematic than seeing the Etoudi Palace Emperor called Paul Biya. And yet, this is supposed to be an environment for promoting academic excellence? Those are the types of things could never appeal to Momany, the free thinker; quite apart from the low or no pay. Thus, pushing the man from lecturer-in-law to "lecturer of love," just as most of his own students have since been clamouring to leave the hole; taking us to *Mpakofrancization*

Mpakofrancizationing the Trancing Cultural Shocks in Limbo

Mpako Francis N. is one of Momany's students at the University of Buea, who also interestingly had this to say in his September 1996 letter to "Dear Sir":

It has been a long time since we last saw, touched and felt or heard from each other. Sir, it is with a deep hearty response that I am sending you this manuscript as a medium of communication. I am sure with elaborate conviction in me that you are fine health-wise and your academic career is moving smoothly. As for me, I am now at home totally confused, in short I am in "Limbo". I graduated since March as 1st batch of the Buea University with a 2nd class lower (2.7/4) degree. Since then I am at home helping my parents to push the younger ones in front. Sir, I am still thinking on what to do next. I thought of entering a Law Chamber to practice but I finally concluded that my background is weak financially and so my accommodation and means of living before I become a full practicing Barrister will be a tough affair. Secondly, since we were studying in Buea University with a lesser means to survive and no textbooks normally as you understand, I will find it difficult to accomplish my mission, taking into consideration the economic quagmire. So this is my present condition and situation that I am facing. Please sir, I am really in a trance.

Sir, our Convocation ceremony will be on the 6th of December 1996 on campus and it will be very colourful and prestigious as you understand very well. Sir, after this glaring episode, that is the graduation ceremony, what next? Well, I am still [keep]ing my fingers crossed and waiting to hear from you in grand style. Sir, this is really the first time I am formally communicating to you but I beg for your indulgence to allow me explain the reasons which are but obvious. I did not write to you specifically because of academic undertakings, especially if you consider the cobweb nature of the U.B. calendar. So, this is my fervent wish and hearty greetings to you, my teacher, and I feel you are living well and everything is fine.

Please sir I will like to be in touch with you from time to time and if you reply me from there, through contacts one can know whether there can be a way to survive over there. Sir, if anything is available on my advantage, tell me all what to do so that I can also benefit from it. Sir, my greatest hope is to study right up to PhD but how can I with this limited means over here? I want to be that way so that I can be managing to live and study. If there is any headway you better inform me, sir.

It has been Mpako Francis. Thanks. Signed.

N/B: Write through this address: xxxxxxxxxx. Sir, if it is hand-mail, you can send it through your wife who will give it to her neighbour who can then give it to me. Signed.

Mpako could not be exaggerating, nor could he just be describing the cobweb situation in just his own Department of Law because Scholastica Achankeng Fossungu (as she then was) of the Department of Sociology and Anthropology also tells this story in her 7-paragraph letter of April 8, 1996 to the husband. Here is the 1st paragraph of her letter: "Dear! You can't imagine that I got your letter three weeks ago and have not been chanced to reply it. This semester is very bad for me, my timetable is very strenuous. I go to school everyday and come back only in the night. I always sleep very late, struggling to read for tests or to do assignments. Would you believe that it is 2.30 AM that I am writing this letter? I have made up my mind to reply it today." Relating to the law student, whoever said a person who is not shy to ask questions and directions cannot miss his/her way must have examined the position well to reach said conclusion. This student's determination to succeed despite all the odds was just so impressive and could not have failed to move someone like Momany who, by the way, perfectly grasps the matter. Being someone who has taught him and known Francis Mpako's penchant for wanting to decorate (embellish, to be more high-sounding) his language – which is also seen in his use of 'manuscript as a means of communication' – Momany would obviously understand the student's first sentence better than most Westerners, who would blindly rush to reading non-existent things into it. Correct me in this *Mpakofrancizing* business, if you can convince anyone at all that what you have just read from him is truly a 'manuscript' (as publishers understand it). Or, perhaps it is, just because it is in a potentially publishable manuscript? Manuscript is not defined *only* by the manner publishers see it since it could be any 'text,' 'document,' 'copy,' or 'script'.

If the foregoing demonstration does not quite do the job, then take also this fastening case from Momany's personal experience in Edmonton, the 1991 send-off party to which you can get a sneak preview in Photo #38. The event in question occurred during the first party thrown at the University of Alberta to welcome them, new students. Many of the East African male students were enjoying the party more than any other person or group, freely dancing together and even going *bal-à-terre* and *soukousing*, as well as doing the 'Haitian-dance' or *coller-coller* together. This is 1991, mark you; with most of the white guys not believing what they were witnessing. Openly gay guys at a time when even the likes of Elton John, Rossie O, Ellen D. (name the rest for me, please) had not even thought of leaving the closet! A bunch of them then approached the joyful Africans and demanded if they were 'gay'. The latter sonorously responded "Yeah!" Why not, these Africans must have been wondering how anyone would not even see how gay they were. Coming from the 99-sense land with a lot of certificateless intellectuals,[30] Momany knew

---

[30] "Those old village women could then really be with ninety-nine senses? Who, for instance, will accuse Professor Delancey here of ignorance or superstition? If not veritable intellectuals, how could they [the village women] have known this ('no-change') right back then when the bulk of us – drowned in the euphoria of 'change' – couldn't? Aren't they then right in that particular rebuke of those of us who claim to know so much simply because we have been to the formal school and obtained a chain of certificates; and yet cannot tell that 'new' is not at all new if affixed to the same Old thing? And that 'federal' is not at all federal if

precisely what was happening and had to speedily intervene to calm down the 'gay-thinking idiots,' telling both sides how they were ignorantly using the same word but understanding different connotations assigned to the word. That the Africans were just accepting that they were gay (happy) people socializing, like you see them doing in Photos #38(a)-(c), and not the gay (homosexual) people that the others were taking them for. The wondering on both sides was huge or *gigantically titanic*, to please lovers of *Mpakofrancization*.

That enormous cultural amazement might also result from most western civil servants following this discussion and discovering some "innovations" of Cameroonians to beat the worrisome socio-economic-educational bog. When graduating student Mpako talks of a colourful graduation and other aspects of the Buea University, he states just a minute portion of the *Cameroonian Quagmaticking Show*. Stephen Z. Fomeche (Photo #9) has smartened and substantiated it with a lot of survival strategies employed even by those working (civil servants) to attempt 'beating Cameroon is Cameroon' (thus confirming its everlasting place as an undeveloping "developing nation") as you peruse his letter of January 7, 1999 to "Dear Power" (or Momany). Opening with "Happy New Year!," Fomeche went on to give "Many thanks for the beautiful card to us and the kind wishes contained therein. Hope you are fine and studies on progress. We are fine for now and life is just bearable." He then plunged into the matter, beginning in paragraph 3, with:

I thought of several possibilities when I got this opening to come to E.N.S. Yaoundé. Many colleagues who come in as civil servants usually disappear between the ministry and school to pursue their interest. Some use it for private business; meanwhile others go out for further studies. The advantage here is that while in school, you earn salary and secondly you are not under any authority of your ministry. In this way you undertake whatsoever interest of yours

---

attached to the same Old Unitary state? And, above all, that there is no independence for a people who 'negotiate independence rather than buy it with the currency of their own blood'?" (Fossungu, 1998, citing, for the quotation, V.T. Le Vine, "Political-Cultural Schizophrenia in Francophone Africa" in I.J. Mowoe & R. Bjornson (eds.) *Africa and the West: The Legacy of Empires* (New York: Greenwood Press, 1986), 159 at 160).

without fear of query from a boss. Since all the possibilities to go out of the country did not work out well, I am open only to business. For now I am poised to embark on some little things, no matter how mean. Primarily, I thought of running a taxi of my own, myself as the driver, but the initial amount needed for the purpose gets more than a third of the previewed cost. If God permits, I will become a broker for state contracts. I have already got the headway. I just need some money to start.

We were at Schola's graduation. It was the first time I was attending an occasion of the Buea University. The crowd I saw was the first of its kind – colourful, thick, joyous and promising. It helped me, Power, to forget about my struggles, failures and disappointments of life. So many young promising Cameroonians who may have had the sky as their limits are compelled to soar and join the market of job-seekers. We are indeed in Cameroon. That notwithstanding, our occasion was good. We feasted with your kinsmen from Douala and Muyuka.

I will write a more detailed letter next time. I just hope I will get you on the line when next I call. Accept the love and wishes of Jacinta, Yeye and Zisuh. Bye! It's Fomeche Stephen Z. signed.

The Wonders of Family Instabilities and Academics

The graduation and some of the kinsmen and other acquaintances of the couple are seen in Photos #39 (a)-(d). An appreciation of Stephen's frustrations is enhanced by knowing that his unwarranted family splitting superimposes itself on *The Marriage That Almost Didn't Take Place*. Stephen's point made above on family splitting due to academics has been very instrumental to understanding Scholastica's entire love and marriage behaviour as I have briefly outlined above. In the meantime, the lecturer on the curious marital union that almost never was is no other than Fomeche from the *Quagmaticking* School again who, on December 15, 1995, asked Momany a question on death and marriage that I want us all to share. You get it in his narration that runs as follows:

Hi Power, Many thanks for your letter which, as you rightly guessed, met us in good health. Hope you're fine too and studies okay.

There have been many developments since your departure. First, we are blessed to live under the same roof together after four years continuous separation due to academics. She completed her course in June, validating all her courses. In late September she was engaged by Seat of Wisdom College to teach English and literature. If all goes well, we will be given a house in the school campus where we will be opportune to enjoy electricity and good water supply.

Another development has been our official marriage. We had the traditional marriage on the 10/11/95, the council marriage on the 17/11/95 and the marriage in church on the 18/11/95. Power, indeed, I leave the aspect of their grandeur to some other tongues and pens and to the best of your guess. God was so much in our favour for the 10/11/95 planned for the traditional marriage almost failed because my father-in-law was admitted in the hospital just the day before. My parents insisted and had things done (financial transaction only) deferring the ceremony later when he was to be sound. There in the hospital, 20/11/95, the family assembled for the nuptial blessing which my father did and expressed much satisfaction. Behold on 21/11/95 those who came from out of Fontem left to their various destinations. On the 22/11/95, my father-in-law stopped talking and died on 23/11/95 (natural causes). The same persons who return from my marriage were called back few days later for burial and death celebration which took place 1/12/95 and 3/12/95, respectively. What do you say Peter?

Life is still the way it was. Preparations are on the way for municipal elections and constitutional reforms. The improvement of living standards is the bleakest speculation. We however do our work conscientiously with the fear of the lord. We hope to hear more about Quebec, your school and your course. Happy Christmas and New Year in advance! Wish you the best. Accept greetings from Yeye. Sincerely yours, signed. Fomeche Steve and Jessy.

Divine Wonders in the Complexity of the 2007 Cameroon Deaths

What a marriage story! I don't think anyone would need that I say anything further regarding it other than to continue with one more intriguingly puzzling case before we wrap up with the Cameroon mess and dive into serious love business; love being a kind of affair that you can often only engage in correctly with sincerity as the watch word. You have just seen how everyone wants to leave the bad situation in Cameroon and go abroad where they ignorantly think everything is just so rosy. Many failed to do so. But Scholastica had the "privilege" to do so. You have equally heard her hot and strong love expressed in some of the communications above. One would normally expect that a (wife's) love that is this strong "at long-distance" would simply choke when the distance is eliminated. Not at all with Scholastica or anyone feigning it for that matter.

Queenta is such a simple and down-to-earth sweetheart who is not really good at love-*letteristic* communication. She could be rightly fashioned instead as a very efficient *loveracticists*. That is, someone who shows much loving more in the practice of than in writing about it. That is, the 'I-Just-Did-It,' as a popular version would put it. If you want to be more 'love-vocabulary' fashionable, then just call them the *Ejudidists*. If you ask my opinion (and I have to remain only on one side of the fence), I would follow the *Action-Speaks-Louder-Than-Worders* and posit that *loveracticists* provide better love: especially so if you also factor in the *monologuing* critiques. You have just seen a lot of 'long-distance' love talking here that would end up in Canada not being any love at all; very unlike some of the deprived and aching spouses. But let's continue *Queentalizing* love with the ideal Bafut wife that never was. Queenta (Photo #28) could also represent Momany's arguments to Panda's insistence on marrying a virgin of his own that you will meet in chapter 5. That is, if you know that most of the Fossungu Royals that loathed her marriage to Momany cited the fact that 'Everyone in Nwangong has slept with her' with Momany's response always being to find out if "I told you I was going to marry her because she was still a virgin?"

Queenta is as well the best of the *letteristically* wanting lovers. For example, in an undated handwritten letter posted to Momany, Queenta could not even fill the page, simply saying "Hello Dear, How are you at moment. I hope everything is well, especially your health. With me, I am well. Mum is also doing fine. I have sent a photocopy of my birth certificate and the passport photos. Stay well. We shall discuss more over the phone. Thanks. Signed." And in a no-subject email of July 20, 2005 at 7.16 AM Queenta wrote: "Hi dear, How is life that way? Hope fine. Please try and call me before

Saturday 23/07/05. I have so many things to discuss with you. Your wife. Queenta." So, if the *loveracticist or practical lovers* can feel so much and, yet, not be able to exquisitely express that feeling *letteristically*, could that pose a significant issue? Generally speaking, the 2007 'Voyage to Bafut' puts this type of lover on the positive side. But Queenta's great handicap, unfortunately, laid only in the fact that she fell in love with someone who was living very far away from her, thus, her not being able do what she is so good at doing in the sphere of love (Chapter 3 below will give you an idea of what I mean here). It is almost similar to 'the wonders of the Scholastica Question,' with the difference being on the type of parents involved and the fact that Queenta never even got to the spouse level. This problem of hers was aggravated further not only by the intervening death but also by the wings to the 'Bafut Star-Trek Voyager' being *London-Courtfully* chipped off as soon Momany returned from the first Bafut Discovery Trip. That London strategy significantly contributed to the flop that deprived Queenta of spouseology, not anything to do with her *letteristical* inabilities.

There seems to be no other way of actually explaining the surprising detour of Scholastica, the author of the above sweet and informative letters and many more of such adoring letters after her much talked about 'miraculous, swift, and joy-bringing' arrival to Canada. The amazing diversion in Canada renders Scholastica's Cameroon showings to be clearly not what can accurately be described as love since we have seen several others who never even reached the spouse level with Momany still in love with him, irrespective of whatever that caused the breach preventing marriage. Here is someone actually married and singing love 'at long distance' but comes over only to screw up the life of the man who is almost wholly responsible for making her what she is today. To think that such a person ever was in love with the one she is now treating like that would be to give a totally different meaning to love, and a highly abusive one too.

Not to stay with the popular cases already covered (*Odilimomanyism, Momanijanism* and *Queentamanyism*), take Anna (Photo #34) to briefly illustrate. Momany miraculously reconnected with her in January 2013 on the phone. 1983 to 2013, how many years? Exactly 30 years of her captivity, with no sign or hint of the whereabouts of her first love. But that never caused the evaporation of that love, the circumstances of sequestration notwithstanding. Add to all that also the fact that neither of these mentioned women would even be having a child with Momany, and the wonders of love would only be magnified a billion-fold. How do you reconcile Scholastica & Co's advice on the house building (while she was still in Cameroon) because of Momany's mother's failing health with her quickly rushing back to court in 2007 to have child support *augmented* "because he is building houses in Cameroon"? So, was the beautifully appreciated work she did over there worth the appreciation or just a scheme meant for crossing the Atlantic? And the return to court thing was the more so puzzling when she knew quite well what had happened (and almost occurred) to Momany during that 2007 trip?

It is like 2007 was a year for travel and marriage within the Momany circle. Georges' wish for his friend to get what took him to Bafut wasn't met.[31] The marriage with Queenta fell apart most probably because of the intervening death; being the death of Fon David Foncha Fossungu (Photo #41) which occurred on the same

---

[31] Georges Neba (Photo #40) in his email of February 22, 2007 inquisitively wrote:

> Hello: Tell me, what were you really going to do in Bafut (Niko)? Hahaha!!! I hope only that you succeeded in whatsoever you were going to do there. I come from Manji, not far from the palace. Mubadang and Evodia all also come from this Quarter. The hottest spot of the place is called "Nsani," and maybe if you asked of me around the area, you might have found one or two people who know me.
>
> I'm happy that you came back alive and that you're in good health. Have you resumed work already? I'm sure you should be broke since you had to travel impromptu to Cameroon. Did you see Mama? How is her health? Hmm!!!!!
>
> I hear cold is whipping your ass in Montreal (-30°C???)
>
> I will be back in Montreal around the 1st of April. A date has been given by the council of Montreal for my marriage. It will be on Saturday the 7th of April 2007 at 11h30. You know you will be my Best Man for the occasion. I intend to invite around 10 to 12 people. We will have to talk about the details later.
>
> I also intend to move to LaSalle. So Christine is now busily looking for a 41/2 in LaSalle, if you happen to stumble on one nice apartment, please inform Christine. I will be coming only for 2 weeks and I will have to marry and change my apartment. I think I will not have much time to do other things. I wish you a nice day and please take care of yourself. Sincerely yours, Neba [this paragraph altered].

day that Momany boarded the plane in Canada with him only knowing about it while transiting in Switzerland. Death did not stop Neba's marriage but it is also like Georges Neba (unlike Scholastica) was happy for Momany's safe return and good health while death was doing just exactly what the Death Theorists of the Fossungu Royal Family cautioned us about. I am talking particularly about the theory from Chief Foletia[32] which found its application in the case of Georges Neba who died on Sunday, January 19, 2009 in Cameroon in a motor accident on the Douala-Limbe road.

Georges Neba and wife, Christine (both in Photo #40), met in Germany where they were both studying. They later moved to Montreal and establish residence. Georges then got a job in Germany and went there alone. After his marriage, he went to Cameroon two years later to see parents and in-laws, most probably to also brief them on the event that took place in Canada. From there he was then to return to his job in Germany but he never did, most certainly because of the recklessness that abounds on our roads, just as in every corner and sphere of the *quagmaticking* country in which "One man is worth more than 20 million people" (Ayah, 2013). Death did not stop the Neba marriage but it did the worst that could ever happen to anyone.

If anyone wants more explanation of the obvious (some things are never obvious to those who have not tasted it though), then Patricia Temeching-Etukeni (Photo #42) is here to help. Just listen to a single mother of two kids that are now in and out of university. She herself works in Cameroon and is studying for her PhD in Nigeria. Answering the query from Momany as to how she has been able to balance and survive the terrible loss of her husband all these years, on October 15, 2015, Patricia (who has now remarried) counselled: "I pray God will grant us the grace we need to continue

---

[32] Chief Foletia had advised that "You can never know when exactly to expect death's knock on the door. Therefore, if there is anything you want to do, just go ahead and do it and stop procrastinating and saying 'I will, I will, I will'. Because, while you are doing that, death is calculating your days and laughingly saying on its part: 'He doesn't know my calendar and can never be aware that I am coming for him this very night'. So, my brethren, as we are here gathered to bid Chief Forbehndia farewell, my counsel to you is that if there is a piece of kola nut in your pocket, do share it with the one next to you and don't say you will do so only tomorrow...." (cited in Fossungu, 2015c: 74).

to 'accept' the things that come our way. It wasn't easy for me taking the decision I took especially as my kids and siblings were all opposed to it. It actually tore us apart but thank God they are gradually accepting it. I had gone for 15 years as a widow with the last 10-11 in total celibacy. I was lonely and hurting inside and being the introvert that I am, nobody knew what I was going through."[33] Even introverts

---

[33] Your understanding of Momany's perplexity with his own lackadaisical family people to take advantage of pushes he gives them for bettering their live would greatly benefit when you know how he usually responds to others (call them strangers, if you like) who take initiative while requesting for his push. That nagging issue would be greased with a similar request from a PhD student-mother for Momany to help his son with admission into a Canadian university and feeling sorry that she was troubling Momany with such request for aid. On December 30, 2014, Momany fired back to that sorry-concern and others as follows to "My Dear Patricia," making it known that:

It's never late to achieve anything, especially what one wants and is determined to acquire. It's a passion thing doing a PhD and without that zeal no amount of pushing from others or the availability of the cash can do it. Once more, congratulations for not letting the passion die out. You are certainly on top of it and I love people like you a lot. Therefore, quit thinking that you're adding any problems on me by seeking to do what is best for your child or any child whatever. I live for the wellbeing of children, my numerous books testifying to it. Now, let's get to your son specifically. I am sure he is/will be just as passionate about what he wants to achieve in life. It is very easy to aid those who already know what they want to do with their lives. I speak from the heart and with lots of expibasketism (new terminology from my most recent book on Midnight Politics). I will throw out a few options that I can think of and both of you can select from them.

ONE: Here is a list of some Canadian universities. I do not have the exact websites but just typing the names on the search engine or googling will lead you to their sites where you can find out more about their course/programme offerings, etc. Begin with my current institution, University of Windsor, Windsor, Ontario; University of Alberta, Edmonton, Alberta; University of Calgary, Calgary, Alberta; McGill University, Montreal, Quebec; Concordia University, Montreal, Quebec; Dalhousie University, Halifax, Nova Scotia; University of Manitoba, Winnipeg, Manitoba; University of Saskatchewan, Regina, Saskatchewan; University of Victoria, Victoria, British Columbia; McMaster University (Ontario, I think); University of Ottawa, Ottawa, Ontario; University of Toronto, Toronto, Ontario. NOTE: the province is important to look for because city names here in North America are repetitive in different parts, e.g. Montreal is not only in Quebec but also in several parts of the U.S.A. or Britain.

can open up a lot; you just need to know how to approach the issues with them. We need to often hear these kinds of stories a lot, not to hide them in our 'closets'. Just like this book is doing, because they can help a lot of other persons. Some people go to the length of killing themselves or some other person (or such other nonsense) when they happen to have a *penny* problem; not realizing that people *with a billion* problems are still living. That might sometimes be because they never knew these 'billion problems' guys are there.

TWO: To be on the safe side and ensure that he does not have to waste another school year, let's not carry all our eggs in one basket. Therefore, while pursuing admission in any or some of the institutions in option one, also try these non-Canadian institutions. 1. University of Malta, Msida, Malta: This is obviously less expensive than Canadian Universities, and easy to gain admission into all-year round, and it is European, of course. Only hitch may be that, for undergraduate studies, he will need to pre-study their language called Maltese (see observation below though). 2. European University at St. Petersburg, St. Petersburg, Russian Federation: Studies are in English, I don't quite know the comparative cost but it will surely be cheaper than Canada and has worldwide recognition, with visa conditions less strident than for North America. 3. Greek State Foundation Scholarships: Here he will need to study the Greek Language first before continuing to his course of study. With the recent financial problems the country has faced as member of EU, I am not sure if the possibility is still as rosy as before. A lot of Africans are unaware of some of these openings since everyone thinks only of North America these days. 4. Try getting admission for studies of Chinese in a Chinese institution. Also an easy route out of the continent as seen in the remarks on this option. OBSERVATION: Once enrolled in any of the cases of this Option, the candidate can then easily apply to be landed in Canada. It becomes very easy then compared to doing so, or even obtaining a visitor/student visa, while still in Africa. THREE: Get admission for a diploma in a Canadian college: An example is canadacollege.com in Montreal, Quebec: It will be very easy here for you to prove more than sufficient funds for the course/programme, most of them being six-month to one-year programmes. Take a close look at Canada College's website (canadacollege.com) and see what they are offering that ties in with his likes as well as possible reasons for his wanting to pursue the course (for visa interview purposes). Admission is all-year round. When he is already here, he can then apply for university admission and extension of his student visa, etc.

What are you researching on in Calabar? Are you still into theatre arts? Do I still get your daughter's name correct? Is it Wilma or Reema? Have a blessed New Year 2015 in advance.

Chief Fotale'eh

Come on guys! Empty the closets and let's move ahead through *frantalkism*.

God's Positive Use of the Devil or Anything like a Good Satan?

Some Christian would feel uneasy with this query but there is no need for that. Is God not frank and true, as we are told? Anyway, listen to the narrative and decide for yourself. It is only God who just did not think it was time for the bridge-builder called Momany to be completely wiped out. Having gotten him out of the public view into their killing spot, there was divine intervention just at the moment of firing. Because his so-called brother called Elias Akendung (Photo #24) had refused (despite all the pleading) to pick him up from Bonaberi, Momany got out of the bus and was heading to the spot from where to board a "clando" to Village (Douala). The waiting assassins were three in number and immediately sandwiched him with cleverly drawn out knives and other weapons, telling him not to try anything foolish and just move along with them. Being that late in the night (about midnight), there was almost no one around to be shouting for help from, so he just obeyed. They led him into the bushes and far off from the main road. They got everything he had on him including all the money that was still in dollars. (Because of the intervening death, he had hurriedly gone to the village on arrival without doing what he normally did.) It was now time to eliminate the guy as planned when God used one of them to save Momany. The God-chosen killer-thief told the others to let the guy go because they had gotten more than enough money from him (many credit cards being some of the credit sources of said money), not to even talk of the electronic and other photo and video apparels direct from Canada.

That is what began the argument between them, leading to the delay in cutting off Momany's penis for him to quickly die while they were gone. The penis cutter was obviously distracted by the heated argument between the other guys and was not concentrating on just giving a one blow of his dagger to the penis. The guy on the same side as the penis-cutter was telling the lone other that their "leaving with Momany alive was not at in the plan." Plan! With whom could a *plan* have been made with them, when Momany had been thinking these guys just got him by chance? These were some of the quick puzzles that were crossing Momany's mind but he was not even concentrating on them as much as on the slow and hesitant cutting action of the third guy, momentary slicing that still was so painful that Momany just involuntarily wailed out: since at that point he had concluded that obeying their rule of silence was not going to change his fate. And low and behold! One attentive *bend-skinner* (motor-taxi driver) just happened to have been returning home through a footpath not far away. Hearing the desperate cry from the bushes, he quickly directed his headlight to the direction of the wailing. It was a terrible surprise for them (and Momany himself) that saved Momany's life. With that sudden appearance of the light, each of them grabbed the bags and money and took to their heels.

Thanks to God who was working further through the bend-skin guy. Otherwise, Momany wouldn't still be alive today. This guy was just too brave to have been any normal person. He continued all the way into the bushes and then carried Momany on his motorcycle all the way to Elias Akendung's residence at Bonne-Dix in Boko, Village. And all what he asked for was just 1500 FCFA. A sum which one would have expected someone whose 'brother' had just been save from death by the total stranger like that would even quickly have paid and still go on to "add dash". It was not the case at all. It was not until the airport incident about a week later that the fact that Elias Akendung had been so shocked to see Momany that late night began to fall perfectly into place. On that night itself, Momany had thought the shock was just because of the shocking story that Elias was being told. But not so; the shock must have been connected to the fact (as the thieves' argument can show) that the *plan* had either not been executed yet, or done but not well done. "Let it be the first," Elias must have then assured himself, "and this time around I will by-pass the uniformed rogues and get that money through another means while having my colleagues put him behind bars, if the grave has surprisingly refused him as tenant." That might well help to join the missing pieces to get to the airport incident mentioned in Bernard Mbancho Fossungu's "Terrible Ladies" message to Momany on Sunday, August 16, 2015 in which states in the 4th paragraph that "Chief, I happened to have overheard some of our village ladies after my wife's burial in the village talking about the problem between you and Elias Akendung and how he even went as far as informing border police officers at the Douala Airport to arrest you during your departure from the country, Had things gone that bad?"

Because of that incident, everything that took Momany there, including even his marriage plans to Queenta of Bafut and the University of Douala enterprise, failed to materialize. As you can see, Momany was even very lucky to still be alive. He divinely survived the plot as has been the case in several other life-threatening situations. But 2007 was just a year of obstructing deaths in Momany's circles. It was the intervening death of Fon DF Fossungu that led to his fateful return from the village via Bafut that conducted him smoothly into the hands of the waiting hired killer-gang in Bonaberi. At the same time in 2007, the Head of Department of the Common Law Department of the Douala University who was supposed to receive Momany as per the communications that you would be perusing shortly also died during that period (January 2007) while the man himself very narrowly escaped death. Amazing! As to the Douala University dossier, just a few communications between him and the Head of Department of Common Law who was very instrument in securing the position since mid-2001, would tell you what it consisted of.

In 'Availability' of March 2006 Momany wrote: "Hello Dr. Nyambo, I hope you and family are doing well at moment. It's been quite a while without any communication from this end. It is a very long story that I wouldn't want to go into here. I am writing now just to find out if there is still a position for me at your Department because I will be ready to come home by the end of this year. I wish to know so as to make alternative plans in case the position is no longer available. Take care. PAF" In his response of March 24, 2006 the Head of Department wrote: "Thanks for your interest in the Department. This time around, I just hope it is final. I will give you final outcome by March ending. But you had better come and taken service so we can see what it can look like some years after. Let's be in touch by end of this month. Joe." On of July 18, 2006, Joe again wrote: "Just to greet. We are on exams now. When exactly should I be expecting you? Bye. Joe." To that Momany said "I am looking at December this year tentatively, but I must be out of here for good at the latest June 2007. Bye now. PAF." On August 3, 2006 Joe said: "Thanks, I suggest you come and assume service before going to tidy up your things over there. Joe." Momany then said "Point very well taken. Thanks. PAF" That was the arrangement that was to be taken care of during that January 2007 trip which was to be the longest in duration before the going back to tidy the rubbish in Canada for a final move-over to be educating students. The tidying being talked about you already know how the mess came about. But would dragdownism just let that happen? No! The next chapter studies their strategies of the dragdowners.

Chapter 3

Intriguing Family Deaths and the Poverty Eradication Projects

This chapter has two main parts, both of which would *Queentalize* love and marriage with deaths. *Queentalization* comes from Queenta Ngum Afanwi (Photo #28) who tried in vain to save the Fossungu royal family from *dragdownism*. Once more, *Dragdownism* is the noun for the act of dragging someone down and is akin to intrigues. The first part scrutinizes the wrong questions being raised within Momany's extended family and these would be related to the declaration of his intentions after obtaining the qualifications that took him abroad. The Second then shows how, as a consequence of the wrong approach adopted, a lot of voices would be heard in the wilderness loudly crying out for help to no avail: because those who could have competently and selflessly gone to their rescue have been prevented from doing by the *moneyintriguists* and *dragdowners* that the Fossungu family itself has in unacceptable quantities.

The surprising *reply* Solomon talks about in his message[34] may tell you how/that Momany always tries to resolve problems within his own home without singing about them to the outside world, and that includes even his own extended family who are wont to pose questions inappropriately, as seen below. But he would also not lie about them if a friend or relative asks to know. In answering the phone query of Solomon (who is also called 'Power'), therefore, in his "Re: How Was Your Trip Back Home?" of Sunday, October 22, 2006 at 5.59 PM, Momany explained to his bosom friend as follows:

Power, Sorry I missed this one for so long. I have not changed address. I merely dropped the home phone and internet. Even the cell phones (514-686-7660 or 514-573-5509) sometimes are not

---

[34] In "Re: How Was Your Trip Back Home?" on September 11, 2006 at 2.14 PM Solomon had written: "Power, I am now in Germany and will be here for the next two weeks. I called your number and it didn´t go through. I don´t know if you have changed address. Please, let me know. Solo."

available: that is, when credit is out because they are both pay-as-you-go.

I have been struggling to come out of the legal mess I have been dragged into by the lady in London, Ontario. It is still ongoing and I cannot be okay until it is over. Just imagine driving from Montreal to London (Ontario) (about 800 km) almost every week! Do not think of just the cost of the trip alone. Put in wear and tear of the car, three days of work lost, fatigue, etc. and you can begin to comprehend what I am going through here. I am going to come clear though, as usual. That is why I am called Power.

Keep in touch. PAF [this paragraph altered]

What a marriage! What a scheme that has not only easily moved a lecturer-in-law to a lecturer-in-love, but also imprisoned him abroad! With what you are witnessing here, who is still not lending support to anyone who is audaciously poised on expanding and restricting the frontiers of love? Do you just have to forever eat shit from someone simply because you have the money-making tools they call 'children' with them? That appears to be the reasoning of many in the Fossungu Royal Family (Royal Indeed!) who ask the wrong questions, very unlike chiefs: according to the *Josephizationing* gospel. *Josephization* is from Joseph Njumo Fossungu's infamously famous letters to Chief Forbehndia, his father. To quote directly from Joe's famous Letters, "You are not a chief because you let people advise you instead of you advising them" (cited in Fossungu, 2015c: 106). You will have to correctly assess Joe's thesis after perusing the reaction of those who Joe described as "foolish Fosungu people" to the death of an intriguer.

Death of an Intriguer Raising Intriguing Questions

As indicated earlier, the great importance of constantly having news of what is happening at home while you are abroad cannot be overstated. Many of Momany's family members have accused him of not communicating when some deaths have occurred, most probably because money would need to *pass* through their hands and the like. Most of them do so without in the least talking about their own role in the breaking of contact; that is, that communication needs to be a two-way affair to be effective. The Fossungu people only come around, when they do at all, to raise or talk about things whose causes and implications they do not even know. This wrong questioning image you clearly get from the letter of Fon David Foncha Fossungu (Photo #41) dated February 17, 2004. In it Fon DF Fossungu stated:

Dr. Nkemtale'eh Peter A.,
I am indeed grateful to write you this letter just to let you know that the death of our in-law, Mr. Asahchop Peter, passed here successfully. I was surprised to see your wife, Scholastica, without having any information from you. You know that according to our tradition when you lose your in-law you have to give a blanket and a crate of beer (20 bottles), I gave it with Madam Zinzi Lucia [Photo #26]. All these expenditures cost me 18000 francs. You will then write to me and explain to me the situation of your wife since you are no longer staying with her. Although I asked her, she told me that it will be very difficult for me to judge the case from one side, except the two of you are present.

I have only been hearing [about] it from people and no information from you and I don't know why; whether you don't consider me like your father. Since you left home now it is almost getting to two years and you have not written to me. I saw the pictures you sent to me through Tanangmock Calestus [Photo #43], there was no letter attached to it. Since I crowned you as nkem direct you promised that you will reach Canada before you will send a message to me. I have been waiting for long. If the two of you agree that I should come to Canada and maintain peace between the two of you, write and tell me.

Signed. His Majesty FONCHA I, Fon of Nwangong Fondom.

The first sentence of the Fon's letter obviously should read like this; "to let you know that the funeral and burial of our in-law, Mr. Asahchop Peter, was successfully carried out." Love knows no peace-maintaining officers to solve its problems because love means peacefulness and understanding dialogue in relations. For, what happens when the officer has left, as he must do? I will take the Fon's letter and the photos issues briefly before getting into the death in question.

The fact of the disunity and distrust in this family comes out in the Fon's talk of "whether you don't consider me like your father";

an issue beautifully cemented by Chief Forbehndia's Will which ordains in paragraph 3 that "The whole family should recognize Fon D.F. Fosungu as their grandfather." The issue of father or grandfather is discussed in the second part of chapter 4. As far as the photos question goes, it is amazing that nothing exists to show what happened from when Chief Forbehndia's corpse was removed from the mortuary to when it got to Dschang like those of Regina Akiefac, exemplified by Photos #45 (a)-(c). It is only from Dschang on that you may have any traces of the matter to put in front of anyone who was not present; knowing still that even those present cannot recall everything that happened, let alone the details. Ngi-Nyam has already told us how important some of these things are for posterity to have. In his reply (to Ngi-Nyam) Momany also affirmed the value of photos and videos. That was in the 2nd paragraph of his letter of May 7, 2006 that told "My dear Ngi-Nyam" that "I have always trusted the power of pictures in telling stories that hardly fade away but your present letter has come not only to confirm this belief but to concretely cement it. Here, then, are two more pictures that could tell a portion of my happy-sad long story that you wish to know – one of my two very young children here in Canada, and the other of myself."

You could also have been told that, as a young child, aeroplanes always fascinated Momany and he wanted to one day fly one; the reason he took his lessons in the sciences (especially mathematics and physics) in secondary school very seriously; becoming one of the few students selected on merits to do additional maths in Saint Joseph's College, Sasse, Buea (see Fossungu, 2013a: ix). If there had been any doubt about that in your mind (since he is not now *Einsteinistically* killing you with formula and laboratory experiments), then, 'believe you me' (as the popular saying would put it) doubting would not have even been the case with a picture (like the one below) attached to the statement. Not to ignore Abongwa Fozo's (2015b) warnings regarding the notorious Biya-Dead Soldiers honouring farce though, you clearly get the picture from this picture that one of Momany's classmates posted on their class forum on November 21, 2011.

By: tfofung
File Name: photo.JPG

Posted: Nov 25, 2011
Resolution: 480x358
Size: 59KB

njakaromanus Fri Nov 25 19:36:10 UTC 2011
Fosungu Peter (aka Figaro cinq), Titus Fofung, Ayuk Collins and Ayah Paul (not Ebine)' These were the Einsteins of our time! They registered for all the Maths subjects available (Math and Additional Math)

All what anyone could ever hear of the Chief Forbehndia burial and funeral would be possible only because that portion of the show (from Dschang down to the end in Nwangong) was ably immortalized, thanks to Momany who also made sure to distribute both the endless amounts of photos and DVDs to particularly Bernard Mbancho Fosungu (the successor) in South Africa and Marie-Claire Efuelancha Afueh (née Fossungu) in the USA; sending all these bulky materials to them by registered express courier. The Fon, as well as many others in the family, also were similarly served. When they complain sometimes, it is hard to comprehend them sometimes. For instance, having returned to Canada, on December 12, 2002 Momany had written this letter to HRH Fon D.F. Fossungu, elaborately telling "His Royal Highness"[35] that:

---

[35] This designation of 'His Royal Highness' (HRH) was formerly reserved for just the Fon (at the time called the Paramount Chief) with the non-HRH users being then known as Sub-Chiefs. The chieftaincy dynamics has since changed in Bangwa land as a whole, with the abolition of the nomenclature of 'sub-chiefs' in

I am writing this letter for three principal reasons. First, I would like to let you and the entire Nwangong people know that, through your prayers and the guidance of the gods of Nwangong, I arrived here in Canada safely. The numerous problems we had with the car when we left the village did not, in themselves, prevent us (my Mafor, Nkwetta, Asa'ah and myself), in any way, from reaching our diverse destinations safely. The breakdowns were simply due to some normal mechanical malfunction with the car. It was duly taken care of in Douala.

Second, I would like to specially thank you and your wives, and the Nwangong people for the wonderful performance during both late Chief Forbehndia's burial ceremony and the second celebration regarding my biological father who died a long time ago. You people really put forward one of the best performances Nwangong has so far known. My only regret is that I do not have the second ceremony on videotape. Ever since my return here we have been watching everything that took place at home during the burial. I very much look forward to the day we can all sit together with some of the children that are still to be born and watch Chief Forbehndia's wonderful burial ceremony over and over again. I haven't printed the photos of both ceremonies as yet and would be sending copies to you as soon as they are available.

Thirdly, I would like to break some good news. On October 19, 2002 there in the village, we all saw Chief Forbehndia, who had left us, returned as a young man. Chief Forbehndia came back then to the entire village and clan. But that is not all that there is to it. Chief Forbehndia has specifically chosen to be a distinguished member of Dr. and Mrs. Nkemtale'eh's family, come March 2003. My wife and I had decided long ago that our next child would be named after Chief Forbehndia, if a male, or after my mother, if a female. Two

---

preference of Chiefs who are now kept apart from the former 'paramount chief' by the grassfield (or Graffi) Fon designation to whom the monopoly of His Royal Majesty (HRM) now belongs. During this book's narration, you will notice (from most of Momany's emails to the Fon that still use the faulty 'HRH') which betrays the fact that most of us outside of the country were not yet aware of the evolution on the chieftaincy institution. So what does that tell you? Of course, among other things, it signifies that paying regular visits to the homeland is a very important exercise since it is quite clear that just travelling around accords a kind of education that no amount of formal classroom lecturing can even provide.

days ago, the hospital report told us that Chief Forbehndia is the one coming into our family next March. Isn't that a wonderful blessing for us? It actually shows that the Gods of Nwangong are working together to make things better for Nwangong in particular and Nweh-Mundani in general.

As I said last time, I am with you all the time although the physical distance between us is too much for actually counting. I have enclosed some photos taken long ago when Chief Forbehndia was still alive. Once more, extend my greetings and thanks to your wives and other village dignitaries that made my last visit home very worthwhile.

Sincerely yours, Dr. Nkemtale'eh. Signed.

So where is the Fon of Nwangong coming from with his talk of not having heard from Momany since he left Cameroon in 2002 after the burial of Chief Forbehndia? Talking of burial, they were also spending the 18,000 CFA francs (which is normal) but the abnormality is that they were never even told by the man's wife (Elizabeth Asahchop) that Momany had *directly* sent 500,000 (five hundred) CFA francs to Mrs. Elizabeth Asahchop (née Njuafiac Elizabeth Tendongafac) for the purpose through Western Union MTCN #610-524-1226 of February 8, 2004; agency Doreen, operator 493; the sum being equivalent of CAD $1402.18. This money was not just hidden from the Fossungus but also the dead man's own family members. Again, Scholastica Achankeng Asahchop justifies well her not talking about the issue to the Fon of Nwangong. But it also raises stiff questions relating to when 'Momany was present' when she did talk (lie) about it to her own parents (and other relations)? What was she actually hiding this time? Momany's Letter of November 4, 2001 to his friends in Edmonton (Nancy in Photo #44 particularly) seems to give an answer when it theorizes in the 2nd paragraph that:

I think I'll try to avoid being so *dependent* on this woman by letting her live her life in peace and without having someone like me being a parasite. It is funny the manner and degree Schola has taken her task of blackmailing me and making sure, according to her estimation, that I should never set foot on Cameroonian soil. I am not in the least surprised that she's been calling people all over the world to do this dirty job but never called people like you or my friend Paul [Takha Ayah in Photo #12] right here in Montreal. She knows you people know the facts and are therefore not going to buy her stories even for nothing.

It seems like the death of an intriguing figure always raises intriguing controversies. One would say this because the death of Peter Ngunyi Asahchop has raised a lot of hell for Momany even within his own extended family members who seem to be asking the wrong questions at the wrong time. You have already read Fon DF Fossungu's letter on the same subject. But he is not the only and neither will the next speaker even be making it just two. In an undated letter (but certainly written after February 2004, month of Peter Ngunyi Asahchop's death) Richard Ngufor Fossungu (Photo #36) wrote:

My dear brother, I am happy to write you this letter, to know about the situation of your family at present. But I think you and the children are doing fine. For us in Cameroon, we are sound; it is only hardship which will kill us. In fact, we were surprised to hear that your wife got to Douala and passed straight away to the village for her father's burial without contacting us, meanwhile we were waiting for any of you to come with the burial programme so that we go together. Brother, even if you are living apart from your wife, you should have sent a message to us and how we will represent you there, because you are having children with her. It was at Muyuka that I heard from Dieudonné that he called to know what should be done while waiting for you or your wife and there was no positive answer from you.

I don't know what is actually going wrong with you that you didn't want to communicate with your own family. You know that at the moment I cannot call you through phone, but I have written two letters to you since you left us last year 2002 after Papa's burial and no response. I thought that it was your studies that were disturbing you from writing to us. Now that you are not studying again you can't write, there is no problem in that. I did not think for one moment that you can stay for up to two years without knowing of the situation of my family or myself. You know fully well that I don't have a job I am doing; I am still as you met me last two years and you don't care to communicate with us. Since the beginning of the second term my children are at home because of fees.

Have a nice time with your family. We are sound for now. Accept their greetings and know that we have a newborn baby in the family by name Sanotia Zifac, a girl, given birth to by Maria.

Ngufor Richard. Signed.

N.B.: Peter, if you are still the Peter I know, I want the reply of this letter through your friend Elias [Akendung] because I don't have an address now or you call me through him. If you hear that I am not living don't doubt; it is frustration and too much thoughts. I am getting paler and paler every day.

Efuelanchakendungism Means a Family against Itself Must Fall

A few points on this unimportantly important letter are essential. First, on the burial programme, these people would be waiting for Momany and the like for an in-law's burial and funeral programme and going together and so on. But what happened when Chief Forbehndia died? That question brings us squarely to the happenings of the October 2002 journey and *Akendungism* and family conniving, distrust and disunity. *Akendungism*, of course, comes from Elias Akendung (Photo #24) whose mother is also from the palace, a Fossungu princess, that is. Momany arrived at the so-called Douala 'International' Airport on Thursday 17th October at about 8.00 PM. What is just so 'international' about that airport except Shame? There at Cameroon's International Shame, Momany learnt that the initial programme he was working on had been changed. Looking at the new schedule, he wanted to cross to Debundschazone as fast as possible after a bath and some food so as to catch up with the others perhaps in Yoke. But Elias Akendung who was the only person waiting for him at the airport told Momany that going to Yoke was out of the question because the corpse and convoy would already have left and on their way to Nwangong by the time they (from Douala) would have reached Yoke. To Elias, the only thing to do was for both of them to go straight to Dschang where the others would already be by early next morning. The mere fact that the programme had been altered without bothering to consider his own input or situation told Momany that he was not only to be naïve to be arguing with his informant on the spot but also that his coming to Cameroon actually meant nothing to those who had done the change. And that included even the one with whom he was talking right there at the airport.

Just hear the full story of *moneyintriguists* and truth haters that this royal family is *brimatized* with to know why the family is incapable to advancing as it should normally have done by now. When the news of Chief Forbehndia's passing got to Momany, he immediately called Marie-Claire (Photo #18). Let's not even go into the fact that she already had the news but never cared to call Momany. On her not being sure if permission would be granted her at her job side, Momany made it exceedingly clear that, come what may, he must have to travel to Cameroon for this particular burial and funeral. As Momany was struggling to arrange his means of travelling, he kept constantly calling to know where Marie-Claire stood on the issue. All through she was still "uncertain" until Momany left for Cameroon. Momany thus arrived in Douala without Marie-Claire having come out clear on where she stood. Elias Akendung would then be travelling all that distance (Douala-Dschang) with Momany and asking questions about Marie-Claire's coming or not: when both of them (Elias and Marie-Claire) had their secret deal! She had sent money instead to Elias in connection with the funeral which the latter tied to hide from view, like Elizabeth Asahchop. But Marie-Claire had also secretly told the girls in Limbe, including Scholastica, her own blood sister (all of them seen in Photos #46(a)-(e)): which is why the "secret" came out when Momany was surprisingly putting every Fossungu on the spot in Nwangong and asking for what their contribution was. How did it all happen and why?

Already in Letia in Nwangong, the situation of 'No-One-in-Charge' just degenerated to unacceptable proportions because those you would have thought were in the driver seat were all just loitering and kind of 'hiding' in their various small beer-drinking hide outs and privately 'doing their thing'! The corpse of Chief Forbehndia had arrived there a few minutes past noon and their changed programme indicated that he was to be buried on that Friday and the funeral held the following day (Saturday). But it was at about 4.30 PM on that Friday that Momany told himself that God alone knows why and how he had been able to make it to Cameroon. Otherwise, there would have been no burial and funeral of Chief Forbehndia worth writing about. Not even the fact that "He lived a successful life, having helped a lot of people, quite apart from his children. I think he did a lot and I thank God for that." That was his successor (Chief Forbehndia Mbancho[36]) talking to the video-man that Momany hired from Dschang to cover the event, in response to the question, "Can you say a word or two regarding his life?" That interview was toward the end of the jammed up programme of Saturday but let us concentrate on the Friday drama.

At this point on Friday, something very serious just had to be done to savage the catastrophe. Momany asked for every Fossungu and other related persons (from out of the village) to gather in front of Chief Foletia's compound, stressing that it was an order. It was clearly an order directed to all, including the so-called 'untouchables' in uniform. Momany then commenced addressing the gathering by seeking to know the person who altered the programme. It was the Douala Nwangong Meeting to which Chief Forbehndia was a devout member (even though not resident in Douala but in Yoke and Limbe), he was told. Okay, we are now here in the village: what is the plan now that even the schedule of the new plan itself is not being followed? Nobody would now take responsibility as representing that Douala union, not even Elias Akendung who was champion of the talking of programme change! Put the Douala shameful Meeting aside! Concentration on the 'insiders' instead, was the idea.

Momany then put each person on the spot by calling out names and asking what they have to contribute in the village in regard of the burial and funeral. Bernard was the first. He said he had bought the coffin in Limbe and to the question of further action, nothing was forthcoming. Very unacceptable indeed because Momany made it clear that it was what was then at hand that was of interest to him; not whatever that was done before getting to Nwangong: since the corpse could not just have been brought there to be thrown at the

---

[36] By the first paragraph of his Will, "The whole administrator is Fosungu Anastasia. She is assisted by Fosungu Justine and Fosungu Maureen. The successor (next of kin) is Bernard Mbancho Fosungu. The Nkwetta is Njumo Joseph. The Asaba is Nkengafac Therese Fosungu. The Mafor is Fosungu Justine. The caretaker for all the farms is Nguazong Nicasius [Fossungu]."

villagers and that was it!. Next in line, Commandant Michael Njumo (in Photo #47) claimed that he had done so and so in Limbe and on further probing as to what he still had to do, he contributed fifty thousand or a hundred thousand francs, if my memory does not fail me. Someone had been commissioned to note down the contributions and since I do not have that piece of paper, let us just take the higher amount. All the girls – Therese (Photo #48); Anastasia and Maurine (Photo #46a); Quinta (Photo #46b); Beatrice (Photo #46d); and Justine (Photo #50) – who were present advanced silly excuses and Momany had not been particularly interested in their contributions.

He just began to question the contribution from those out of Cameroon who were not present there in Nwangong, beginning with Joseph Njumo Fosungu. The sad story was that nobody had any message from him. The next name was Marie-Claire Efuelancha Fossungu (now Afueh). At the mention of this name Elias Akendung found himself actually hiding naked in public! He mentioned a certain amount of money sent to him by Marie-Claire, and hell broke loose, with all the girls from Limbe, including Marie-Claire's sister (Scholastica Nkengafac Fossungu – Photo #46c), who all began *yahkghegh* or shaming the man (in Bangwa), saying that Marie-Claire had clearly told them that she had sent 400,000 FCFA, not the meagre sum the police man was claiming. Whatever the case actually was, was none of Momany's business as he continued to ask for what is to be officially put down as contribution from the conniving woman in Bowie, Maryland. Elias began justifying how he had used this and that amount to do this and that at her own *cry-die* house in their father's compound which is very far off from Chief Forbehndia's residence in Letia, and other such rubbish. Momany just had to cut off the stupid narration, insisting that whatever that was happening or not happening privately between people was of no interest to the point there and then. What was of importance was what was being contributed to the official ceremony taking place at the official *attehttah* (theatre of action in Bangwa). Elias then said all what was remaining of the money was thirty thousand francs which he was tendering as Marie-Claire's contribution! Not even near to half of what the video man covering the occasion was taking home to his family! (The coverage of the event cost 150,000 FCFA, for those who want to know.)

But it was still something, considering the fact that, but for the staging of the "embarrassment show" no one (except the Limbe girls – and perhaps a whole lot of others called from Bowie) would be aware that four hundred thousand francs flew from there to the *Akendunging moneyintriguist*. The Bowie-Douala Conspiracy against Momany's stand on positive-progress (because in Cameroon's Advanced Democracy regression is still measured as progress) was thus exposed if you also remember the two of them (Elias & Marie-Claire) again in the Police-Family Thesis (meaning people who only take and take and take, never giving in return). As mentioned before, nobody was actually expecting this bold action from anybody. But I think the "surprise" was necessary because it is not understood just how/why the corpse of someone like Chief Forbehndia should have been brought to Nwangong for burial and funeral without anyone being in charge of coordinating the lined up activities, actions which must also have been well mapped out and respected to the letter. But if you find all that surprising, I ask you to hold on until we have also elaborately found out a few things. In asking the questions about Marie-Claire, was Elias just out to hear what Momany had to say and then pass it on to the US partner in *dragdownism*? And yet these are people who call themselves 'your brother/sister'? You can see that giving Momany a bad name for nothing is not just an *Asahchopination* thing.

Mamiteelization and the *Frederickeugenic* Theory

The bad-name story is not new and it is neither not old enough because Joseph Njumo Fosungu of Dallas, Texas (USA) did the same thing in 1992. To acquire his cheap and useless popularity with them, this is what Joe would tell the son of Solomon Tangwa ('the technical adviser to the whole children'[37] in Photo #49) called Ernest that he

---

[37] That is from the 3rd paragraph of the Will of Chief Forbehndia which entirely says: "Mr. Ntemgwa Solomon is the technical adviser to the whole children. He should be crowned as nkem. Nkengafac Therese [Fossungu] should own the house at Yoke near the Yoke water. She should use the farms but she has nothing

(Joe) wanted to bring Ernest to the United States but Momany had to first invite the Tangwa son to Canada from where Joseph would take over and get him to the USA. What a stupid way to acquire fame with stupid people! And Joseph went ahead fooling all these people without having even suggested anything of the sort to the "key-holding man"! Joe is obviously correct in defining 'your Fossungu people' as stupid; and that stupidity does not quite leave Joseph out even if he denounces being a Fosungu as he has done in his *Josephinizationing* letters: the full contents of which can be found in Fossungu (2015c: chapter 3. Three persons that Joe cites incessantly as having poisoned his father's mind are 'Therese and Catherine [who] poison your mind to the extent that you abandoned my mother and caused her death.'

While you will find one of the accused, Catherine Fosungu (in Photo #50), I must say, unfortunately, that I have not been able to lay hands on any photo of the 'victim' (Thecla Anangfack Fosungu, née Njumo). None of Momany's siblings of the household that has been contacted by email or phone for the purpose of acquiring a photo of her (their biological mother) has responded at all. It is kind of strange, but not so to anyone who understands what *Mamiteelization* signifies. That is, the idea put into their heads by their birth mother (Mamie Thecla) that Momany was "an outsider" who should not be trusted and associated with whatsoever. This royal family is made of a lot of people who think in similar lines and thus give *Mamiteelization* the boost that should have been lacking. Marie-Claire being a clear case, considering that she has taken her birth mother together with her blood siblings to the USA without in the least thinking about those others that brought her up to where she is today. But that is not all. At this point, know that *Frederickeugenism* is the worst form of narrow-mindedness.

There is no need for me to give you Eugene Lekeawung Asahchop's lengthy and perplexing letter to Momany on the issue of Marie-Claire asking for the return of "her" things because she and Momany are having problems. I say no need for that since what you really need now is just the confirming letter from her brother,

---

to do with other properties. The whole family should recognize Fon D.F. Fosungu as their grandfather."

Frederick Temenu Fossungu. Dated June 3, 1999 and addressed to "(Mr.) Brother Peter and Sister Schola," Frederick's letter entirely went as follows:

It's a great pleasure writing [to] you people again. How are you at this moment, I hope everybody is alright; back home at this moment everybody is fine. We thank the almighty God who gave sister Scholastica's visa last month.

Here in Dschang, everything is okay despite the fact we are suffering in the hands of Francophones. All lectures, assignments, practicals, field studies are all carried in the French language. Out of the 15 courses I am doing in level II, none is taught in English. Brother, I wish that you should do me a favour and look for any document i.e. any magazine concerning the European Union there in Canada and send it to me. Such a document is very important to us especially concerning Human and economic geography of Europe, with special focus on European agriculture. Here in the French cultural centre one is being sold at 6500 francs. I hope that there it is cheaper.

Last month Sister Marie-Claire asked me to go to Buea and collect her bed, mattress and wardrobe. I refused going. She said that she is having problems with you people, so I told her that she cannot ask me to go and collect her things from my friend and, of course, a student as myself (Eugene). I wrote a letter to Pa Peter and he said I should wait.

Brother, as I did mention in my last letter, if you happen to see rotring pen variant over there brother kindly send it to me. It is very important during cartography and especially thematic cartography. Such pencils are not only scarce here but also expensive and difficult to see. Goodbye brother. It's me Temenu Frederick. Signed [this paragraph altered].

You see the ways of people who never look beyond their noses? *Mamiteelizalists* or *nonoselfists!* Nonoselfists are those who really do not know what they stand for in life, wallowing with the wind. Assuming even that they (Momany and Marie-Claire) are having problems, in acting as she has done does Marie-Claire ever think of what Momany too can then be asking back from her? Put differently, as soon as Marie-Claire has some problems with her birth mother would her mother not then be entitled to ask her back into her womb and to refuse to give birth to her again? Small minds can never think big. Full stop! But if you want it to continue, then let's ask Marie-Claire what else she actually wanted Momany (who is already a declared enemy to both of them) to be doing in their intra-selves problems? The question is appropriate especially if you know that what she considers as the problem is 'that Momany did not show interest when she was having problems with her husband'. Get the exact thing from Fon NN Fossungu (Photo #57). In a paragraph of his "Greetings from Cameroon" email of September 29, 2008, Fon NN Fossungu made it clear to Momany that "Sister Marie-Claire told me that she is not in good terms with you because when she had those problems with the husband you showed little or no concern. Please know that you are a man besides being a senior brother to them and so you have to always keep that possibility of keeping us together both at home and abroad...."

I cannot here go into discuss her definition of "show concern" except to ask if some of these people ever think of anyone else but themselves? Just another method of giving Momany the usual bad name, eh? What a complex family of complex schemers and *moneyintriguists*! Wouldn't it just be miraculous for a non-scheming member of such a family to successfully accomplish straightforward plans? Imagine the type of farewell ceremony that Chief Forbehndia would have received if all the four so-called children abroad (two in the USA, one in Canada and one in South Africa) actually collaborated and coordinated the show, whether or not all were physically present in Cameroon, and you would have realized what the theory of trust and unity in family dealings entails.

It would be those same traits that are responsible for your not having a portrait of the architect of the decried *Mamiteelization*. Nevertheless, just looking at two of Mamie Thecla's daughters – Josephine Forzi Fosungu (in Photo #51) and Annastasia Chamo Fosungu (in photo #46a) – would not be far from according you a good representation of her facial image. While you are getting her physiognomy as directed, I will be addressing Joseph (whose photo too could not be obtained) and his baits in Debundschazone. Momany was very clear when the naïve persons in Limbe called him to talk about the issue of their son being invited, making it exceedingly clear that, if the scheming and bad-name-giving brother in the USA was anything but serious on doing what he had told them he would do, then he would not at all need to put in the Canada hook because Canada is no road by which people leave Cameroon to the USA; the other way round even being a little bit more convincing, if one *must go* through the one to the other at the time, viewing that Joe got to the USA in 1985 and Momany to Canada only in September 1991.

These demonstrations from the United States bring us back to Douala to find out why the programme could have been changed without the knowledge of those who were travelling that far to be part of this important event? Or, was it only Momany that was in this darkness? Who was it that actually changed the programme but was no longer taking care of the programme so changed and why? These are just some of the questions that were burning Momany's head, especially as they had arrived Dschang the next morning very early but only saw the arrival of the rest of the convoy from Debundschazone with the corpse at about 90 minutes to mid-day! And then the hasty drive from there to Nwangong without anyone at all having given him any briefing. While they had been waiting for the others in Dschang, Momany had contracted for a video/camera man to cover the occasion for four days, not being sure that some such professional was already accompanying the convoy from Yoke. Thank God he did that!

"Operation End-of-Poverty" from the Willing of the Gift?

As to Richard's second paragraph, that particular letter was responded to through Momany's letter to Richard Ngufor Fossungu dated March 24, 2004 which needs to be fully discussed here, it constituting, as it were, the centrepiece of the strategies for ending poverty in the family. After Chief Forbehndia's funeral ceremony in October 200, the first thing Momany began with doing was the 2003 Maurine-Calestus invitations (as well as Bridget's in 2009); followed up by a lot more that could be coming up from time to time. He was doing all these things without having seen or heard of the contents of Chief Forbehndia's will; a will that only got to his attention, thanks to Mafor Justine's Canada College Files of 2008-2010. Already in the course of realizing this particular Canada College project, at one point (as in the just noted case of asking for photos) he asked for certain documentation from Justine so as not to rely solely on what he had in his head as her essential information. Precisely, he wanted her birth and academic certificates to be sent to him. Justine sent the requested documents while also including a copy of Chief Forbehndia's Will, a paragraph of which touches directly on what Momany was even then doing without knowing. Could Justine just have included that Will simply because it mandated what the man was doing? I am talking about the 7th paragraph of the Will which ordains that "Madam Justine Fosungu should take her studies very serious and be careful the way she uses her money (finances). Peter Ateafac Fosungu, Marie-Claire Afueh, Mbancho Bernard [Fosungu] and Njumo Joseph [Fosungu] should take proper care for Justine M. Fosungu for her education problems."

The Justine File (Canada College Project) is thus so graphical in exposing Momany's 'ignorant' clairvoyance, which is not limited thereto but could be detected also in (1) the unknown fight with *midnightism* or midnight politics (see Fossungu, 2015a: chapter 3) and (2) the defending of the Julie Fosungu underdog who was not strong and experienced enough like the accused Madam Catherine above (see Fossungu, 2013c: chapter 3). That was the 'dead and unknown' Will that was 'being ignorant executed'. The question that remains is that of what the gift being willed consists of. All the answers you need you can get from a classic Letter to the Whistance-Smith family (Photo #33), dated Monday, January 5, 2004, in which Momany wrote:

Dear Andrew, Nancy *et al*,

WHAT A GIFT! I had become almost speechless before this gift's arrival but now I am completely flattened by it. What can I say? Thank You? Would that be enough Enough? What a nice and wonderful way to begin the year 2004 after the likes of 2002 and 2003! Your letter is jammed with a lot of interesting things that have happened to your entire family in the last year or so. But the gift of writing off my enormous financial debt to you has overwhelmed me and I do hope you will understand why I can hardly talk now about any of the other things you have written about.

Despite how sad and heartbroken I have been, especially in the last two years, some small and clear voice inside of me has, of late, been incessantly telling me that 2004 was to be the year that I have been waiting for to "re-blossom". I didn't know, until today, how exactly that was to be. Now, of course, I do know how and why that voice has kept "pestering" me with its unrelenting consolation.

I think I just have to get ready to hang up the heartache of the past two years, gather myself up, move on and start my life all over again. I must tell you this. No winning lottery ticket of any amount of money would mean as much to me as your GIFT. I wasn't expecting it. Yet, I can't say NO, THANK YOU. My intention has always been to honour my word to you by paying back the debt. The only troubling issue has always been WHEN (not WHETHER) I would be able to do so. This issue has been haunting me a lot, considering the predicament I have had to find myself in since Scholastica's surprising attitude began.

Now you have just turned one of my greatest worries into my greatest gifts of all and I think the best way for me to say Thank You enormously will now be to fearlessly move on and not, in any way, let the unfortunate gap created in the last three years stand in my one-way journey. ALL THAT I DO NOW HOPE AND PRAY FOR AS I MOVE ON IS THAT I BE GREATLY INFECTED BY YOUR ABUNDANT GOODNESS.

Sincerely yours, signed. Peter A. Fossungu.

You cannot correctly appreciate the above missive without the full contents of the gift-making letter. It was attached to and on their traditional yearly Christmas letter recapping the year as concerns the activities of each and every member of the family of five (two boys and a girl, in addition to the parents). It was precisely on the "Christmas 2003" one that the message was 'untraditionally' affixed:

Dear Peter, Thank you for phoning and passing along your new address. I imagine that you chose to move out because things were going very poorly with Schola. I do remember you in my prayers and hope the children are well and that you and Schola are doing better with some distance from each other. I'm sure this whole situation is very difficult.

Andrew and I have decided that you no longer owe us the money (approx. $20,000) we lent to you. Please consider it a gift.

May God richly bless you in 2004.

Nancy & family.

The bill that was then attached to that wonderful note was crossed, with the words "Paid in full" and signed by Nancy Whistance-Smith in December 2003 would show the entire debt of CAD$20,610 broken down by months.[38] This particular letter from Edmonton is principally responsible for and reflected in many of Momany's letters since its reception, epitomized notably by this one to Richard Ngufor Fossungu which was dated March 24, 2004 (being in reply to his letter under discussion):

Dear Nkemngu Richard, It's been quite a long time. I must say that I have had all the letters you sent to me in which you indicated your desperate situation and requesting my assistance. That much

---

[38] This is the breakdown

PETER FOSSUNGU		
[1997]	2000	
	1500	3500
	500	4000
	750	4750
	1560	6310
	900	7210
	1000	8210
	700	8910
	700	9610
	700	10310
	500	10810
	1500	12310
[1998] 31 March	700	13010
April	700	13710
May	700	14410
June	700	15110
July	700	15810
August	700	16510
September	700	17210
October	700	17910
November '98	700	18610
May 2000	1000	19610
October 2000	1000	20610

needed aid did not come your way from here; neither is it now coming. But I have you always in mind even as I am currently unable to extend a helping hand. I just do hope and pray that you can continue to hand on nothing and still not fall flat to the ground.

My main purpose of writing at the present time is this. What do you think you would do (as business) to get out of your current situation and sustain yourself and family independently: if you wake up one day and discover that you were a millionaire? This is only hypothetical but I would like you to seriously consider it and let me know what business plan you have should that become reality. In other words, let me know what you foresee doing (if you had it) so as not to be poor thereafter again. As I have just said, this is just hypothetical and I want to be the only one you discuss your plans with. Make it as detailed as you can.

Extend greetings.

Sincerely yours, signed.

That represents just a minute portion of the operation meant to eradicate poverty in the family. The expectation was to make sure that his case (like many others) is taken care of once and for all so that Momany is no longer distracted by him when he starts the process of aiding another person. This has been described as *Scholasticalization*, deriving, of course, from Scholastica Achankeng Asahchop (Photo #1) who took advantage in meeting the requirements so well that she, very unlike the others, speedily got to Canada. Lined up in the 'Operation End-of-Poverty' in the Family were Dieudonné Asongu Fossungu (Photo #31) – businessman and landlord in Alou; Vincent Awandem Fossungu (Photo #52) – businessman in Ekona; Esther Asongnkeng Fossungu (Photo #53) – businesswoman in Ekona; Richard Ngufor Fossungu – businessman in Douala; Calestus and Bridget Fossungu (Photo #43) – landlord and businesswoman in Douala; Quinta Alonche Fosungu (Photo #45b) – very successful seamstress in Limbe; Odette Ateafac (Photo #25) – businesswoman in Douala; and Therese Nkengafac Fosungu (Photo #48) – restaurant-operating businesswoman in Yoke. And there was **Project Canada** which specifically caught in Kelie Fossungu Tsopzem (daughter – Photo #4); Queenta Ngum Afanwi (wife-to-be); Regina Akiefac Fossungu (mother); Justine

Mamefat Fosungu (sister); and Mitterrand Tale'eh Fossungu (nephew – Photo #54).

The phone problems in Cameroon at the time and persisting,[39] would tell you why Richard has been talking all the time of being contacted through Elias Akendung. As regards Richard's further communications in that regard, take his letter of June 23, 2003 to Momany & wife:

Dear Mr. & Mrs. Nkemtale'eh, I am indeed sorry to inform you that I lost my daughter, the last born of Mary, on the 5/6/03 after a brief illness, and we took the corpse for burial in the village. Another sad [piece of] news is that of Ernestine Tendongmo, the daughter of Pauline Anangafac, the Fon's wife, on the 29/5/03. Since you left us, I have not been able to write due to financial problem; that is, money to buy a stamp to write to you. I hope Ngunyi and the small brother are all sound, and their mother too? Greet them for us. In case of any message to us call through your friend Elias [Akendung].

Thanks. Signed.

---

[39] In the 4th paragraph of his cited 2006 letter, Ngi-Nyam stated that "Here in the village, we have not yet had the Network to enable us communicate with cell phones but before long, we will have it. Thenceforth we would be able to talk to each other frequently. However and for now, continue to rely on letter-writing. This being my maiden letter, has, of necessity, got to be brief, later ones would be lengthier. So long then and with all the best of wishes and God's choicest blessings Peter." The telephone question is not just limited to Ngi-Nyam's village. Many areas of the country are still 'un-networking' even as the arrival of cellular phones (thanks so much to murdered Colonel Gaddaffi of Libya) has reduced a lot of the unnecessary communication problems that Cameroon is well known for. I say: 'Unnecessary' in what sense? The hands of a multitude of candidates are up; but let 'Power' Solomon Tatah (the closest of them all to Nginyam) powerfully explain it to you. In the first paragraph of his letter of February 2, 1998 to Momany, he made it known to "The Most Powerful [that] I received your powerful card and letter on 30/01/98. We thank you for having us in mind as you entered the year 1998. We too have been thinking about you despite the break in communication between us. Unfortunately, we don't yet have a phone which could have facilitated communication between us whenever it is impossible or difficult to write. The bureaucracy here at P & T is making the acquisition of a phone more difficult than putting an elephant through the eye of a needle. Despite the fact that we have 'played their game,' there is still no headway, I'm just fed up now because of the numerous visits I have been making to 'ACTEL' without success. Nevertheless, I keep hoping that one day we'll have it. So they tell us. That is Cameroon. Take it or leave it. The decision is ours."

Just imagine trying to aid a desperate person like that through passing through someone like Elias Akendung and you would have sufficiently appreciated the necessity for direct phone contact that is being evoked here. You must still remember the matter in chapter 2. I am talking about the comment from Chief Forbehndia Mbancho made about "Terrible Ladies" (and 'Gentlemen,' I would add) in regard of the airport problem. The foregoing situations clearly demonstrate why Momany chose to go personally in January 2007 to settle Richard Ngufor's case on the spot as well as take care of other important academic and marital businesses that required his presence in Cameroon. All that because Richard gave an interesting response to the letter seeking to know what plan he had for becoming self-supporting with a million francs at his doorstep one morning. It is worth mentioning that Calestus Nkemanang and wife (Photo #43) would vouch without hesitation that they got their own million francs before then and had equally invested it well. They are not as fine today as would be expected simply because both of them do not quite synchronizing in their handling of money.

Anyway, the ill-fated 2007 journey to Cameroon was then Richard's turn because of his reply of May 12, 2004:

My dear brother Dr. P.A.F., It was a great pleasure when I received your letter of 24-03-2004 and all its contents were well understood. How are you and family? I hope everybody is in good health. As concerns the question you asked me that if I awake one morning and find myself a millionaire, what will I do with the money? In case such an opportunity falls in my hands, I will rush to where the second hand vehicles are sold and take a 19-seater Toyota Hiace, or a pick-up double-cabin, for transport. With a pick-up, it's good to buy oil from a neighbouring town as Edea to sell in Douala on retail and wholesale.

On the other hand, when things will be moving smoothly, I can also integrate a store for articles around my quarter or buy plots to construct studios, another way to plant the money.

You know fully well the story of the 10-seater Liteace which our late father bought. As you saw it yourself, I hadn't free hands to manage the bus as earlier planned by him due to the house he built for his wife, Catherine. If not of that I would have not been what I am today; due to much respect that I gave to our late father, following the promise he gave me but later on he didn't fulfil [for more on that unfulfilled promise, see Fossungu, 2013c: 31-34].

I wish you a nice time and your family, while waiting to hear from you. I am still hanging around waiting for your opinion. Accept greetings from me and family. For now we are sound. Bye-bye.

Nkemngu Rich. Signed.

Very impressive the way Richard wanted to use a million francs to come out of "the harsh discipline of poverty" (as Ngi-Nyam would put it). But, unfortunately, when Momany went over in January 2007 in order to try (among other things that took him there that year) setting up something for Richard thieves were sent after Momany not only to seize the money but to kill him as well. The important thing here is to note that Richard Fossungu's letter (in relation to the Asahchop death that is being discussed) is not used here because he is one of those who do not communicate until they have a death or sickness through which to have money sent via them. It is instead used for the persons telling him in Muyuka that they called and Momany gave no positive response (that is, the channelling of the money to them). Dieudonné Asongu Fossungu (Photo #31) is Momany's only full blood sibling. But he never communicates until there is an occasion for money to get into his hands.

Just listen to his only letter ever written to Momany, noting well the inconsistencies of his claims. Dated February 17, 2003, late Dieudonné wrote:

Dear Dr., How is it going? I hope everything is moving on successfully. This letter is just to apologize for the fact that since you left I have not written any letter to you. It is just because I was not having any address that I could use to have the reply. And the address you used to write to me is very good because the letter took only 18 days to reach me.

With regard to our mother, she is now living with Mamie Lucia in the village. I heard from one of my friends who came from the village that she is quite well now. SORRY Why?

DR. this is also to let you know that I had an accident in Penja with my bus on 14-2-2003, knocking down a woman. It was on the same day I received your letter to me and since then I am detained at the Gendarmerie Brigade.

Greet Sister Schola and the child for me. If you want to phone, you can use this number XXX XXXX.

N.B: Please DR I am begging for your help. I am in difficulties. I am in a very bad condition now.

I am yours Asongu Dieudonné.

In the Wilderness Crying for Love and Understanding Dialogue

You can see that most of these people think communication only in terms of asking for "help" or "cry-die" money and the like. Not so with Richard Ngufor Fossungu. If there is one Fossungu name that has the highest number of letters with Momany, it is no other than Richard. He is right in his observations but all that only goes to make the point of advancing in *moneyintriguism* and *dragdownism*,[40] especially as many of the mishaps in his family particularly came to Momany's attention as clearly seen in the announcement to the Fon of Nwangong, after which the *dragdowning* problems or obstacles began pouring in, in a more accentuated and complex fashion. I am referring to Momany's letter of October 30, 2000 to Fon David Foncha Fossungu in which he announced what he was looking forward to doing with his latest achievements, not actually knowing what the *dragdowners* were plotting:

His Royal Highness D.F. Fossungu,

There have been several deaths and other mishaps in the family since I left the country five years ago. I have so far been hearing of most, if not all, of them. I have so far not been able to write and talk about some of these things and about my own state of affairs here in Canada. It is not because I am not interested in these things. I am very up to date with what has been happening back home. The simple reason for my silence has been that I got so caught up in things here

---

[40] For example, before *dragdowning* assumed enhanced proportions, Momany had tried to aid him resolve some the enormous difficulties confronting him by sending to Richard Ngufor Fossungu the sum of 200,000 FCFA on August 8, 1999 through Western Union #790-071-7301 (being CAD 535.91), with Agency being Peel 612's operator 134.

that I wanted to devote most, if not all, of my little time and financial resources to achieving what brought me out here in the first place. It has not been easy at all. But today I am very happy to inform the entire family and village through you that you can go ahead and rejoice because I am now (since October 26, 2000) known as Dr. Peter Ateh-Afac Fossungu. In other words, this family has a doctor now and, with God's grace, things will never be the same again in this village which must hereinafter have to assume its rightful place.

The gods of Nwangong in particular and of Cameroon in general have all through been with me. I am very thankful for this and hope they will continue guiding me in my efforts to change, for the better, Nwangong, Lebialem, South West, Cameroon and the World.

I have enclosed a photo of me holding Ngunyi Fossungu when she was two (2) months old and another of Ngunyi alone at 5 1/2 months old.

Once more, go ahead and celebrate in your own way while waiting for my arrival home sometime early next year, 2001.

Extend my greetings to everyone at home.

Sincerely yours, (signed) Dr. P.A. Fossungu [this paragraph altered].

Note well the year of planned triumphant arrival to Cameroon and that Chief Forbehndia (Photo #19) received a similar letter too, as it is the home-coming "reconsideration" that he would be talking about in his own pleading letter to be read later on. Oh! What an *Asahchopination*! 'Chief Forbehndia' in Bangwa means a "chief who is the foundation of the house," 'the one who sustains the family or community from downsliding into ruin or disrepute'. Here then you find that same Chief Forbehndia in the wilderness crying for help, to no avail, because of the very Scholastica that he has been so instrumental in advancing. Who, with a sound knowledge of who this man is and what he represents, would not cry a river just reading his desperate letter? Of course, only a *moneyintriguing dragdowner* wouldn't. And should one just stay in a marital union with such a person just for the sake of the children that they are merely seeing as money-making tools?

Some Fossungu royals would appear to think so. For example, Momany's sister, née Esther Asongkeng Fossungu (Photo #53), aka Mafor Nkemtale'eh, wrote to him on January 2, 2003 as follows:

Dear Nkem, I am sure that you went back very safely. How did you meet the family?

I have tried on two occasions to get you by phone but failed.

Have you reconciled and are living together with your wife? If yes, then praise the Lord; if no, then you are a man, try to do everything possible for you people to reconcile.

One native doctor told us that if Nkwetta is left at Lobe he will die. This made my husband and myself to struggle to bring him and his family from Lobe to Ekona. He is still very sick. The small money we had is gone on medicines and he is not well yet. There is no money to take him back to the hospital. My husband is still down as you saw him.

Accept warm greetings from Foncha who did well in his first term examination. He is begging you not to forget that his thing he begged from you. Accept warm greetings from all of us and share with the family. I am eagerly looking forward to hearing from you.

Yours sincerely, Mafor Nkemtele'eh.

A letter from Vincent Awandem Fossungu (Photo #52), aka Nkwetta Nkemtale'eh, confirmed some of the contents of the one above. Also written on February 2, 2003 Nkwetta Nkemtale'eh told Momany:

Dear Nkem, I am happy to tell you that I am now living with my wife and child with Mafor and the husband at Ekona. I was surprised one morning in Lobe to see Mafor come in. She started parking my things and said that all of us must leave Lobe for Ekona. Well, I had to give in. We are now in Ekona.

I am still down in health. That cough is my problem. It needs serious and immediate treatment. The small money sister had is finished. I don't have money to continue treatment. And with the illness, I can't do any hard labour. Nkem, I am pleading for financial assistance to enable me cure myself.

Justine [his wife] has sent greetings and says that you should not forget that her promise. Extend warm greetings to Madam and child.

Yours faithfully, Nkwetta Nkemtele'eh

That was merely confirming the message of Mafor Nkemtale'eh who was also pleading "for you people to reconcile." Enter Chief Chief Foletia (Photo #23), the *grand style* reconciliation advocate.

Foletia's letter of February 21, 2004 refers to Momany as "the husband and father of Scholastica while she is your wife and mother," pleading with the parties (like the other personalities already seen, and more) to "call off the matter and keep me informed." Chief Foletia's communication is not only significant because it was addressed to his nephew, Momany. Quite apart from the fact of his also being the Chief Celebrant of the Nwangong Marriage in question, his letter is so instrumental in giving more education to the issues of this book:

Dear Nkem Tale'e h,

I am writing to believe that your journey back from Cameroon was safe. I was hoping to hear from you since then.

Your wife was with us for the burial of her father, Peter Asahchop, your father-in-law. I expected a note from you to the bereaved family but all was in vain. In the course of finding out, I was told you are not pulling well with your wife.

Even if you had some problems with your wife, situations of death and burial could suspend the problem and eventually end up the matter. Over there you are the husband and father of Scholastica while she is your wife and mother. I am by this [letter] appealing that you call off the matter and keep me informed.

The health situation of your mother needs your regular calls, contacts and some preparations before it is too late. I doubt whether you are aware and have prepared.

Greetings to you and children and others over there. I am waiting to hear from you as soon as possible.

Chief Foletia. Signed

P/S: Our mission station church house has collapsed and I have been commissioned to appeal for some financial assistance from you and other sons and daughters of Nwangong over there. Do well to communicate with Marie-Claire and others. You people can always communicate with us through B.P. 257, Dschang, Menoua Division, Cameroon.

Thanks in anticipation and best wishes. Signed

Queentalizing and Forbehndializing the Dieudonné Asongu Irresponsibility File

Chief Foletia might be right in the theses he advances. Take first the "The health situation of your mother [which] needs your… preparations before it is too late". Obviously predominating here is the house issue which Elizabeth Asahchop, as well as Scholastica herself, would already have talked about in one of their letters above. Effectively trying to take care of these concerns began in June 2004 with the impromptu visit that was prompted by the mother's health condition, a trip that is also a classic in the *Queentalization* of most of the Fossungu and other Files. As noted in previous chapters, Queenta's interest in Momany's family is impressive and reminds me of the words of the main character in a Nigerian movie, *Beloved*. To his girlfriend (fiancée) who was advising they quickly elope from the inhibiting [Nwangong] village despite the cries of horror coming from the girl's compound, Ezimba (if I got the name right) theorized that "I cannot truly love you and don't care about your family!" Unfortunately, though, he died in the process of trying save the lives of the parents of his love, leaving the woman to bring up his unborn child all alone. These are parents who, by the way, were stiffly against their marriage (like Nwangong's Royal Family stupidly was to Queenta's), a stance which provoked the eloping enterprise.

That would be a clear opposite to Jane's parents, leading to Momany's thesis that "he has never regretted his not having Jane as his wife as much as his not having her parents and siblings as his in-laws" (Fossungu, 2014: 57). Momany can scarcely be wrong as can be demonstrated in Jane's father's letter of October 8, 1998 that he sent to Momany.[41] Translated, the letter could read like this:

---

[41] Paul Jiomeneck (Jane's father) could not have put it any better in his letter of October 8, 1998 that he sent to Momany from Yaoundé (this is the Original text whose translation is found following in the text):

Bien Cher Monsieur Peter,

C'est avec un très grand plaisir que je vous écris cette letter en reponse à la carte de veoux que vous avez bien voulu m'adresser pour me souhaiter une très boone guérison suite à une terrible maladie qui m'a frappé. Au moment où votre carte arrivait à Yaoundé j'étais au village où j'ai passé un peu du temps, raison pour laquelle je vous responds avec un retard et je vous demande de m'en excuser. Une fois de plus je vous dis

My dear Peter, It is with enormous pleasure that I write this letter to you in reply to the 'Get Well Quickly' wishes you sent to me after the terrible affliction that visited me. Your letter arrived while I was in the village and that explains why I am replying a bit late. Once more I thank you from the bottom of my heart for this message that made everybody in the house so happy. As to my illness, it is just as my children (who are all your brothers and sisters) have already explained to you. I had a stroke and God has worked his miracles and I am now about 80% cured and, with a little of more time, I am sure I would completely recover. I know that you pray a lot for me and I ask that you continue doing so, for God is going to answer our prayers.

How are you faring with your studies? I know you to be a fighter and am therefore convinced that nothing will stop your coming back soon with your Ph.D. I want to also thank you for being so dependable to my family, not to leave out your unmatched assistance to Barthelemy in the domain of admission and scholarships for studies abroad. I am hopeful that God will not allow all these efforts to be in vain and that he will succeed in the matter. I am here also extending greetings from my wife and everyone at home and wishing

---

merci pour votre carte de souhait qui a rendu tout le monde très content dans la maison.

Pour ma maladie, tout est comme mes enfants qui sont vos frère et soeur vous ont expliqué. J'ai eu un STROKE et le Bon Dieu a exercé ses miracles sur moi et me voici guéri à environ 80%. Je suis sûr qu'avec le temps je vais retrouver toute ma santé. Je sais que vous priez beaucoup pour moi. Il faut continuer ainsi et le Bon Dieu va nous recompenser.

Pour vos études comment vous vous y prenez? Je sais que vous êtes un grand bosseur et rien ne va vous empecher de rentrer au pays un de ces jours avec le plus gros diplôme de votre formation.

Je vous remercie aussi d'être si reconnaisant en vers ma famille. L'aide que vous faites à Barthelemy pour l'aider à trouver une école avec une bourse est incomparable et je crois que nous allons réussir à lui obtenir quelque chose grâce à vos efforts et à Dieu aussi.

Je vous transmets ici les salutations de mon épouse et de tout le monde à la maison.

Nous vous souhitons un grand succès dans l'aboutissement de tout ce que vous entreprenez.

Bonne chance
Signé
Paul Jiomeneck

you success in all your undertakings. Good luck. Signed. Paul Jiomeneck.

This is my translation of the original text which will later also aid us in chapter 4 to get into the heads and logic of the *moneyintriguists*. So, with just this minute part of it, is there any reasonable person that would wish more than more from God who has given them in-laws like members of this family? Is this not the type of family that would already have propelled Momany to already be doing, if not even completely done what he promised the world through Fon David Foncha Fossungu and which Jane's father has also made mention of? Very unlike the *Asahchopination* that gets everything but everything is never everything to them until the provider of everything ceases to exist, just hear all the praises Momany is getting from the Jiomenecks and others for just doing what he does so well to anybody who cares to want to progress and he possibly can be of any help.

Queenta Ngum Afanwi (Photo #28) would surely have made a perfect spouse to the Fossungus if they were not as shortsighted and "stupid" (as Joseph Njumo Fosungu puts it) as to join hands with the Asahchops to chase her out of Nwangong and marriage. Grateful people (and those truly in love too) do not require 'Heaven and Earth' to say thank you. In her "My Health Now" of April 10, 2007 at 12.05 PM Queenta would also be telling "Dear" Momany that:

I will not stop thanking you for your kindness towards me especially during this tough period of mine. In fact, you are God given. I went to the hospital as earlier mentioned and some drugs were given to me for now. The doctor says I will come again in a week's time for check-up. Also, the echography was done and the doctors said that I should take the drugs first before they know the next step. Actually, Dear, the bleeding and pains are subsiding now, Glory be to God. I don't know if you finally called through the number I gave to you because I was not around. That same day I was called back to the village because thieves broke into the house and stole the VCD [you brought for us] but there is serious investigation going on now.

Dear, hope you are fine that way. My number is available now so please I am expecting your call any time after reading this mail of mine. Matilda extends greetings and wishes you the best of life. The latest number you gave to me is quite inaccessible. I don't know if it is actually network problem or something else. Nevertheless, you will clarify this to me when you call next. Please keep on praying for me. HAPPY EASTER IN ARREARS!!!

You just cannot love someone and do not care about their family relations. Thus, you also see the cordiality even in Momany's sustained relationship with Odilia's sister that became very instrumental in his reunion with Liza. Those of you with a 'Long Memory' would now be privileged to know that Pat is actually Odilia's senior sister in *Janodilism* who might have caused or contributed to the failure of the Odilia-Momany marriage. But also note well (previous and later communications apart) that on January 22, 2006 at 9: 23 AM Pat also wrote to Momany in "Re: How are you?" as follows: "Hello! Thanks for replying. It was good reading from you again. We are all fine this way. Sorry for the winter. Home is really home as you say. I pray for grace for you to get used to your second home. Thanks also for the forwarded message. In Africa we say *"black man nodi die dirty"* but I think we ought to be more careful. I'll send it to as many friends as I can. Hope to read from you again. My regards to Schola and the babe(s)." We have already had more in this direction when we examined ex-lovers' reunion in chapter 2.

What we need to harp and focus on here is the fact that, with Queenta in Scholastica Achankeng Asahchop's shoes, a lot of Momany's extended family members will still be alive today and especially Chief Forbehndia who you see in Photo #19. It wouldn't even have gotten to that stage. But, finding that Momany could not travel, Queenta would have quickly jumped into the plane the next morning heading to Cameroon to ably replace her husband in the tasks that needed performing. When he didn't descend into the level of hatred in Scholastica's regard the day Momany received his own father's letter desperately needing urgent help which he was not able to give, thanks to Scholastica's machinations, Momany confirmed to himself that day that God never ever gave him that hating-ability for a reason. That is, that God instead gave him just the things he needed to accomplish the task that was his to realize. Imagine Chief Forbehndia dying, not because he didn't have the means like Richard Fossungu, but solely because the only son who could have easily fulfilled his desire for obtaining medical treatment in Canada in 2001 was himself helpless. Handicapped in the sense that he could not travel to Cameroon!

In the end, it is certainly not the sick eyes that killed Chief Forbehndia but the frustration, which was further aggravated by the unreliable people he then had to rely on as "his eyes". Even his letter of May 11, 2001 was not written by himself as usual. It was written by someone else but signed by him (with 'father' written by himself immediately before his signature in different ink). Note the "father" designation too well for the confusion thesis in the Elephant Money Fight lecture in chapter 4 below. Chief Forbehndia's letter earnestly pleaded:

Dearest son, your letter of 14 March [2001] was received. Greetings to the family. Your promise to visit us shall be reconsidered [because] I am facing a serious medical help. My eyes are not seeing. I proposed to ask your opinion if I can take treatment with you in Canada. Write and tell me (or by phone) about the formalities needed to come to your place for treatment. Eyes specialists in Cameroon have said that my case is beyond their medical care. I am taking eye drops treatment for now. Medical doctors have advised me to understand that I may soon be completely blind. Phone to me as soon as possible for means of treatment in Canada. The last vision of my eyes will soon disappear if specialized care is not administered.

My last consultation was on the 2nd of May 2001 when the medical report proved my case as increasingly abnormal. We are waiting and I am to finance my trip to Canada. I am ready to take the treatment in Canada through your able directives.

Pardon me for any misgivings and reply me as soon as possible.

N.B. Write to or phone Madam Marie-Claire for the worst tension [worsening situation?] of my eyes and [that she] should help financially for my medical trip to Canada.

Thanks for remembrance

Fosungu Emmanuel, father. Signed.

What a loss! All that happening because Scholastica who knows, like everyone who knows, how Momany (let alone herself) could not have come to Canada in the first place without Chief Forbehndia's enormous push. Imagine that Momany was already a permanent resident when that letter came in, then you begin to see the point more clearly. At the time the father's letter arrived, Momany's passport with which to travel was with the immigration authorities since, because of the so-called wife's refusal to sponsor him, he had to file for his own asylum (again, based on Scholastica's lies?[42]). The sponsorship would never have required his being at any time without his passport. Chief Forbehndia had his money available that he was ready to spend to treat his eyes but there was no "able" child to work him through the process of obtaining the visa. And this because that able child had been imprisoned by the very person Chief Forbehndia's money has inestimably advanced. What a shame!

Momany did all he could to instruct his sisters back home on how to go about it to no avail. What else then could Momany be able to do in Cameroon while still in Canada? I just don't want to attempt even getting into these cases of Momany's siblings of the Household because that would be enough material to constitute a different forthcoming book altogether. But you can get an insight or idea of the frustration and incomprehensibility encountered with the Chief Forbehndia Canada-coming question from this email titled "Be Serious and let's know what you really want to do!" that Momany sent to Mafor Forbehndia Justine (aka Justine Mamefat Fosungu – Photo #46e) on Saturday, October 11, 2008 at 11.25 PM:

Mafor Justine,

People who really want to succeed in going abroad do a lot of serious work to get themselves out. It seems to me that you are thinking that everything will be done for you. That is not possible. Earlier on I had sent you details about the email account created in your name (XXXXXXXXXX) which I am using to secure admission and other things for you here. Though you are not to use this email to send out any communication, it is important that you check the

---

[42] "A few questions will suffice here to wiggle your mind. What was Schola making of her husband's own safety in Cameroon too [by refusing to sponsor him]? Was her claim of persecution there because of the husband's critical writings true or false victimhood? Was she really coming to Canada as someone's spouse or just using that spouse *status* as a bridge to get here to *only* realize the schemes they (she and her parents) had cooked up back there: at the expense of the children and supposed spouse?" (Fossungu, 2015b: 50)

email regularly to acquaint yourself with what is going on and keep up with the development of your case. I forwarded communications received through this email to your present email and all what you could do was forward it to me without a word. I don't understand what you mean by this. I had, before the forwarded message, sent you an email explaining how you should get yourself prepared for the eventual visa interview at the Embassy there in Yaoundé but have heard nothing concerning this issue until now. Know that I can do every other thing regarding your coming to study here but **I cannot attend the Visa Interview for you. And without you succeeding in this interview, every other thing that would have been done would have been done in vain**. Please, if you are not serious about this matter, just let me know just what it is that you want to do with your life. To me, it is what you are serious about doing that is important. **So, what is it that you really want to do: study here in Canada or study in Buea (Panafrican Institute)**? I will send the password to the email again if you want it. Make up your mind and let me know. Thank you. PAF

It is this same kind of attitude that could not get the father out of there into Canada for treatment despite all the efforts from here. How could anyone back there (who has never been out here) have been able to understand the fix Momany was in? So, like Richard Ngufor, Chief Forbehndia just could not believe that it was Momany of all his children that was not doing anything to help him out. What was the use of having sent this boy to Canada if now that he so badly needed treatment that can be offered there and that same boy is not doing anything effective to get his wish fulfilled? No way else to understand it than that the boy is simply being wicked; the more so as they can all see the wife's parents and siblings being flown to all corners of Europe and then to Canada? Momany has no problem at all with the flying all around the place. That is all part of the progress that he works for. The problem only relates to why they want to be doing all that but also doing everything to thwart any other person from ever being assisted by the same person that did same to them?

Not to go back there and cry a river all over again, I will use just Dieudonné's case which, again, would take us back (even as we don't want to go back) to Joseph Njumo Fossungu's "chief-theory." Dieudonne fell sick in Nkongsamba in Wourizone where he then was living. It was so serious that he was advised by some people, perhaps, 'to go back to the village to die there'. He got there and was just lying there waiting for that day. Momany only got news of it from someone, not even a Fossungu at all. The informant, Paul Njukang Morfaw (Chief Fonjenachop – Photo #55), was ready to help take him to a private clinic in Dschang, if the means were there. Momany assured him that things were not as rosy as they should be but that, together, they have to do all that was required to save the man's life.

For a start, Momany sent a sum of money (about two hundred thousand francs, if I remember well). Dieudonné already at the clinic in Dschang, news came from the man in charge that his sicknesses were so numerous and included those that would not warrant operation or even the cutting off of the rotten toe since the wounds wouldn't heal. AIDS/HIV and diabetes were among the enumerated afflictions. Momany gave the go ahead with the alternative treatment suggested, promising to send more finances later, not on the spot as was desired. A day or so later Momany called his man on the spot and in charge but no one would answer the call. He tried the number of the man's wife (a Fossungu princess!) and got the same no-response response.[43] Even Dieudonné's number wasn't going through anymore. Wow!

---

[43] The talking of 'no-response reponse' reminds me not only of 'no-title title,' a subject that also distinguish Odilia and Liza in a way. Unlike Odilia, except when Liza is responding to Momany's email by hitting the Reply button that creates a 'Re: XY' message title, Liza's emails (as you could have amply noticed) are usually *titleless*, assuming, of course, that 'No-title' is not a title. Perhaps *'titlefully titleless'* would better handle the apparent title contradiction here? Doesn't it sound very much like Cameroon's certificate story, about which some experts have already made some sense (see Fossungu, 2016a)? Whether or not there is any sense with Cameroon's nonsense, here are examples: In a no-subject message of August 20, 2004 at 1013 AM Liza had asked her *"Chéri, Comment vas-tu? En ce qui me concerne: côté santé 100% bon. Il n'y a que mon téléphone qui ne fonctionne plus bien car l'eau y est rentrée. Tu sais que c'est la saison pluvieuse ici. J'aurais souhaité en acheter un autre; bisou à toi."* No-subject message of March 6, 2005 at 2.50 AM: *"Good morning my Dear, I hope you are doing well! Eli."* Again, in another no-subject message on May 19, 2005 at 10:00 AM Liza greeted and informed Momany that *"Mon seul et unique frère est décédé hier à 30 ans. Ma mère n'avait que 2 enfants. Je l'enterre le Weekend prochain. Bonne journée."* On January 17, 2004 at 12.41 PM Liza wrote in No-subject email: *"Peter, Merci pour les conseils. Je suis malade et ne travaille pas depuis ce matin. Je suis en repos médical pendant 4 jours. je t'écrirai plus tard. Je t'embrasse."* On March 15, 2004 at 4.01 AM Liza stated in No-Subject email: *"S'lut, Malgré ton silence, je voudrais de dire que mon papa de Manjo est*

> **CONTRACT OF EMPLOYMENT**
>
> BETWEEN
> **Dr. Peter A. Fossungu** (The Employer)
> AND
> **Ms. Queenta Ngum Afunwi** (The Employee)
>
> I, **Dr. P. A. Fossungu**, a native of Bangwa – currently residing in Montreal (Canada) – do hereby undertake to pay Ms. Ngum Afunwi a basic monthly sum of fifty thousand francs (50,000 Frs.CFA) for taking general care of my mother (Mrs. Regina Akiefac Fossungu) while I am out of Cameroon.
>
> I, **Ms. Queenta Ngum Afunwi**, a native of Bafut – currently residing and working in Nwangong (Lebialem Division) – do hereby undertake (in view of the monetary consideration from Dr. Fossungu to me) to generally take care of his mother, Mrs. Regina Akiefac Fossungu, just as I would do to my own mother.
>
> Signed at Bamenda this Wednesday the 21ˢᵗ Day of June 2004:
>
> ....
> The Employer   The Employee

It was then that it came to Momany's realization that the Hospital Enterprise might have long ended abruptly and Dieudonné taken back and dumped where he had been before. Momany then thought of no one else that could help him understand what was going on in the Nwangong Theatre of *Moneyintriguism* than Queenta Ngum Afanwi, with whom he was still having the obstructed employment contract you see above. Very willing to aid was Queenta who had already been chased out of Nwangong and out of her two jobs by the Asahchops for daring to take care of Momany's birth mother. Just see them again together in Photo #29 and also compare the body language with that in Photo 56. It must be noted, even if only in passing here, that Momany and Queenta were in love with each other. But Momany had still entered into a formal contract for Queenta to take care of his mother.[44]

---

décédé jeudi dernier. L'enterrement s'est bien passé à Bafoussam. Bon début de semaine! Liza" Whatever you make Liza's emails, the Dieudonne Question certainly puzzles a lot.

[44] The terms of this employment agreement being as just shown above, thus making it hard to comprehend why Queenta would later (because of the inhibiting problems on his return, consequent on the attack in Douala in 2007) declare that she had always known that Momany just wanted her to be babysitting his mother (Fossungu, 2014: 129). Anyway, that was long after the Dieudonné File under discussion now.

Momany thus called Queenta who was very happy to be of help. Money was speedily sent to her through Western Union (as generally shown in Table 3) and the next day she was on her way to that same Nwangong where she was already an outcast, to literally carry the lame Dieudonné to Bafut where the man was diligently treated by having the toe that was rotting and expanding cut off. He spent quite a long time there but started walking again (thanks to a lot of the money transferred in Table 3), whereas others had already concluded that he was incurable, having created all sorts of illnesses as his just in order to have an inflated endless flow of the proceeds of all the banks in North America to them there in Nwangong. Oh! *Moneyintriguists*! You think only in the *Asahchopination* you would find them?

Table 3: Western Union Money Transfer to Queenta Ngum Afanwi				
Money Transfer Number	Amount (FCFA)	Amount in $ (CAD)	Transaction Date	Agency
055-448-6213	30,000.00	80.45	February 4, 2008	#0620, operator 397
207-901-9010	40,000.00	102.59	January 3, 2008	#0620, operator 423
206-572-8315	30,000.00	80.21	December 14, 2007	#0620, operator 397
240-935-7783	40,000.00	100.73	Nov. 16, 2007	#0629, operator 381
859-090-7693	100,000.00	234.63	October 27, 2007	#0620, operator 381
257-707-4284	30,000.00	75.95	October 23, 2007	Doreen, operator 001

012-255-5520	40,000.00	98.52	October 18, 2007	#0620, operator 397
007-654-6330	260,000.00	593.40	October 5, 2007	#620. Operator 363
278-772-5264	40,000.00	99.65	September 22, 2007	#0620, operator 381
187-207-1621	40, 000.00	100.84	September 14, 2007	Doreen, operator 001
815-326-7615	70,000.00	176.83	September 7, 2007	#0620, operator 381
456-669-0054	100,000.00	242.07	August 23, 2007	#0620, operator 381
387-797-7999	50,000.00	130.31	August 16, 2007	#0620, operator 411
678-181-4661	40,000.00	101.99	August 9, 2007	#0620, operator 411
051-166-8792	100,000.00	243.52	August 2, 2007	#0620, operator 301
872-707-1882	40,000.00	102.22	July 28, 2007	#0620, operator 411
833-137-7375	100,000.00	244.08	July 13, 2007	#0620, operator 381
NT1870706769*	20,000.00	51,95	July 6, 2007	NTE Head Office

783-617-4740	30,000.00	83.25	April 12, 2007	#0620, operator 388
001-595-2367	20,000.00	59.41	April 7, 2007	#0620, operator 397
929-834-2290	50,000.00	129.02	October 16, 2006	#0620, operator 188
496-602-9660	500,000.00	1333.56	May 13, 2005	Doreen, operator 001
554-312-8923	30,000.00	91.78	February 17, 2005	Doreen, operator 001
527-133-1074	105,000.00	287.70	September 30, 2004	Doreen, operator 001
326-067-6309	65,000.00	188.73	July 3, 2004	#0620, operator 102
Grand Total:	**1,970,000.00**	**5222.12**		

* This is NT Express, not Western Union.

Here then is the funny stupid part of the story of someone who was practically not able to even move his own body around. As he was recovering, Dieudonné started sending for cigarettes and beer while still on his hospital bed. Queenta would then advise him not to start smoking and drinking until he was really well. What does she get in return for thank you? Dieudonné who is still very much dependent on this so-called stranger's goodwill barks back out: "Who are you to tell me what to do or not to do? Who are you, by the way? It is Scholastica that I know!" Yet, all that insult would not push Queenta to just stop cleaning all the mess of this ungrateful man who is passing for Momany's brother! Who can define that with anything other than LOVE? She would still be doing all what needed to be done to see Dieudonné (her brother-in-law) up and doing again. How could Dieudonné (to leave out the other Royals in the village) not even ask himself the simple question: "Where were all these relations of Scholastica Achankeng Asahchop when I was lying there helplessly?" There is no need even going into the case of Momany's mother that had provoked all what Queenta was then undergoing: except to clearly mention that after Dieudonné she went further to get his mother from Nwangong to Bafut where she (Queenta) could be able to continue looking after her, as she could no longer do so in Nwangong. Yet, you would continue to think this man called Dieudonné was actually God's Gift as his name implies?

But for the timely and purposeful intervention of his own friend and age-mate, Nkemanang Calestus Fossungu (Photo #43) Dieudonné would have perished in the cell in Penja or Mbanga, if you recall his only letter discussed above. With the sum of 120,000 FCFA (being CAD $340.00) sent to Nkemanang through Western Union #790-330-3356 on February 25, 2003, he was able to save Dieudonné's ass. It is not even necessary mentioning the 250,000 FCFA (being CAD $673.93) that was also sent to Mafor Nkemtale'eh on May 8, 2004 through Western Union #098-569-9064 (with Agency #0620, operator 308) for the purpose of settling the formalities for a wife that Dieudonné had himself looked for. All these transactions were beautifully handled for his benefit by those to whom the money was channelled.

That talk of channelling money brings us squarely to the Nkemanangs. The issue comes up here not only because (like Queenta) they stayed with Mamie Regina. But also because a lot of people (within the family especially) do think that Nkemanang and wife have made and are still making a lot of money from Momany by having his mother with them since 2008 till when she died in June 2014. That is not at all true and provides the necessity for including in this book a table like Table 4.

Table 4: Money Transfer (Western Union, Except Otherwise Indicated) To The Nkemanangs - Calistus T. Fossungu (CTF) & Bridget Manifuet Fossungu (BMF)

Money Transfer Number	Amount (FCFA)	Amount $ (CAD)	Recipient Name	Transaction Date	Agency
64092455*	203618.52	487.00	CTF	June 7, 2016	TR248372
70850565*	200002.46	487.17	BMF	October 2, 2015	TR523752, Valérie
49553556*	220,005.10	509.62	BMF	September 5, 2014	TR282529, François
778-408-0827	600,000.00	1443.70	BMF	July 8, 2014	#1826, oper. KAM
331-343-4337	100,000.00	257.00	BMF	March 25, 2014	#1826, oper. KRI
767-465-2717	99.873.00	261.66	BMF	February 18, 2014	#3115
740-041-9953	100,000.00	253.30	BMF	March 6, 2014	#1826, oper. KAM
964-181-7247	100,000.00	254.20	BMF	April 17, 2014	#1826, oper. KAM
851-452-5694	100,000.00	220.98	BMF	May 2014	#1407,
726-292-4112	200,000.00	473.23	BMF	February 7, 2014	#3115
018-461-0310	200,000.00	422.36	CTF	Nov. 22, 2012	#1407, oper. MAC
061-285-4199	100,000.00	231.75	BMF	Nov. 28, 2011	#1407, KIM
47759674*	56,730.00	122.00	BMF	July 20, 2011	Joshua
76733902*	450,002.05	1023.83	CTF	June 17, 2011	TR182973, François
847-289-8592	90,000.00	210.98	BMF	April 23, 2011	Doreen, oper. 001

859-343-7400	250,000.00	538.92	CTF	January 6, 2011	Doreen, oper. 001
68036839 *	200, 002.27	521.61	CTF	February 5, 2009	TR1004227, CEL
790-024-6007	50,000.00	150.97	CTF	March 13, 2003	Doreen, oper. 003
790-330-3356	120,000.00	339.88	CTF	February 23, 2003	Doreen, oper. 001
790-378-3369	150,000.00	361.55	CTF	September 5, 2001	Doreen, oper. 001
TOTAL	3,490,231.22	8571.71			

* MoneyGram

This Table 4 does not even include the Nkemanangs' own one million francs tendered to them in the context of Momany's little known Poverty Eradication Project that has been sparingly discussed above. And they obtained this money through the intermediary of Momany's Tiko-based friend who travelled home from Canada long before there was even the need and idea of the Nkemanangs living with Momany's mother. That alone could, without doubt, make you to begin to see that those coming up with such unfounded stories in regard of this humble family in Photo #43 would be clearly telling you that they themselves would not venture to assume such tasks unless all the money in the banks of Canada would have to be transferred to them. Have many of these people (notably Margaret Akendung in Photo #24) not even shamelessly walked up to Madam Nkemanang several times to advise her to keep sending messages to Momany "to the effect that his mother is so sick and requires lots of money for this and that hospital this and that just to get the money flowing"? (You abundantly see the same trend in the family when Momany tries to aid someone: the person would then begin to fabricate plots for more money to flow.) Of course, being the genuine people that they are, the couple's response to all these suggested machinations always was: "If we say that now that Mama is not sick, what are we going to tell him when she would actually be ill?" The couple would certainly have been greatly laughed at by these crooked people; but the same crooks would still go ahead and formulate this and that story on how the Nkemanangs are profiting from taking care of Momany's aged mother.

Also, many of them would view the figures in Table 4 without taking into consideration that most of the amounts therein are sums channelled to the couple simply as the most reliable means of getting those funds effectively reach others that could not be accessed directly. The case of Fon Nicasius Nguazong Fossungu (Photo #57) already exemplifies these numerous situations. In his "Greetings" email to Momany on November 11, 2014 at 9.50 PM, the Fon of Nwangong, HRM Nicasius Nguazong Fossungu, would write to the newly crowned Chief Fotale'eh as follows: "HRH, Accept greetings from Cameroun. Once more, thank you so much for the timely assistance during my wife's burial. For now the children are doing well and the rest of the family too. The wife of Nkemanang Calixtus wants to talk to you. She will like you to call her. She has been trying your number to no avail. Wishing you all the best. Extend greetings to the rest of the family out there [altered paragraphing]." The 200,000 FCFA sent to the Fon as assistance for his wife's burial and funeral was channelled to Bridget by MoneyGram transfer #49553556 in the amount of 220,000 FCFA. The additional 20,000 FCFA was Bridget's transport from Douala (in Wourizone) to Limbe (in Debundschazone) where the Fon resides for work purposes. It was the Fon himself who suggested the sending of the money through Bridget because of his national identity problems at the time. There is no use even going near talking about the hospital and other expenses relating to Momany's mother's chequered life and death; but one would like to also add situations like the 450,000 FCFA meant for the burial of Dieudonné Asongu Fossungu which was dutifully handled by this exemplary and selfless family.

But just let money meant to take care of another person get into Dieudonné's hands and be very certain that the said person has already died: unless some other sum is again redirected otherwise. A clear case in point relates to Nkwetta Nkemtale'eh's letter above. For the purpose of his treatment, Momany sent two hundred and ten thousand (210,000 FCFA) on April 9, 2003 by Western Union (#790-344-5613) to Calistus T. Fossungu (Nkemanang) who was to take it to the Limbe General Hospital where Nkwetta Nkemtale'eh from Ekona was admitted. Nkemanang was not then in Douala, as made known by George Ndemaza through whose phone Momany then used to contact them. Because of the urgency of the case, Momany asked George (who he had not personally met) if he could help receive the money and channel it to its destination. It was okay and Momany then change the recipient, putting George's name. Remember that on March 29, 2003, just about twelve days before, money had also been sent to Dieudonné (then residing in Douala) who had "some missions" to attend to in Dschang, as seen in the first column of Table 5.

Table 5: Western Union Money Transfer to Dieudonné Asongu Fossungu				
Money Transfer Number	Amount (FCFA)	Amount (CAD)	Transaction Date	Agency
790-130-0503	50,000.00	148.84	March 29, 2003	#0620, operator 216
477-262-8369	250,000.00	689.06	Dec. 10, 2004	Doreen, operator 001
028-407-2815	80,000.00	196.27	June 7, 2007	#0620, operator 388
463-132-8939	60,000.00	168.69	June 8, 2007	#124, operator EBU
483-283-7726	50,000.00	142.82	July 14, 2007	#124, operator EBU
935-852-2773	25,000.00	68.08	Sept 7, 2007	#620. operator 381
489-566-3690	20,000.00	54.32	Oct 13, 2007	#0620, operator 397
619-456-0977	35, 000.00	91.37	Dec. 1, 2007	#052, operator 423
177-771-0206	100,000.00	253.05	January 20, 2008	#124, operator EDU
256-473-3520	40,000.00	103.95	February 28, 2008	#0620, operator 363
980-993-5815	485,641.00	1270.00	March 29, 2008	#0620, operator 397

274-919-2546	100,000.00	266.44	April 5, 2008	#0620, operator 422
122-188-0084	60,000.00	168.88	April 17, 2008	#0620, operator 397
635-154-4620	40,000.00	108.34	June 2, 2008	#124, operator JAC
Total:	**1,395,641.00**	**3730.11**		

Before you know it, Dieudonné appeared from nowhere with pranks of mother's serious illness in the village and got half of that money before its delivery to Limbe. He then came back shortly again with a further story that the half taken had also been taken from him by thieves at the Bonaberi motor park as he was about going to the village! If this Dieudonné was not as irresponsible, then why would others be the ones looking after his mother while he himself is right there? I wouldn't even want to venture near the wife-marrying troubling cases that Mafor Nkemtale'eh and Nkemanang could better narrate to you. Dieudonné's tale is just too long and useless for exhaustion here and I am sure he died in June 2011 simply because there was no other Queenta Ngum Afanwi then who could have helped in passing on the information of illness and also again go and take him to hospital to get more insults for "thank you". What did Dieudonné's "known Scholastica" do even when Dieudonné "passed on" in the village where he was supposedly thriving in the motor-taxi business?

Talking of intrigues in Mwangong also leads us to the much talked about village house issue, with the name of Chief Fonjenachop (Photo #55) standing tall. I think the House Factor cannot be discounted in the entertainment differences between the Chief Forbehndia's funeral in 2002 and Mamie Regina Akiefac Fossungu's in July 2014. The Chief Forbehndia's entertainment aspect was hijacked because in 2002 Momany did not as yet have his own house in the village. With his own compound, as was the case with the July 2014 event, all the preparation of entertainment would have been under his control and done in his compound by those selected by him for the purpose. All these conditions could not be satisfied while there was no compound of his. The dynamics only changed because, like with Queenta, Momany had to also use a contractor to at least get the building up, after all the torments from family members. You will realize that members of Momany's large extended family have been spoiling Chief Fonjenachop's name simply because he was aiding Momany to somewhat by-pass their extreme exploitation. Even if this contractor has eaten millions as they claim (do they even know what arrangement was between the two people?), at least the structure is standing there for all to see, just as Queenta's love against their preferred Scholastica's lovelessness. What structure did the complainants ever put up before this man came into the scene? And why did he even have to come into play if they were so competent in doing the job? (Ask the same for Scholastica about Queenta and you wouldn't be wrong for doing so.) It is hard for me to buy any of those stories and you too wouldn't if you consider that what had been sent to Chief Fonjenachop in Table 6 includes the contract price for the execution of the work which was a million francs.

Table 6: Western Union Money Transfer to Njukang Paul Morfaw				
Money Transfer Number	Amount (FCFA)	Amount (CAD)	Transaction Date	Agency
448-444-9372	905,000.00	2019.42	November 9, 2008	#0620, operator 423
333-943-4875	600,000.00	1397.58	July 16, 2007	#620. Operator 381
921-956-4978	205,000.00	519.87	March 29, 2007	#0620, operator 397
377-700-3408	205,000.00	531.61	March 17, 2007	#0620, operator 383
033-139-2867	1,900,000.00	4628.95	December 4, 2006	Doreen, operator 001
283-179-5613	600,000.00	1427.62	Nov. 20, 2006	#620. Operator 388
705-100-1505	500,000.00	1156.00	October 15, 2006	Doreen, operator 001
886-648-5564	500, 000.00	1141.17	April 21, 2006	Doreen, operator 001

090-851-0673	1000,000.00	2322.12	January 11, 2006	Doreen, operator 001
710-547-9000	150,000.00	418.67	March 6, 2005	Transworld, operator BAN
475-843-3242	250,000.00	684.68	February 18, 2005	Doreen, operator 001
Grand Total:	6,565,000.00	13,421.84		

And also that the amounts sent were not directed all the time only to the house project. For instance, to leave out the Dieudonne hospital amount which is also included there, take the 500,000 FCFA sent on April 21, 2006. Only 400,000 CFA francs would actually be intended for the house, with the hundred thousand in addition being to be used as follows: 50,000 FCFA given to Mamie Lucia Zinzi (Photo #26) who was then staying with Momany's mum as pocket money, 20,000 to Momany's mother, and 30,000 for the contactor's newborn baby. Are there any further queries from the blind money talkers? How much of such sums sent through Dieudonné himself ever got to their destinations? And would Momany have had to be paying someone else to coordinate and supervise the building of the house if Dieudonné was as responsible as he should normally be? In your response try to use the financial figures in Table 5 to show proof of what he actually achieved with all that money and living in that uncompleted house in Nwangong until his death on June 16, 2011.

The June Monster: The month of June appears to the month of death in the Fossungu Royal House. Table 7 gives you an idea in relation to the month of June and the number of deaths in the Fossungu Royal Family that I have been able to track.

Table 7: Some Recent Deaths In The Fossungu Royal Family				
Name	Date of Death			Relation to Momany, if possible
	Day	Month	Year	
Josephine Fossungu	19	April	2016	Fon NN's wife
Elizabeth N. Fosungu	15	September	2014	Sister-in-Law
Erica Fossungu	02	September	2014	Fon NN's wife
Regina Akiefac Fossungu	16	June	2014	Mother (biological)
Dieudonne Asongu Fossungu	16	June	2011	Brother
Nkemngu Richard Fossungu		June	2007	Uncle
Joseph Njumo Fossungu	06	June	2007	Brother
Fon Foncha Fossungu	22	January	2007	Grandfather: Fon DF
Chief Fosanoh Joseph E. Fossungu		April	2012	Uncle
Esther Manyinkeng Fossungu		December	2003	Fon DF's wife
Annastasia Chamo Fossungu		August	2004	Sister
Beatrice Ngwika Fossungu			2003	Sister
Ernestine Tendongmo Fossungu	29	May	2003	Cousin
Richard's child	5	June	2003	Cousin
Emmanuel Nguajong Fosungu (Forbehndia)	11	October	2002	Father
Thecla Anangafack Fosungu			1998	Mother (upbringing)
Constance Tumekong's mother		June	1998	Aunt
Valentine Nwochianwo Fossungu	25	October	1998	Uncle
Manchuah Fossungu (Elias' mother)		October	1995	Aunt

Again, what did Dieudonné's "known Scholastica" and Momany's 'wife and mother in Canada' do even when Dieudonné died? Even leaving Dieudonné aside, I wonder if these Fossungu people ever found out also what Momany's 'wife and mother in Canada' did when Chief Forbehndia died in October 2002 (about a year earlier than Peter Ngunyi Asahchop), let alone the death of Momany's biological mother. And why did these 'situations of death' not as well lead to a suspension of the (court) matter? "Stupid Fossungu People," as Joseph Njumo Fosungu has said in his *Josephinationing letters*? It is even very doubtful that "situations of death and burial could suspend the problem and eventually end up the matter" where there is just no desire or willingness on the parties to genuinely talk things over, like the case of Henriette Flavie Bayiha (Photo #2) exquisitely shows (see Fossungu, 2015d). Or, when one party takes dialogue or compromise to mean that the other party must just *kowtow* to his/her wishes or else there is no dialogue, like the case of Scholastica Achankeng Asahchop (Photo #1) exemplifies. This twisted version of dialogue is even found, for example, in the contents of the father-law-law's letter of October 7, 2003 to Fon DF Fossungu – and not to Momany who is on the spot and knows the facts. And all that being done in the process of illicitly grabbing money while dragging down the money-maker at the same time.

Chapter 4

Getting into the Heads and Logic of *Moneyintriguists* with the Confusion on African Tradition

This chapter focuses on studying and analysing the calculations of *moneyintriguists*, squarely taking us inside their heads and logic and has three main parts. The first circumscribes the freezing of the Canada Project of the Poverty Eradication Programme; the second deals with Scholastica and the impressions given that would suggest that it is not Momany who has been responsible for training her and the third treats the general scheming comportment of the *Asahchopination*. It must be noted and stressed though that the Asahchops cannot be entirely saddled with the fact that the Fossungus have not also filled the corners of Canada. Although the Canada Project cannot be fully discussed here, you can get the baseline from the *surprising* reaction of Bernard to what can rightly be regarded as the philosophy of the Canada Project.

What/Who Is Stalling the *Fossungunization* of Canada?

There is no better expression of the said philosophy than Momany's 2008 communication to and with the current head of the Central Family of the Royal House, Chief Forbehndia Mbancho of the Republic of South Africa (RSA). Momany's message to Chief Forbehndia Mbancho on Tuesday, July 1, 2008 is captioned "Immigration to Canada" and is one of those classic cases of members of his own family not paying the deserved attention to his farsighted and helpful advice, but merely expecting him to both chew and swallow for them. Here is what he gave to "Hi Chief," theorizing lengthily how:

I think you should apply to immigrate to Canada. For people like you, it is very easy. I do not know exactly how beneficial whatever you are currently doing in the RSA is; but I can assure you that the benefits for you of immigrating to Canada are very immense, especially for your family. I think I had suggested this to you before but I am again doing it now and hoping that if you had not thought of doing so for yourself then you would do think of doing so now for your family, especially the kids. When your entire family is here as permanent residents, you can always get back to the RSA and continue doing what you're doing there, if that is indeed what you are really interested in doing. Nevertheless, you would have, at least, given your children and wife the opportunity that a lot of people are seeking and have never got. Just the fact alone that I (your brother) am a citizen here already gives you a lot of points. Your educational level also scores you a lot of points. Your professional background as a translator and interpreter, coupled with your work experience with the Cameroonian government would bring you exceptional and unparalleled additional points. You are so eligible to emigrate here that it is just a question of you taking the time and initiative to apply. For details visit wwww.cic.gc.ca

I am now trying to see how I can get Justine and the others over here. Problem is that I just can't get any of them over there to be serious over these things. I will forward to you an email I sent to Justine requesting some information but haven't heard from her till date. I also talked to Maurine about a week ago and she promised to send me an email so that I could get her postal and other information but nothing has been done by her as yet. Some of these things, as you may already know, are so time-conscious and do easily elapse with time. Could you, please, talk to them and get them to respond immediately when a thing is demanded of them? And can you yourself take this immigration to Canada suggestion as seriously as it deserves?

I remember very vividly making this solemn declaration to myself on 7 November 2006. That is, when the gravity of the personal and family problems that have for so long embroiled my life here seemed to be subsiding and my professional prospects began to show a lot of prospects, especially in Cameroon and elsewhere (out of Canada and the USA). This is exactly what I wrote down as my motto on the aforementioned November day: THE PROFESSIONALIZATION OF A FOSSUNGU IS IMPORTANT TO ME. BUT THE FOSSUNGUNIZATION OF CANADA IS EVEN MORE IMPORTANT AND CRUCIAL TO ME. Now is the time for concretization. And where else do I begin than with Chief Forbehndia's portion of the Fossungus?

Stay blessed and bye now. PAF [this paragraph altered]

P/S: It is better to communicate with me using the address ....[omitted email] because the present address ....[omitted email] is often jammed with group emails from associations such as Goodwill Montreal and the Association of Cameroonians in Canada (ACC). Goodwill Montreal is an association that I and a few others created here in 2003 and which is now flying very high and has been doing a lot to help integrate new (especially English-speaking) immigrants from the motherland. For more on this association, visit wwww.goodwillmontreal.com

Also in addition to the cases mentioned in the above mail to Bernard, in his email titled "Passport Photo" of November 3, 2009 sent to her, Momany told Mafor Justine (Photo #32) that "I need you to quickly send your recent passport size photo so that I can enter you for the American DV-Lottery. Send the photo as an email attachment. Tell the photographer to make the photo 600x600 pixels; with a clear background (these specifications are very important). If you could let me have the photo by this weekend the better. Extend greetings. PAF."[45] Did Justine ever do that, let alone in time enough? The cases are just so many that trying to give several of them is plainly futile. Yet, the cases of non-family persons motivationally sending their photos and earnestly requesting such services from Momany is legion too, with a lot of these cases having succeeded in the said lottery.

As I have prefaced this discussion, a lot of *nonoselfists* would jump to thinking that Scholastica Achankeng Asahchop got to Canada in April 1999 simply because she was Momany's wife. Not that alone.

---

[45] In her letter of December 1, 1996 to Momany, Scholastica stated: "Power, do you know something? Let's take this American lottery visa thing seriously. It is really helping people. Many people have gone through that way. We shall register it seriously this year because we are really behind in our life and can never do anything if we stay in Cameroon. Imagine that we do not have anything and owe people some money. The only thing is that you should struggle and have a green card. I don't know how difficult or easy it is in Canada. The green card is really necessary." It must be noted that emails for speedy sending the required documentation was practically unavailable at this time but Scholastica would still do everything to send it by regular post.

She worked hard in the sense that she was motivated and easily took advantage of the resources and other timely information Momany put at her disposal like he does to every person that can help him/herself with his non-discriminating push. Affi Wodong Penn, for instance, would clearly clarify some few things to you. First, that she and Momany have never personally met each; second, that she too got admitted into Canada College through Momany's aid; and, third, that the man even sent her 40,000 FCFA (Western Union #919-589-4305) to help with the documentation acquisition processes back in Cameroon that were proving difficult for her.

Bernard's case here (like Justine's that is, again, topically exhibited in the Canada College File outlined above) is hard to comprehend: except, perhaps, in the context of *Mamiteelization*. If so, then the further questions raised are many. For instance, do you really need to be my trusted brother for me to use the help you put at my disposal to better my situation in life? What about the non-family 'strangers' that are taking advantage of these same opportunities and forging ahead? Is it truly a case of nonoselfism or that of *Mamiteelization*? Are the two concepts in any way intertwined? It is just important that I mention here that Momany's email signature at the time of the above messages was "No idea is completely useless except one that is not expressed or made known. Goodwill Montreal, in my view, is an idea that was, and is still being, duly expressed." And here are some of those ideas that must have to be further expressed.

As soon as he was out of the country (both first and second times), Momany always tried to work together with his siblings and other family relations in order to ameliorate the lot of the entire family. The very first letter he wrote to any one when he got to Calabar, Cross River State of Nigeria in the early 1980s was to Joseph Njumo Fosungu. This is someone who left Cameroon for the USA in 1985, but has never written a letter to Momany until his death in June 2007. Momany has always been desirous of working as closely as possible to alleviate hardship in the family without distinction as to who is blood or no-blood this and that to him. But he always has met only with this inexplicable leg-dragging comportment. Listen to Bernard Mbancho Fosungu himself on April 18, 1997, for instance, to concretize the theory. His letter of the said date told "Hi Cinq" (his preferred nickname for Momany) that:

I regret the fact that I couldn't reply [to] your letters before today. When I received them, I had to travel to Yaoundé for my University transcript and this process took me about two weeks. I also went to the Canadian Embassy in Yaoundé for some enquiry; all I need now is the admission letter and the immigration form for, as I was told, I can't do the medical test without the admission letter. I have also sent letters to Sweden for admission letters before writing to the address you gave me for scholarship.

I am first interested in [the] McGill autumn session before seeing how Montreal winter session can look like. It was not possible for me to get my transcript from Buea because they could not lay hands on our Year 1 marks. Maybe the former disgruntled Deputy Director went away with them but I hope with the transcript for Ngoa Ekelle you can obtain an admission letter for me from McGill so that I can begin the other procedures at the Embassy against the fall session. Hope to receive it as soon as possible. Accept greetings from Takwi Caroline. Everybody is fine both in Limbe and Yoke. I wish you the best.

Ben Fosungu.

Well, Bernard's first apology-seeking letter had a lot of persuasion as to why he never responded to a lot of the time-sensitive opportunities and Momany's letters generally.[46] This time around: it

---

[46] Just hear what Bernard Mbancho Fosungu's (Photo #8) desire of 'leaving at least a fiance behind' did to him, to better comprehend the intrigues of love being studied here. You could style it *The Child-Complication Message from Douala-Wourizone*, if you will. The issue of being backstabbed by friends and also of women using children and pregnancies as instrument of blackmail and intimidation would not be unique to Momany. Other members of the Fossungu Royal Family also know these stories heartbreakingly well. This is very much the case with Bernard as you hear him trying to explain to his brother why he (Bernard) had not responded to the brother's many letters. October also appears to be another heartbreaking month to the Fossungu Royal Family. Written on October 31, 1996 Bernard's letter went on to interminably expose that:

> It would just be proper to begin this letter by humbly tendering my sincere apology for not having written to you despite your two letters to me. Thanks a lot for your concern especially with regard to your sympathy card.
>
> In fact, just one reason has been responsible for this poor attitude: intense frustration. The past eleven months have been the most frustrating in my thirty years here on this earth. This frustration had been manifesting itself both financially and emotionally. At the financial level,

I had sold all my belongings to travel to Italy on November 6, 1995 only for me to have my air ticket stolen two days before by a very close friend of mine. The matter has been dragging in the Buea Court of 1st Instance since April 16, 1996 without any solution because I have not yet received a franc out of the 557,000 [CFA] francs not to mention the over 150,000 [CFA] francs that I have spent on Gendarmes, State Counsel, lawyers and magistrates. This has completely rendered me broke despite a substantial amount that Dad had given me to travel to Italy. All that has been lost and the matter is still in court and I can't just retrieve this money from this guy without promising a 30% kickback to magistrates. This is the approach I adopted yesterday: whether I will still succeed, let's wait and see. The country is damn corrupt.

Emotionally, the stress has been very devastating. I began an arrangement with one girl in Douala, hoping that before leaving the country last November, I would have at least left a fiancée behind. My abortive departure was the first setback. Secondly, in one of our early sexual dealings, this fellow got pregnant and for reasons best known to her, she hid the pregnancy from me for three months. I can't still decipher what she had in mind. It was only in February 1996 that she informed me of the pregnancy which, according to her, occurred in November 1995. Cinq, you should count yourself lucky to have understanding in-laws. While I was struggling with my case at the court, the pregnancy matter cropped up and the initial calculation of my in-laws was the complete abandonment of their daughter to me. The full responsibility of her everything was mine coupled with the preparation of her delivery. What further aggravated the situation was the serious illness and death of the father. He died in June and she delivered on August 13 (a baby boy). Thanks be to God that the delivery was very smooth because had it needed the intervention of a gynecologist then things would have been different. In all these instances, that is death and delivery, her parents were expecting too much from me. My frustration at the financial level coupled with these unforeseen events orchestrated much emotional stress and at times I thought all was lost for me in this world. The parents have all along been pressurizing me to go to the village for the traditional celebration of the marriage. They first programmed it for March 1996. I turned down the proposal and this led to serious problems. But despite their worry that I am not serious and that I will subsequently abandon the girl, I intend standing my grounds to brave all pressures irrespective of their origin. My prime concern is my court case and the amount that I can recover. I am afraid that this marital issue might cause many problems to both parties. In short, these financial and emotional problems have left me in a mess but I am gradually plucking up courage to brave the two with much serenity.

As for us here, everybody is doing fine apart from Dad who is still ill, but it is our wish that God should grant him good health because he has sacrificed much for me within the past one year about 1 million and is a doubtful mystery, as to just what held him back not to appropriately react to two letters again. The issue of transcript-issuing is surely a very thorny one with Cameroonian universities and we all know that. But, for anyone really bent on getting admitted to a university programme out there, there will always be a way out. And that way out is all the making of the determined person. To concretely illustrate, take Momany's most recent attempt to study for a master's at the University of Windsor. He created two important documents that tore down the two Hercules (1) of academic references and (2) of transcripts emanating directly from the University of Yaounde (UNIYAO or Ngoa-Ekelle).

Let us have just the shorter second requirement concerning which Momany told the Windsorians through his write-up titled **"Why Transcripts Cannot Be Coming Directly From The University Of Yaoundé"** that:

By this note I wish to let you know that transcripts of my studies at the University of Yaoundé cannot be "official"; with official meaning that these documents are mailed by the institution directly to you; that the documents have never been handled by me, a friend of mine, a relative, or any other individual I know personally; and that the envelope they come in bear proper seals, signatures and postal markings. As you can see from the <u>Nota Bene</u> (N.B.) at the foot of the institution's transcripts that I enclosed with my application, "ONLY ONE COPY OF THIS TRANSCRIPT SHALL BE DELIVERED. IT IS IN THE INTEREST OF THE OWNER TO

---

as usual rumours are rife in Douala that I have instead duped him. This keeps the two of us worried and my greatest wish is for me to improve upon my situation and refund his money as soon as possible. Cinq, I am very sorry that the job opportunity you proposed in your first letter was not exploited by me. I am still interested. I tried to get in touch by phone but I was told that the number was a wrong one.

In case of any opportunity, you can phone me on XX-XX-XX Buea, it is my neighbour's number (Mr. Maimo Henry). Tell him you will like to talk to me. For fax, use XX-XX-XX Kumba c/o Zemenjuoh Etienne. We are constantly in touch with each other.

I wish you the best and may God bless you abundantly in all your endeavours.

P/S: Extend greetings to Joe and Marie-Claire. Tell Joe that things are rough and if he can help I would be grateful. I am no longer with the Governor's office.

MAKE AS MANY CERTIFIED TRUE COPIES AS HE/SHE MAY DESIRE."

In addition, the University of Yaoundé in which I studied (1984-1989) is no more, having been replaced by two separate universities, namely, University of Yaoundé I and University of Yaoundé II.

I hope the copies of the transcripts that were included in the application will serve the purpose. Or, should I have them certified before sending to you again?

I requested those from the University of Alberta, McGill University, and Université de Montréal; and I am sure you have already received the transcripts from them directly.

Thanks. Signed. Peter Ateh-Afac Fossungu (ID# XXXXXXXX) [this paragraph altered].

That is what I would call self-help, something unknown to nonoselfists. Would Momany have been admitted if he stayed uselessly crying over the University of Yaoundé's unusual and *dragdownist* academic politics? Chief Forbehndia aside, Richard Ngufor Fossungu (Photo #36), without whom Momany might not have been Momany today (see Fossungu, 2013c: chapters 3 & 1), is one of the biggest victims of *dragdownism*. And he is one of the few who have actually admitted and explained themselves when they could not stay in contact as expected. Take for example the 2-wives-man's letter of August 8, 1996 in which he told "Dear Mr. Ateh Peter" that:

I am indeed sorry for not replying your letters sent to me on the 10/5/96 and 10/6/96, respectively, due to lack of time. Since you left us, I have been working alone, with no helper, and later on a series of family problems I faced immediately you left us.

I am sure you left here when Mary was hospitalized because of her stomach. In fact, Peter, her sickness cost me over two hundred and ninety thousand (290.000) francs but I don't regret because the sickness was removed; and immediately after that, pregnancy started developing. That was again another series of expenditures that I encountered. Shortly after that, my car engine went dead ('knocked') on the 23-10-95. I almost collapsed because of the engine but thanks to the almighty god as that our monthly contribution at Boko was still operational.

Well, Peter, my congratulations to you for your restless [relentless?] performances. Once again, I was indeed glad to read from you about your results. Let's give thanks to the almighty god. Concerning the matter of your wife, I saw your letter of the above [date or matter?] but she met me on the 2nd of July, I struggled and gave her the sum of fifty-five thousand (55.000) francs to go and register for the visa, she told me her father had already made her passport

I don't have much to tell you for now. Accept goodwill greetings from my family, they are all in good health. Mary gave birth to a bouncing baby girl on the 23rd May 1996; she is named after my mum – Mangeh Joyce. Accept her greetings. If you are free, kindly keep Marie-Claire informed of a new baby girl into my family with the name of Mangeh Joyce, born on 23/5/96.

Stay well. Signed. Ngufor R. Fossungu

First of all, a word or two on what Richard refers to as "our monthly contribution." *Njangi.*is the way Cameroonians generally call this monthly contribution idea. As Richard's interesting case shows, this is a very crucial self-help mechanism for Africans. I actually love this *Njangi* topic a lot because of what once transpired in the General Assembly of SOBA-Montreal about three or four years ago. It was during the first Assembly of the year and several projects to be realized during the year were being selected and discussed. There were so many giant or kingly projects like building a sick bay in St. Joseph College, Sasse in Buea; the college library, you name them. Momany was sitting there truly wondering if all these talkers were not just talking for talking sake, because the impression was clearly given that we were to be running the college but not reaping the profits as proprietors. Momany's contrary contribution did not see why we should be contributing financially to Sasse College when we were not standing on any good financial position here in Canada. Rather than be talking big projects for Sasse College, Momany told us, we should be looking at the *Njangi* option through which to aid ourselves and family right here. It was truly a wake-up call and, until date, SOBANS (Sasse Old Boys Association members) here have never stopped appreciating the positive effects of the CAD$200.00 per month that each *njangizer* contributes monthly for one member to take home and help his family with. Momany's *njangi* suggestion was not to say that we shouldn't entirely look at helping the community back home though, just that we should first be in a comfortable position to do so before doing so.

The Lying Machine of Momany's Financial Efforts?

Even Richard's talk of who made Scholastica's passport was enough to ring bells because it is Momany's doing, not Scholastica's father's. Why was Scholastica lying about it to the man's brother from whom help was being requested at the same time? Must she have lied to Solomon Enoma Tatah too, perhaps, that Momany sent her to him for money? The question is asked because in the 6th paragraph of his 4-page letter of February 2, 1998, Solomon noted that "Another mishap was the failure of a plot deal we contracted in July, 1996. In January 1997, it was discovered that we bought a bad piece of land. The matter is now with the gendarmes for our money to be reimbursed.

In sum, 1997 is a year I will like to forget if possible. But since I am still immersed in the misfortunes of that year, I can't easily do so. Due to all these, I've not been able to render any assistance to our darling, Schola. I did explain everything when I saw her last week and she understood. Let's hope this year will see changes and be a better one. A sign towards the direction is my appointment in a committee to co-ordinate development assistance to Cameroon by the P.M. on January, 6th. We are still to start effective work because it is a new structure." It is quite vague but, viewing other instances, one is pushed to start reviewing things that might need no reviewing just to see if there is a message missed, including her/their lying about the fact that it was Momany who was doing everything for her since marrying her until September 2004 in Canada, date when she moved away to Ontario to commence working and still taking the court action for more long-distance sucking of the man 'Canada-Dry'. You know by now just how good she is with long-distance dealings.

Talking of long-distance and Scholastica's coming to Canada, the debts and other financial undertakings do not just end in Cameroon and Canada. On March 29, 1999 Momany had made a money order in the amount of USD $350.00 to Jackie Goodchild of the Congress Secretariat, being Scholastica's registration for the IFTA Conference she was supposedly to get there to attend. The Royal Bank of Canada money order #16495451-111 was expedited to Akron (USA) by Purolator using Bill of Lading # 4008-833-6116 of March 29, 1999, also costing CAD $26.25. Scholastica was just so lucky (as seen in Table 1 above) that Western Union, for example, had begun operating at the time in Cameroon. Until the advent of Western Union and other popular money transfer agencies, Momany used to go through a lot of hell just to get money to his wife. Issuing international money orders to and from Cameroon was only possible in French francs. For example, on December 7, 1995 Momany sent by a bank money order in the sum of one thousand and ten French francs (1,010.00 FRF) to Scholastica Achankeng Asahchop. The Royal Bank of Canada money order number is 13278119, costing CAD $291.93. Momany also sent eight hundred and two French francs (802.57 FRF) to Scholastica Achankeng Asahchop on February 13, 1997 through a money order issued, again, by Royal Bank of Canada with #13337172 and costing CAD $256.50; all that money coming largely, if not exclusively, from the monthly CAD$700.00 loan from the Whistance-Smith, following their undertaking of December 26, 1996 that also graphically enabled Momany to obtain his Student Authorization for the doctoral programme at the Université de Montréal.

Written on his professional letter-head and addressed "To Whom it may concern," this very important document to Momany's academic evolution stated that "Please be advised that I, Andrew Whistance-Smith, will underwrite any expenses that Mr. Peter Fossungu may incur while schooling in Canada up to and including the amount of sixteen thousand dollars ($16,000). Sincerely, Signed. Andrew Whistance-Smith, D.D.S." As I have theorized on numerous occasions, when you are authentic, there is no need to struggle with expressing yourself for that authenticity to be known to your addressees. I say this because there was an earlier "Affidavit of Support for Mr. Fossungu Peter Ateh-Afac" that Momany's so-called family in Maryland, USA, had provided to him on December 10, 1996 that could not even do the simple job of acquiring the preliminary Quebec CAQ (Certificat d'Acceptation du Québec). Lengthy as it was in providing so much more details about the undertakers' citizenship, loaded jobs, inflated bank accounts, properties owned, and what have you, and being sworn before a notary public of the District of Columbia, the document was clearly lacking in believability and clarity as it merely "certified" "That we will provide support for my Brother-In-Law Mr Fossungu Peter Ateh-Afac for his schooling." Where that schooling was to take place is a whole lot of mystery, let alone the dollar amount of the support. Anyway, the Edmonton white friends (Photo #33) did not only furnish the paper document but also the money in excess of what is even mentioned as the upper limit stated. It is from that money that Momany's wife's activities in Cameroon were also being financed through sending her money by the means being examined.

The money orders as well as travellers' cheques (see below) were usually sent to her by courier and some of the cheques used to be stolen as you can see in Momany's request for refund of October 8, 1996. Directed to the attention of 'Accounts Receivable' of Purolator that is housed on 6969 TransCanada Highway in Saint-Laurent in Montreal, it told 'Dear Sir/Madam' that:

I sent a package containing certain documents through your corporation as shown on the enclosed copy of the international bill of lading. The letter was delivered but without the documents (travellers cheques). The Purolator tracing number is 131256; and the police report number is 31960913. I am hereby requesting a refund of the charges I paid Purolator for transporting the said package. Sincerely, signed. P.A. Fossungu (paragraphing altered).

As for the sending of already endorsed travellers' cheques by express courier services, some examples of such travellers' cheques are in Table 8. As noted already, theft of some of them was often registered as you hear, for example, in paragraphs 4-6 of Scholastica's very interesting 20-paragraph Letter of January 7, 1997 which fascinatingly captures so many other issues of this book that you certainly would have to patiently go through all of it:

My dear husband: I got your letters on Monday the fifth. I like the card you sent to me with its symbolic red rose. Those are the things which occupy me here when I am feeling lonely.

Table 8: Samples of Travellers' Cheques Sent to Scholastica Achankeng Asahchop

Visa Traveller Cheque Number	Amount (in USD)	Date of Purchase	Date to be Cashed (if specifically noted)	Where Cashed (if specifically indicated)
152-2020-788-076	100.00	March 25, 1997	April 15, 1997	
152-2100-832-536	100.00	June 17, 1997	July 5, 1997	
157-2035-507-707	300.00	July 22, 1997	August 14, 1997	
152-2100-848-141	100.00	October 29, 1997	Nov. 15, 1997	
152-2100-869-036	100.00	December 8, 1997	Dec. 20, 1997	
155-2039-928-590	150.00	January 4, 1998	April 20, 1998	Muyuka, Cameroon
157-2035-558-428	300.00	January 27, 1998	Feb. 14, 1998	Buea, Cameroon
155-2039-858-750	150.00	March 12, 1998	March 31, 1998	Buea, Cameroon
155-2039-879-408	150.00	April 16, 1998	May 1, 1998	Muyuka, Cameroon
155-2039-928-668	150.00	May 25, 1998	June 10, 1998	Buea, Cameroon
155-2039-979-467	150.00	June 1998	July 10, 1998	Buea, Cameroon

Power, how are you going to do with your school fees? I felt worried when I read that letter. I don't know why things are proving to be very difficult on us for a very long time like this. Nothing of ours is coming easily. Why so? Even while you were here I struggled to take in but did not succeed. Why should our own destiny be delayed for long like this? I know that you are very hard-working and if things are proving to be difficult like this, it is not your fault. Let's keep our fingers crossed and keep waiting when our own things will start being easy as those of others.

I heard what happened to you as concerns the pot that almost got burnt. Thank God that you people came back early. Had it been that it persisted, the whole house and maybe neighbouring houses could not have been safe. God was really with us that day. It may be he was the one who brought you people back so early, without which I don't know how things could have looked like exactly. Say hello to Paul when you go back to Canada or when you people communicate.

Power, I saw the [travellers'] checks. I am very grateful for that, though one of the checks was not seen. I saw but 80 dollars. The last check N° 152-2100-869040 was not there. I doubt if it was removed or you forgot to put it there. Even one of the letters was incomplete; you started the letter and ended as if you continued on a different page and the page is nowhere to be found.

As I told you when we discussed over the phone, I went to the village without seeing it [letter with travellers' cheques]. I borrowed some money from Dorothy before going to the village. Dorothy works now in a certain security (ASA) company in Douala. I changed the money in the bank as usual and excluding their charges, it was 40,000 francs [CFA]. I want to use 22,000 francs for the second instalment of my fees. I shall go and pay it on Monday. [With] The 18,000 francs left there is remaining only [1]3000 francs because I had malaria and went to the hospital yesterday, I used 5,000 francs on drugs. They wrote drips and I shall start taking them today in the school health post. When you call I shall explain in detail. I don't know how I shall live now to the next month, but thank God that my school fee is with me. Now is a very bad time for us. We are preparing for our exams and are even writing tests. I pray that by next week I should be well because this is a very serious time for us. I shall take my treatment for three days. I know it is because of stress, I am even forcing myself to write this letter. Anyway, I am feeling better today because they gave me a certain injection. I asked for drips because I don't want to be sick during exams.

I shall call (phone) Dorothy any of these days to inform her that I shall give her money only in a month's time. Her money is 20,000 francs.

I really managed the little money I had and what I took from Dorothy, I bought Edith a small present, I bought an African wear for your mother and myself as you will see in those picture we took in the village [47]. Your mother was very happy with me and she even said that she will stay longer and enjoy her wife. Anyway, I am not blowing my trumpets. The only thing is that I did not have money to give her. It was my father who even paid our transport back. I thought I shall send her (your mother) some money when I come and receive this money but look at how things are now. I don't even want to think that I don't have money now, because it will disturb me now.

Power, if I have seen somebody who will come and see you like this and haven't sent anything (present) to you, it is because I don't have money. I have some *eru* here for Sister Marie-Claire. I am not sure to write to her, you will just say hello to the entire family. That is all what I can send to her and her family because I don't have money. If you are going to be there in the USA for long, I am sure I shall send something to you. Do not think that you have an uncaring wife, I lack only the means.

Power, I have a problem with my face, pimple is really eating me up now. I don't really know what to apply on my face and my body. As you will see on those pictures, my colour is really depreciating while pimples keep chopping my face. I hope you will not feel that my troubles are so many. You are the only person I can complain to. For the fever, it has gone down but those pimples keep increasing.

Power, the wife of Mr. William Asongu died. I mean your uncle who stays beside the Palace. She died about four months ago. I went to the village and he was asking me if you are aware of it. I mean Christopher's mother.

---

[47] Photo #56 shows Momany's mother (with Scholastica) during the Christmas celebration Scholastica is talking of, one of the best outside Nwangong (one could say) until her arrival in Douala in 2008 via Bafut? Momany's mother had been there in Fontem early that same year on medical grounds, according to Stephen Fomeche's reporting. In the 5th paragraph of his March 4, 1997 letter, he indicated that "Back in Fontem there is no serious problem. We had the pleasure of being with your mother for a short time while she was here in Fontem for health problems. She is now okay and gone back. Your in-laws are okay but for the death of your maternal grand-father-in-law. The town is just what it was many years ago and the like."

Eugene says I should greet you and that he has not yet seen the letter you sent to him. It is still with Brother Romanus. He says he will write to you immediately he sees the letter.

Accept greetings from everybody in the village, especially Chief. He has got married to another wife. Your mother said I should greet you.

Power, as I went to a certain herbalist last time before going to Yaoundé, he asked me to bring 50,000 francs for him to do a certain cleansing rite on me and 20,000 francs for protection. I did the 20,000 francs one and the other one was left. I keep wondering if I should do the other one or not. I thought I should ask you and hear what you are going to tell me. You know my greatest prayer is that I should take in immediately we come together because we are getting late in life. When I see all my friends who got married after me with their kids, I feel so worried. I keep advising that each time you go to the hospital you can make a spermogram test, because things like low sperm count could contribute to the problem we are having.

We were together with Stephen and his wife in the village. They really took good care of your mum and myself. On New Year day, I went to their house with her and they really entertained us well. We also went out from there and he really spent his money on us. His wife Jess is pregnant. She will soon give birth. Stephen is now in higher Ecole Normale; she is there now because her condition does not warrant her to move.

Power, what of those my dresses? You left them in Canada or they are there in the USA? Please, do well to send them because people always leave there to come to Cameroon.

Your sister, Marie-Claire, was telling me that they will struggle and you will remain there in the USA. I don't know how you people are working it out. Please, you can be comparing the two, because it seems as if life is very hard in Canada. Our only prayer is that you should have a stand. Thank God that you have a multiple entry visa, which could enable you to go and finish your PhD in Canada before coming back. The only trouble is your school fees that you don't yet have. I have posted those references.

Power, I am sure I have exhausted everything. Do not think I complain a lot. Last time when you sent me money, I used it for paying my rents. I paid a caution fee of 10,000 francs and three months rents, making a total of 40,000 francs. That is how the money finished, I had only 10,000 francs. The little money I have is for everything of mine. I said I shall try and replace my school dresses, but haven't been able because of financial difficulties. Now that my face is very rough I can't do any serious thing without money. After everything I very much appreciate your efforts. Imagine that you aid me like that out of nothing. God did not create us to come and suffer forever, I believe we shall be fine one day and will have many things to tell our children how we suffered when we just got married.

This jewellery business, I really like doing it but the problem is who to do it out there with. There is another type of jewellery they call Brazilian gold and people are really making money in the USA with it. If I saw somebody who could be selling the things out there for me, I could have loved to do the business.

Don't forget to write to Elias, his child was very sick.

I can write until all the papers will get finish around me and I will still not lack what to inform you. Bye.

Your darling Schola. Signed.

N/B: The Whistance-Smith family wrote a letter to me and sent their family card to me. I shall reply the letter when I am sound. Please, Power, I didn't have enough time to dry that *eru* well. Tell Sister Marie-Claire to remove it from the wrapping immediately.

The banks used to also cheat her a lot in relation to the travellers cheques as you can hear her explaining in paragraph 11 of her 18-paragraph letter of **January 28, 1998**.[48] That is obviously why, in addition to those means of sending money as demonstrated above, Momany also made a lot use of sending her money through people who were travelling to Cameroon as you also hear from her mentioning of it in many of her letters (that cannot all be outlined

---

[48] "Power, anytime I have an opportunity to talk with you for long, we shall discuss how we can change the system you have been sending money to me. They cheat me a lot in the bank because their exchange is very low, and their charges too high. The bank people also trouble me a lot before changing the money, claiming that I should open a bank account. I used but people's account in changing the money and each time I change it, I give something to the owner of the account. Finally, 100 dollars US which is 60,000 francs presently become 47,000 francs or 50,000 francs at the point that 13,000 francs or 10,000 francs each time you send me money is not small money. Canada is too far and it is difficult to see people coming to Cameroon."

here) but notably that of July 31, 1997(which has been discussed in chapter 2). Regarding this alternative, on April 20, 1998 Momany also sent USD $300.00 to Mrs. Jane Alobwede (Tatah Solomon's sister-in-law) who was visiting in the United States, being money to be given to Scholastica Achankeng Asahchop on Mrs. Alobwede's return to Cameroon. This money order to Jane Alobwede was issued by Royal Bank of Canada with #16193803-111 and costing CAD $436.99. Mrs. Alobwede duly confirmed both cashing it and the handing over of the money to Scholastica in Cameroon. That is the same woman who comes to Canada and decides that children and marriage can only be instruments in her hands to bully Momany into everlasting slavery, supported (if not instigated) by her moneyintriguing dad.

The Royal Ultimatum and the Confusion on African Tradition

We have just talked of Peter Asahchop's letter of October 7, 2003 which was addressed to Fon DF Fossungu – and not to Momany who is on the spot and knows the facts. Yet, Peter Ngunyi Asahchop would be bold enough to talk of having obtained his information from 'reliable sources.' His daughter is very *reliable* to and *usably useful* for him, of course. The Fon-ordering letter is important though for schooling people (albeit truncated) in African tradition on marriage and family even as its proponent woefully fails to demonstrate how his daughter's comportment in Canada (such as wantonly aborting consensually produced pregnancies) fits perfectly into that 'African tradition' he is so much invoking. A lot of other things such as this letter contradicting his other letters, like the one blaming Momany for not showing up to talk with *him* (below), the one about using two-sittings in the G.C.E. to enter the Yaoundé University (below) …. In short, here is Peter Ngunyi Asahchop's complete two-page typewritten letter or ultimatum to Fon DF Fossungu:

I have the honour to inform you that I have information from reliable sources that DR. Peter Fossungu left his wife, my daughter Scholastica, and two children and he is renting a house somewhere [since] 01/08/2003.

I have to bring to your notice that the marriage of your son and my daughter was according to our tradition and not the type children meet nowadays on the street and arrange themselves and only to tell their parents this is my husband and this my wife. DR. Peter

Fossungu came to my house one day with his friend, Asah Forsah, requesting to marry my daughter and I told them that they were juniors to come and request for marriage according to our tradition, that if they were serious they should meet his father Fon D.F. Fossungu or his uncle Chief Formbeandia Emmanuel to make the request for him. His Majesty and Chief Formbeandia made the request according to our tradition and I told them to give me time to discuss with my daughter, my immediate family, both my family members and that of my wife.

After all the consultations, both family members accepted without any opposition. I wrote a letter and we met at Alou Market telling you people that we have accepted, the date was fixed for the marriage feast, which was successfully carried out.

Dr. Peter Fossungu left for Canada for further studies and his wife was under the care of Mr. Elias Akendung [Photo #24] with assistance from me as the father, and there was no problem or complaint for the period of three years. She later met the husband and they have stayed for four years. Last year 2002 about April when she was in pregnancy, he abandoned her with a child went and rented a house somewhere until the death of Chief Formbeandia in October, 2002 that he came to the house, prepared and came to Cameroon for burial of Chief Formbeandia. However, by the Grace of the Almighty God she gave birth successfully. He again has abandoned her with two children and is renting a house somewhere.

His Majesty, this is the highest time your intervention is needed in this matter. You find out what is wrong, for him to outline a few points, and the solution DR. Peter Fossungu feels could be done to solve the problem between him and his wife so as to allow my daughter at peace. He should note that human rights are more observed over where they are than here in Cameroon. When DR. Peter Fossungu came to Cameroon his behaviour and attitudes previously and at the time he was here towards me and family showed a clear picture of what was in his mind. I am therefore appealing that you contact him either in writing or phone and let me have the reply in three months' time. I am then sending this very important letter to you through Chief Foletia Vincent of the Royal family to read and interpret in its entities [entirety?] to you and his mother very, very well.

Thank you very much for your understanding, while anticipating your prompt action. God bless you. Signed. Asahchop Peter [this paragraph altered]

That was the directive from Peter Ngunyi Asahchop (Photo #22) to the Fon of Nwangong. It should be noted that if anyone has to mix up Chief Forbehndia (Photo #19) as Momany's uncle and Fon DF Fossungu (Photo #41) as his father, it is surely not Peter Ngunyi Asahchop. Doing so then tells you a lot about what he might have had in mind doing what he did. Why didn't he also refer to Chief Forbehndia in 1993 as Momany's "uncle" but "father"? On December 8, 1993 Peter Ngunyi Asahchop had also written to "Dear Mr. Peter," inquiring:

How was your journey from home to Douala? I hope your trip was safe, and you met everybody at home in Douala in good health.

On [examining] the detail[ed] results of Scholastica, I found that she has history grade 'D' and English literature she had last year she could not make it this year. I have been told by so many people that she could be admitted in the University of Yaoundé with two papers at different sittings. I will like to know your opinion whether she repeats here and go to Buea next year or you can take her to Yaoundé and find admission for her. Immediately you receive this letter consult your father, Chief Fombeh, about it and let me know as I find admission. If you accept this condition then you come either after Christmas or before, also know that if Chief Fombeh cannot come, we meet the chief, his Royal Highness for certain formalities as tradition is concerned.

You accept greetings from every person for me.

Signed. Peter Asahchop

The *Asahndeming* Lecture on African Tradition

The timing of his letter, like his daughter's seen in chapter 1, should be noted too, viewing when the issue of marriage to his daughter was made (July 1993). Going even by the tradition that Peter Ngunyi Asahchop claims to know so much and abide by, Fon DF Fossungu would not be Momany's father but grandfather. That is the tradition that is ably understood by Chief Forbehndia as seen in the portion of his will earlier. And that holds since Fon DF Fossungu is successor to Momany's biological grandfather, Fon Sunday Tedongmo Fossungu who you see sitting in the middle in the following 'story-telling picture' (whose invaluable importance the 'Lion of Judah' called Esambe Lobwede Ngi-Nyam has duly brought home to you[49]):

L-R – Chief Peter Ateafac Fonwancheng, Fon Sunday Tendongmo Fossungu, and Chief Fomellah

---

[49] As the *Lion of Judah* (as Ngi-Nyam Esambe Lobwede Lucas likes to be called) reiterated in the first paragraph of his famous April 18, 2006 letter, "Beloved Doctor, often enough, memories fade fast but as every pictures tells a story, I had been able to locate you with one of the pictures you sent to me from Alberta while I was still in Yaoundé a couple of years ago. How did it all happen? Early this year, while looking at the pictures in my Album, I caught sight of one of the three pictures you had kindly sent to me and then asked myself, where the hell is this man now? As a matter of interest, I removed one of the pictures and sent to my son-in-law, Solomon Tatah currently in Boston with his family being that it has been through him in Yaoundé that we got to know ourselves. It has been through his recent letter of March 2, 2006 received here in my village on April 9, 2006 that, apart from enclosing the picture, gave me the vital information about your whereabouts. He indicated that he had gotten in touch with you and that you were eagerly expecting to read from me. This I now do with confidence and sincere love."

This is so because "a king or chief or fon never dies in Africa. He simply goes on a journey and comes back younger than he went, it is said" (Fossungu, 2015c: 133-134). That is why traditionally, therefore, Momany is now the father of his siblings: as Mafor Nkemtale'eh's husband, Asah William Ndem (Photo #58), who is more learned in tradition than Peter Ngunyi Asahchop, would rectify it for you. In his letter of February 2, 2003, Asah William Ndem, who is looking right at you (together with Momany) in the mentioned photo, addressed Momany as follows:

Dear Father-in-Law,

I am grateful to write to you. I am sure that you had a safe journey back to Canada.

As regards my health, there is a bit of improvement. Let's pray that this improvement continues. Here, we are in need of drugs, so if you could lay hands on rheumatism drugs, you could kindly send them to me.

I am happy to inform you that your Nkwetta is now here with me with his entire family. The sister went and brought them with all their things. In fact, he is not sound in health and needs serious treatment.

Here are the photocopies of the children's birth certificates which you asked for. In this family you remain the main captain and through your assistance the rest of the family can grow. Foncha was driven from school for lack of fees and textbooks. He was at home for three weeks before going back to school. With my poor health, I managed and he returned to school. He came first in the first term examination.

I implore you to consider what I told you about your Asa'ah [that is, Dieudonné] and Nkwetta. You know that one tree can't form a forest. So, they and the entire family are under your canopy.

Have you had any response concerning your job opportunity in Douala? Try to phone the man handling the matter. Again, all what we discussed, take it serious. I am eagerly looking forward to hearing from you as soon as possible.

Extend my warm greetings and New Year wishes to the family over there.

Yours faithfully, Asah William Ndem

P/S: Use the address I gave you when writing to me.

Even Fon Nicasius Nguazong Fossungu (in Phot #57) who succeeded his own father (Fon DF Fossungu) would still be Momany's grandfather, not father as such. If the *Asahchopinationist* logic is that Chief Forbehndia is, in reality, only an uncle to Momany for being the brother to Momany's biological dad, then he cannot at the same time turn another brother of that biological dad into Momany's father. Why do you think he still did so? Well, continue to the capital of Cameroon that breathes and the rest of the rotten country lives on. Don't get me wrong. I am just passing on a vital message that puts you in a comfortable seat to safely dive into the bottoms of the Deep Sea of *Moneyintriguism*. The preparation is coming from Momany's able lieutenant from no other town than Fontem where the money-mindedness is seated or headquartered. The assisting man on the spot is our well-known *Quagmatickism* Show lecturer called Stephen Z. Fomeche (Photo #9) whose June 19, 1996 letter to Momany opened with "How are life, work and studies? Hope with your God-given 'power' you are carrying on well. Back at home, we are still in this 'Slough of Despond' called Cameroon. Any expression of hope is self-mockery. We move from one day to the next with imbecile child-like satisfaction, entrapped in the stoical cliché that 'tomorrow will take care of itself;' how will it? The Lord's prayer, 'Our father,' is now taken seriously, more than ever before, with a ridiculous rotundity on '… give us this day, our daily bread…' My brother, nobody is sure of that bread. The worse is still to be born of the ugly looking and demanding pregnant monster, the O.A.U. Summit. God bless Cameroon!"

The Yaoundéan-*Josephizationing* Lecture on the Elephant Money Fight

There is no doubt that some Yaoundéans like Jane's father are still upright people and would greatly aid us in the tricky journey 'Inside the Head of a *Moneyintriguist*'. For a start, one wonders about the accuracy of Joseph Njumo Fossungu's 'chief-theory' with a further question, namely, since when the Fon's subjects began issuing ultimatum to him under normal circumstances. Also consider Elias Akendung's message sent through the Fon of Nwangong! Tradition has really descended so low in the face of money that anyone can now just order the Fon any how, any way and any time![50] If Peter Ngunyi Asahchop could do it with his well-known ultimatum letter to Fon DF Fossungu (under discussion), who else shouldn't? In an email (titled "Request for reception") of February 25, 2014, Fon NN Fossungu (Photo # 57) told Momany that "Mr Elias Akendung in Douala, intends to travel to Canada and wishes to be received by you. He said I should ask if you can do that favour for him. You can write

---

[50] The imperative need to eradicate poverty in the Fossungu Royal Family cannot need any capacity of the rocket scientist to grasp. But if I must exemplify again how this family is "confronted with the harsh discipline of poverty" (Nginyam's words in his April 18 letter cited above), even if with the most minute evidence, then I would like us to consider the current Fon's email of September 29, 2008 titled "Greetings from Cameroon." It was dispatched to no other than Momany, the one personality in this Nwangong Royal Family from whom so much is deservedly expected. The Fon wrote to "Dear Brother" in the following terms:

> I regret missing you this long. I have tried your phone number for so long but could not reach you. Remember your promise to send some money for me to make my passport. I have been waiting for that. Beside all those *concours* [competitive examinations into the public service professional schools] ended in a failure and the only hope is that we should do all we can to secure a place either in Ecole Normale or ENAM before the end of December. That should be the last hope for me because of my age.
>
> Remember people now disobey me because of my economic dependency. Note that I will soon be reduced to nothing if I continue to depend on the village of which they [give] little or nothing to me. Now we have been accorded a Government Secondary School – GBSS Emollah-Nwangong – to be built around the palace but because the people of Ndencop and Nwencheng feel they have money they are putting up another structure at Nwencheng.
>
> The children at home need their fees and I am still waiting for the dry season to have money from the few palm lands. I do not even have the money to do some things for myself not to think of the mothers at home. Besides, I am planning to have a wife to settle down with... All these things for me!
>
> My regards.
>
> H M Fon FOSSNGU N Nguazong, Nwangong Fondom [omission is original].

Rather than work together to ameliorate the situation, the central figures of this family only exhibit their centrality in dragging the family and fondom down in moves that show clearly that they just want to be the "only eye" around the place. They then go about writing silly emails to those they consider as having insulted the Fon. Do I hear you well, Marie-Claire Afueh? That is surely not the correct way to defend the family's INTEGRITY or HONOUR!

to me or contact him at XX XX XX XX. Remember too the family meeting of the 10th of April and get to the president, Nkemanang Calixtus. I can say all is well here as there is no major illness, hope you are all well too. Accept greetings from this end." The questions are many. Why would Momany now be the one to receive Elias Akendung to Canada when he has another (the other being Marie-Claire in the USA) very important partner in Canada in the person of Scholastica Achankeng Asahchop? Was he just bringing this up as a strategy also to hear what Momany would say or do and then pass the information on to the one whose "ears and eyes" he is in Cameroon? Could the Akendung plan even have been hatched in Canada itself just to give to Momany their usual bad name?

That small North American trip brings us back to the puzzlement of what was actually in the head of the *moneyintriguist* in Fontem. Paul Jiomeneck has unambiguously exposed the schemer in Peter Ngunyi Asahchop with just his one sentence *"Je vous transmets ici les salutations de mon épouse et de tout le monde à la maison"* (from Jiomeneck's letter of October 8, 1998 that has been discussed above in chapter 3). The card was sent to *him* but it is the entire family that was so happy about the gesture which is duly reflected in that sentence of a letter whose full text and translation you can find above. The untranslated French sentence here even clears out in this discussion so that you don't need to go back reading the entire translation, if you like. What is clear from that particular sentence from Paul Jiomeneck is the love and unity within that household. You cannot love someone you distrust. Period!

The Loan-But-No-Loan

In Peter Ngunyi Asahchop's letter of November 3, 2002, he accused Momany and said in the second paragraph that "You discussed with Mamie and not me."[51] Many questions are raised.

---

[51] On November 3, 2002, and viewing what is said in Fossungu (2013c: 98-99), Peter Ngunyi Asahchop wrote to Momany while he was in Cameroon (Nwangong, to be precise), stating:
> Good morning to you and other family members you travelled with from Limbe. I had your letter which states that you may not likely come down to Menji. We had two nights at Menji and the first day many people

How did he know that Momany discussed with his wife? Could he know that without also knowing what was discussed? Why was a private discussion with him so pressingly important? Why, why, why, and why? Let's get into the heads and logic of an intriguing family of schemers, not forgetting those of the Fossungu family already seen above too. For a bright day's start, the main point is the centrality of the supposedly sent money (CAD$1000.00) that Peter Ngunyi Asahchop was eyeing, money that was also the subject of a grand dog-making scheme. In view of the lengthy *Eugenizationing* letter (see Fossungu, 2015c: 27-32), it is surely a complete miracle (*The Means of the Divine*) that Momany could even have been able to be present at the burial of his dad in October 2002. Momany could only make the journey, thanks to the efforts of his colleagues in Edmonton and Montreal. In Montreal, the following assisted financially as shown in Table 9.

---

came to greet you, and in addition you have had several sleepless nights. The second you went to greet others and came in late and we could not discuss anything. Next day you left for Douala with reasons that you were to come and discuss with me before your final departure from Cameroon.

It was a little bit funny when I read from your letter that you may not likely reach Menji, meaning that we have discussed nothing at all. You discussed with Mamie and not me. I wish you safe journey to your station, a few things have been parceled into the box brought for you and family. I have written to your wife that both of you should change and come to be as you were before and that the best principle of marriage is forgive and forget. We shall see next when you come to Cameroon.

Mamie was to come but sorry that she had fever and she is on treatment and I really regret her inability to come 'say' to you 'bye'. We thank both of you for the few things you brought for the children.

The bearer of this note, my child, has dropped the parcel inside the box and left it at Mr. Gabriel Anangfack at Three Corners Ndungateh (Foto) for you to collect tomorrow while on your journey back to Douala and departure to Canada. Since we were waiting for you and finally failed to see you, bearer, my child, will drop this letter and leave immediately because today is Sunday and tomorrow is Monday, a school day, and she cannot be absent from school. Collect box and parcel at Mr. Gabriel's off licence 3 corners Foto.

Asahchop Peter. Signed.

Table 9: Contributions And Loans That Helped Momany To Attend Burial Of Father

Name	Amount $ CAD	Name	Amount $ CAD
Co-workers in Rossy Dollarama[52]	$380.00	Montreal Cameroon Group Total of $395 was broken down as follows:	
Eric Kwati	$20.00	Lysly Ayah	$20.00
Hans Najeme	$50.00	Paul Ayah	$60.00
Dave & Marie-Helene Kometa	$200.00	Johnson & Plebious Ngala	$50.00
James & Emilia Tambong	$100.00	Berri Nsame	$25.00
Denis Alem	$45.00	Wilfred & Yvonne Kangong	$50.00
The Whistance-Smith (from Edmonton[53])	$500.00	Denis Alem	$70.00
LOANS		Ayuk Ako-Arrey Donatus	$20.00
Dr. Tambong and family	$400.00	Dan Mulema	$60.00
Moses Nkwenti	$500.00	Henry Nfon	$40.00
Quinta Asaah	$500.00		
Scholastica Asahchop	$1000.00		
TOTAL	$3695.00		$395.00
GRAND TOTAL $4090.00			

From Table 9, you can see that someone like Denis Alem contributed twice (both as an individual and as a member of the group) whereas all what Scholastica did was to *lend* money to her husband (upon whom she was even dependent while taking good

---

[52] The contribution came with "A message of Sincere Sympathy" card that all of them signed which told Momany that "May the love of those who care, strengthen you during this time of sorrow."

[53] In their sympathy card titled 'Remembering You In Your Time Of Loss,' they wrote in addition to "Dear Peter" that "I hope that you make it to Cameroon in time for your father's funeral. We've enclosed some money as a gift to put towards the cost of your air ticket. With much love, Nancy, Andwre, Greg, Tim & Emily."

care of the *Asahchopination*). I am, therefore, talking of the loan that Peter Ngunyi Asahchop's daughter made to Momany as he was going to bury Chief Forbehndia but called her dad while the 'husband' was still on his way to tell her father that she had sent that amount through Momany to Peter Ngunyi Asahchop. Peter Ngunyi Asahchop's sentence here ("It was a little bit funny when I read from your letter that you may not likely reach Menji, meaning that we have discussed nothing at all") would give the idea that this was the only time Momany has been held back by unforeseen circumstances that have prevented his meeting up with promised meetings. Not correct at all, as other chapters of this book would further demonstrate.

The money (supposedly sent) was so important here because, on an earlier occurrence, Peter Ngunyi Asahchop wrote to Momany on January 8, 1996 as follows:

Dear Mr. Peter, I had your letter of 22-10-95 just of recent, that is end of December 1995. You really expressed yourself how you left without coming to the village. However your journey was successful. I had your letter and could not reply earlier because the Mayor and Civil Status Registrar had gone out for Christmas. Immediately they returned, I discussed with them. They suggested two ways, that is, to send you a certified true copy of the marriage certificate or to send the certificate and you sign and return their copy. I have contacted two witnesses, that is, your witness and that of Scholastica. I have taken Nkweta Elias Fonge and wife as both witnesses and have borne all the cost of this marriage certificate for both of you. Scholastica shall be here on the 19-1-96 and all of us shall move to the Mayor and civil status registrar and sign the certificate and when she returns to Buea she will give you the feedback. I was at the village last week and your mother has improved very well. How are studies that way? I hope things are fine. Hearty greetings from my entire family. Signed. Peter Asahchop.

This letter also shows you how Momany was doing everything in his powers to make life better for these people but all they were seeing was plotting. Otherwise, why would Scholastica's father even be talking of shouldering a mere amount for dressing up a marriage certificate when her daughter and the others are in the Buea University because of Momany? And that is the same marriage certificate that would soon be used to screw the man's life as soon as

Scholastica has landed on the other side of the Atlantic. Could that be the reason he was so pompously bearing "all the cost of this marriage certificate for both of you"? Anyway, let's stay with the other letter blaming departure without discussion. As the saying goes, when two elephants fight it is the grass that picks up the bits (suffer, that is). You can competently continue developing your theory with Elizabeth Asahchop's letter to Scholastica above in chapter 1, the one in which she indicates how the husband never made her know about the sent sum of money until she must have learned of it from another source. Don't forget too to decorate it with the wife's own Western Union money from the son-in-law for husband's burial also mentioned above in chapter 3. Is your theory rounded enough?

Then beautify it with Scholastica's 'Loan-But-No-Loan' blackmail (CAD$1000.00) that may even have been 'chopping off' her daddy so much when he was penning said ultimatum-letter to the Fon of Nwangong to be read to him by no other than his friend, Chief Foletia, the very person calling for 'an immediate calling off of the problem' (by his friend's death). This is an issue they don't even have the slightest idea about. Who is bold enough to find fault with Joseph Njumo's thesis here? You cannot be advising on an issue you know nothing about. As an intelligent chief, you cannot take sides but listen to both sides before rendering a decision. None of these Fossungu royals did that; just working on the stories the other family was busy spreading around the whole place and then jumping in to give orders for Momany to call the problem (which one?) off because of Peter Ngunyi Asahchop's death. It is the only death that has ever taken place on the planet, of course! The Asahchop *moneyintriguist* just could not have been luckier to have such a royal family that is jammed full with self-centred 'Fools'. Joe Fosungu, thank you very much for saying it as it is; although the tone is totally just as out of place as those you are condemning.

Unfortunately, Peter Ngunyi Asahchop's very good 'secret-keeping' daughter was chasing so much money and 'property-sweeping' to London, Ontario, that she forgot their "secret letters" that you are now having the rare privilege of publicly reading and to connect the dots. Get the pleasure of one of them right here to coat Joe Fossungu's thesis on these royals or chiefs that are not advising but instead being badly advised. One of these Top-Secret letters is from "Mr/Mrs Asahchop" and dated December 27, 2003. Here is the content of the letter that must have to shout up the likes of Chief Foletia and speedily bring them to order:

Dear Mrs. Scholastica, Good morning to you [and] children. I wonder whether you had my letter sent to you early September 2003 and really talked [to] you [about] my illness problem and the condition in which we are living and if you have not got the letter then it is unfortunate. I explained [in it] that I have pledged my compound to obtain a loan of 100,000 francs. Now I have also used a part of James' money on my illness and other things. The both of us coming to Canada is really impossible because the other right leg is also developing problems and I may soon be belind [?] as I wrote last time and it is a mocry [mockery?] for you taking a belind [?] to Canada, especially both of us. Please almighty God is there to solve our problems, let us pray that your sister could make the O/L and come to meet you as already proposed. I really sympatharised [sympathize?] your suffering but it is not possible for your mother to leave me at the condition in which I am. You continue to pray for God's guidance and help as usual. Thank you very much for the chairs you sent the money to buy. The money really remove us shame during the celebration of your friend's father and kept us comfortable during Christmas. I hope Eugene [who is in Belgium] is doing fine. I asked Bridget to send to you a copy of the letter your husband wrote for separation and also my letter I wrote to his father his Majesty Fon D.F. Fossungu and if it has not come then it is in transit.

You should not be too worr[ied]. Have a peace of mind and note that you are not the first person to be disappointed. It is regrettable we cannot send you anything because Willingelis [Relindis?] told us that she is not nearer, that can only [be by] post and letter to you. I sent photocopies of letter written by DR Nkemtaleh and the one I wrote to the Fon through Bridget to you and here enclosed other photocopies to you which is faster. Since his letter states that both of you will take care of the children, you should never take him to court, be patient and put everything to almighty God. Please you phone whether the [address] on the letter you sent is your address for now.

Signed. Asahchop Peter

The letter whose photocopies are referred to in his letter (and attached to Momany's name) is the one discharging Momany of the Chief Foletia 'husband-father' duty. It must, therefore, have been in view of the fact that he is considered back in Cameroon to be both 'Scholastica's husband and father in Canada' that Momany was duly discharging and unburdening himself of any further 'husband-father' responsibility by writing the letter of October 4, 2003 whose contents are following:

My dear Parents-in-Law,
It is unfortunate that I should be bringing bad news at this time. But I must let you know that I am no longer in a position to account for whatever is or might be happening to your daughter here in Canada. She is now on her own as you must have already heard. I just thought I should tell you myself. She thinks she doesn't need my input whatever regarding whatever she decides to do. In short, this marriage exists to her only when she can take rights from it but never when it comes to shouldering obligations/responsibilities emanating from the marriage. I cannot here begin to explain anything. The purpose of this letter is just to inform you formally that we are not living together anymore and that, therefore, I am no longer the right person to be able to give you any trustworthy information in her regards. As for the children, I continue to support them financially.
Sincerely, Signed.

If it is not something else, then explain this to me, please. You address somebody but instead of talking back to you he goes ordering those who don't know what you talked to him about. Why did Peter Ngunyi Asahchop not also tell them that his "reliable source" was Momany's letter and even show them the letter itself? Why wouldn't he respond to Momany but instead to the daughter, and copying Momany's letter? And that is someone to be talking reconciliation with? Is that not a way of telling his daughter (in the Lapiro style): '*Go before tara, all the Asahchops are solidly behind you*'? Don't be fooled, therefore, by his counsel on patience on the court-taking. As said, this *moneyintriguism* protagonist knew his targeted audience of the Fossungu family was ignorant of the dynamics at work; the precise reason for going to them rather than to the man in the soup.

Otherwise, why would Momany's discussion with his wife not concern him – unless he wants to privately *discuss* the supposed money: since he did not want the wife to be aware of it?

This thesis is given more impetus and firmness by the useless excuse the husband creates in the third paragraph in the nature of the wife's illness: "Mamie was to come but sorry that she had fever and she is on treatment and I really regret her inability to come 'say' to you 'bye'." Wasn't he just being afraid that Momany could then hand the imaginary money to her? Most probably and there is much to pin the answer on. That was probably his fear and, being the perpetual intriguers that members of this family are, she too wouldn't divulge that fact to him. So, sending but the child is the best option that guarantees his knowing if that money had been handed over since 'he and his daughters don't have secrets' (Fossungu, 2013c: 152). Money-grabbing and thanklessness would seem to be such creeds in the Asahchop household that you can even discern them in Peter Ngunyi Asahchop's talk that is pretending to be thanking "for the *few* things you brought for the children" but 'my *lots* of CAD$1000.00 is still in your keeping,' could be what is actually meant? Does this man even remember why Momany was then in Cameroon in the first place? To bury his father! No! His Uncle, Asahchop's correction! And should he have brought all of Canada to them? I guess someone must have told him just how much 'Canada-USA' Momany had brought along to members of his own large family. Does all that not validate the thesis that it is the supposed CAD$1000.00 that he was not getting handed over and yet not asking outright for it, that was solely blinding the *moneyintriguist* to realities? And how is the theory you were developing doing?

You obviously got to the child-sending alternative, I remember. But even that option, plausible as it is, is still dangerous toward the money remaining a secret between him and the loyal secret-keeping daughter in Canada. Hence, since he cannot go himself because he is belind[?], the daughter (Belinda Chopazem Asahchop[54]) transmitting

---

[54] A family of "secret" dealers indeed! On June 6, 2000 Belinda Chopazem Asahchop wrote to "My dearest sister" (beginning with the second paragraph here) as follows:

> I wanted [you] to remind him [Momany] of the promise he made that he is going to send me to dormitory school because right now my

the parcel must not be able to meet Momany, being the last paragraph: "The bearer of this note, my child, has dropped the parcel inside the box and left it at Mr. Gabriel Anangfack at Three Corners Ndungateh (Foto) for you to collect tomorrow while on your journey back to Douala and departure to Canada. Since we were waiting for you and finally failed to see you, bearer, my child, will drop this letter and leave immediately because today is Sunday and tomorrow is Monday, a school day, and she cannot be absent from school." Conclusion of the money-game is that either he alone (not with wife[55]) has knowledge of the money or it returns "undelivered" for

---

performance in school is not very nice because of house work. You know that one cannot stay in the house without working. So, I was just trying to say that if he has the money he can do it but if he does not have he should not be worried and you should take everything normal. I can do [that] in a different class but if you have I can try.

But sister one thing that I will make [want?] you [to] help me [with] is that [you] don't tell this to papa and Mamie It is a "secret" between the three of us so keep it [in the] "dark". I am also trying to go for holiday in Foumbot in the house of Brother Bernard but Mamie is still saying she doesn't know whether I will go. My pen says stop and I have to stop and obey the lord. While waiting to hear from you, I will also say greet all your friends for me especially the baby. Pamela says I should greet and all [my] friends also said that. Thanks.

Your sister Belinda. Signed.

[55] See what Temenu Theodore Asahchop can help you with here. His undated letter to his sister (Scholastica) goes as follows:

Dearest sister, it is a great pleasure for me writing to you these few words of greetings. I hope you must have been very surprised to see that since you arrived [in] Canada and wrote to me I have never written to you. This is just because each time papa is writing to you he doesn't inform us.

The most important thing you will do is that you will look for me a pen friend there in North America, that is, either Canada or America (USA).

I suggested one thing to papa that I will like to write the O'Levels in form 4. I told him I will write only few papers that I will write only seven namely, English, French, Mathematics, Physics, Biology, Chemistry and either Economics or Geography, but he refused. If you support this idea write and tell me with a support. Even if you like it or not don't write to papa telling him anything. Just reply to me back what you think it can be.

What about Brother Peter, sister Quinta, Ado and Asaah? I hope everyone is fine. Tell Brother Peter that I will only write to him next time. Have this my cards and send to me yours, and also ask sister Queenta to send to me her card. Tell her that Joicy is in a certain non mission private

another more tactful and professional scheming money transmitter like "this other guy called Dr. Magnus Ajong who usually did most of the money transfers (Canada-Belgium) during his numerous trips to Canada and to our LaSalle residence. He still thinks to date that I was clearly unaware of the behind-my-back dealings. I used to just look at all of them and just laugh inside because, as I have theorized, the best way to understand just how far others would go on taking you for a fool is to assume the position of an idiot" (Fossungu, 2015d: 103).

To ally this theory (if Theodore Temenu Asahchop's letter is not enough), make a small trip back again to Mrs. Asahchop's letter to Scholastica (in chapter 1) complaining about the father not showing her the money "you sent to us". The sum in question itself is clearly money sent behind Momany's back. That is what they are even talking about, not the one they regularly sent together. If you are doubting (and at this point you will be crazy to doubt), why would the money to Momany's mother (in the same letter) be referred to as the money "*you people* sent to your mother-in-law" but the one in question being just "the money *you* sent"? Knowing who Scholastica has proven herself to be, could Momany ever be sending the first money with her to his mother without correspondingly sending money to her own parents? How does it all end up then? It simply validates the schemer versus schemer theory, of course. In other words, for those not familiar with the schemer theory, Peter Ngunyi Asahchop failed to openly ask for and obtain his supposedly sent CAD$1000.00, letting the non-existent thing to return to Canada because he was dealing with other schemers in the person of his wife and daughter (Scholastica). Did Scholastica really send the CAD$1000.00 (loaned to Momany) but to the father and yet took repayment of the CAD$1000.00 by Momany? But Scholastica has succeeded in all her schemes that you are well aware of (but this

---

boarding school in Bamenda. John Paul is there in school that is why he is unable to write to you. I hope you know he is in Seat of Wisdom College.

Signed. Temenu Theodore.

N.B: Please sister, take that problem of a pen friend very serious. When writing to me write through our school with the following address: ….[address omitted]. The letter will reach me under all consequences [circumstances?].

CAD$1000.00 palaver that gives the dog a bad name) solely because Momany is not also a schemer. And that explains why Momany's relationship with any non-scheming family is so almost perfect.

That apart, one can see how the entire family would present twisted facts and then give ultimatum to ignorant third-parties to fix 'their solution' for them. Peter Ngunyi Asahchop's talk of human rights being observed more in Canada (in same ultimatum letter) can already tell you where the 2005-2006 London court case originated, because even in Fontem in Cameroon they master very well how Canadian human rights institutions just don't care about the human rights of the millions of children that the scheming *moneyintriguist* women victimize and/or kill everyday (see Fossungu, 2015d: chapter 1). On his part, Momany did all what any reasonable person needed to do in order "to work together for the mental and emotional health of your children," as Nancy Whistance-Smith (Photo #44) has put it in her "Nice Talking to You" email.[56] But all the man got from Scholastica (and her parents and siblings), in addition to all the incidents mentioned above and particularly in the *Scholeugenizing Conspiracy Against Children*, would come live to you from Momany's handwritten letter of September 28, 2002 to 'Dear Andrew, Nancy *et al*' which went as follows:

Now I am stuck as to how to begin. Well, let me just put it this way simply. The above [4864 Boulevard Cavendish, Montreal,

---

[56] Written on August 17, 2004, Nancy titled it "Nice talking to you!" and stated to "Dear" Momany that:

> It was really nice talking to you tonight. I know things seem pretty grim right now, but the time you spend with your children is so important. In the larger scheme of things you still have years ahead to realize your dreams re: Cameroon. I just cannot imagine that God will allow the passion you have for healing your country to be wasted. I will continue to pray that He will give you glimpses of hope for the years ahead. I will also continue to pray for peace between you and Schola and that somehow in the months and years ahead you will be able to work together for the mental and emotional health of your children. You are a very strong man, and although you may choose not to engage in discussions with Schola, I trust that you will continue to treat her with respect if only as an example to your children.
>
> Please keep in touch - I miss hearing from you. Love, NancP.S. Thanks again for the clothing from Cameroon!\
> Nancy Whistance-Smith

Quebec H4V 2R3] is my new address. I'm out of 879 Blvd. Bishop Power #8. I left on Friday, 26 September 2002. Schola has gone too far for my calm disposition that it became a question of move out or you'll be moved out into a cell. She usually picks up the phone and says all kinds of trash to them about me while I am sitting there. I don't do anything, just sitting there as if I was not the one. But she has lately started to, in addition, physically attack me. At this point I can hardly continue to be calm and would have to defend my person against such unprovoked assaults. And this is where the risk of imprisonment comes in. She is currently three months pregnant (I don't want to go into the fact that this pregnancy only came as a means to stopping my travelling to the U.S.A. in search of greener pastures). I am a hundred percent for the baby that is yet to be born. That is why I have had to put everything off. But it now seems all this sacrifice only paves the way to my imprisonment. I would rather have things the way they are now than have Ngunyi (I am not sure of her follower) grow up while I'm behind bars.

Since last Sunday, September 22, 2002 – her [Schola's] birthday – I have not eaten a thing in the house. Schola prohibited me from touching food, drink, etc., since she was the one who bought these things that week. I don't want to start narrating all what led up to this interdiction. Problem is that I cannot be in a house where I principally, if not solely, feed Ngunyi with food that I myself cannot taste. By Friday I was running out of steam. You all know that a hungry man is an angry man. Coupled with the fact that she was surely to come in one day and accuse me of having touched her food and jump on me, I acted in a preventive manner by moving out before I am moved out to where I detest. That's what she's been looking for anyway.

In my new address there is nothing yet. I sleep on the floor for now but the pressure in my head is reducing gradually. It's only tomorrow that I'll call the phone company to have a line here. I'll keep you posted on developments here.

Extend my greetings. Love. Peter [this paragraph altered]

The thing that ought to be quickly noted is that Momany is talking of 'not being sure of the unborn baby' because of a possibility that it might likely be cavalierly aborted again and not that it is not his. With an incessantly provocative comportment like this, would anyone say that marriage was contracted for the sake of getting married or just for attaining some other ulterior agenda? Is home not where love is? What makes for an ideal marriage? The next chapter attempts some answers by further problematizing love, marriage and sex in order to exclude some practices from their definitions.

Chapter 5

Problematizing Love, Marriage and Sex and Expanding the Frontiers of Love: Is Home Where The Love Is?

Lovexpantierilization (or the expansion of the frontiers of love) seems to depend on the triplets of love, frankness and *lettigoolexism* (to be defined shortly). The trio appear to be the cranium for successful marital life as *Odilimanyism* (Odilia-Momany relationship) would want to point to. Permit my audacity again for theorizing that it doesn't seem to be for nothing that this inimitable woman called Odilia has been described as 'the perfect match and ideal replacement for Anna' because she is 'also very unpretentious, deeply unselfish and reverential,' making her coming around into Momany's life 'just like finding some very precious thing that you had lost before' (Fossungu, 2014: 54). Above all Odilia appears to be the female version of Momany when it also comes to *lettingooolexism*.

Lettigoolexism thus defines the uncommon art of learning to properly let go of *ex-lovers* or ex-spouses without letting them go. Oxymoronic, you are saying? Well, you are cautiously advised not to waste too much time worrying over this paradox since it will become clear as you read along. In the theories of this chapter (particularly), *Lettigoolexism* goes hand in hand with triplet and cranium and we need to explain these too right away. For those of us who never took human biology classes, we are made to know that *cranium* is the part of the skull that encloses the brain (Hawker & Waite, 2007: 205), which would become 'successful marital life' in our case at hand. *Triplet* refers to (1) 'each of three children born at the same birth' and (2) 'a group of three musical notes to be performed in the time of two or four' (Hawker & Waite, 2007: 978). So, do we venture to say that the triplets of love, frankness and knowing how to let-go of ex-loves would constitute the essential tripod on which a successful marriage stands? Or that it is the cranium behind which a successful marriage gets protection?

Odilia especially (and the others) could help us find out. You may already be aware that, until their respective marriages to third-parties, Odilia and Momany remained very close, notwithstanding being separated not only by *Janodilism* (or excessive fear of senior siblings) but also by being in the two continents of Africa (Nigeria) and North America (Canada). Unfortunately, though, posterity won't be hearing much from their very enlightening and endearing *letteristic* communications of this defining period in their life. This is because, after marrying Scholastica, Momany destroyed all these precious things, including photos, from all his long historical chain of lovers till then. Like Anna's few *firstolovist* letters (see Fossungu, 2014: 46-47), Odilia's letters of that epoch, too, were jammed with much that would have been seriously desired by wisdom-seeking students of love, family, and marriage. It is so unfortunate that these letters and other documentation were destroyed by Momany who then erroneously thought he had reached the pinnacle of the spouse-quest flight. Regretful as the destruction of the said Odilia-Momany letters, above all, may be, you just don't have to worry too much though, since letter communication (albeit the change in context and tone) has never ended between Momany and some of these lovers, notably the jolly JOE (Jane, Odilia & Elizabeth) Architects of *Janodilism* (which confounds fear for respect) and *Lovanglocardism* (dealing with Liza's conspicuous brandishing of the 'Anglophone Card' as what she sees as her advantage over the 'Francophones' of her college, to be Momany's wife). There is no better preface to all that ebullient and blossoming balancing of love, marriage/family and *lettingoolexism* than by the sampling of these love exchanges(*Odilimanyist* and *Momanyanist* communications) in marvellous *frantalkism* in the first part; exchanges that would exquisitely spice up the enlightening gold-digging (or expansion) enterprise. In the second part we problematize love, marriage, and sex with both the *Janeckinology* (Jane's love philosophy) and *Momalizalism* (from the Liza-Momany side).

Frantalkism Means Love, Love, Love and Nothing But Love?

From the *Scholamanyist* (or Scholastica-Momany) marriage just described in the previous chapters, I begin to see why some people would prefer remaining *celibataires* all their lives than get into such a dungeon. Thank God though that there are lots of good marriages like Chief Foletia's and Ngi-Nyam's out there that can last as long as fifty years plus. Momany's reply to Ngi-Nyam's letter tells us more on this. Written on May 7, 2006, the letter told "My dear Ngi-Nyam" in the first paragraph that:

How nice it is to read from you after all these years! You were never forgotten as you say because I have always kept up-to-date regarding the whereabouts and health situation of the *Lion of Judah*: thanks to your very able and deserving son-in-law and my bosom friend, Solomon. My hearty congratulations on your Marriage Golden Jubilee Celebration held in Baseng on the 3rd of January 2005. Solo mentioned it to me but, as you know, he is not good at praising himself and I am only now hearing of its pomp and pageantry, and other details from you. From the very first day I met Ngi-Nyam, I told myself that this was a very lucky man. Please, the word POVERTY has no place in your vocabulary because you have what no amount of money can fetch for a lot of others – responsible and well-behaved daughters, four in number, and deserving sons-in-law especially championed by no other than Solomon E. Tatah, the one man I have come to consider one of the luckiest guys on earth.

With Chief Forbehndia's case shouting it out the way it is, one could not go far to see just how accurate Momany's assessment of Ngi-Nyam's lot is. You have seen that the Bangwa chief had all the money, even on retirement, but could not have what Ngi-Nyam now has without retirement benefits. Hear *The Lion of Judah* saying it all by himself in paragraph 2 of his April 18, 2006 letter where he stated:

As you must have been already aware, I had since come to roost as all birds certainly do, but without any retiring benefit (Pension) but a lump sum compensation they call GRATUITY. I had not put in the 15-year service period to qualify for a Pension. Since I had been away from home for so many years and had not built a house, my first priority was to build one with the six and half million francs I got as Gratuity. I now have the satisfaction of having a nice house in which I sit to look through all my Albums while breathing God's refreshing air. With the periodic financial assistance from my sons-in-law (now four in number with Solomon being foremost) we, as a couple, continue to live well.

Nginyamanyism defines the philosophy that is captured in the Momany-Ngi-Nyam communications. They appear to have much education and problematizations for the marriage/family specialists and other experts to grapple with, as well as cautionary advice to both prospective couples and those living abroad like 'bush-fallers'/*mbenguists*. Indeed, we are blessed to have some of these exemplary marriages. Otherwise, I am certain that the *Kwankandas* would all have been validated, with the *Nkanés* of *Ashawonism* (see Fossungu, 2015a: 53; & 2014: 110) legitimately replacing the traditional institution of marriage: assuming, of course, that SSM (same-sex marriage) or 'Man on Man' has not already done so in another sense by stiffly questioning God's marriage intention. All what I am saying here is not just *tok-tok*. I am merely interpreting what I once heard Funnyman telling a group of *arguers*.

The story at the root of the argument was a so-called conspiracy against married men by the *Ashawos* who prefer that all men become *Kwankandas* (unmarried men, as men are wont to camouflage their own harlotry[57]). They want it that way because, as Nicole Mara sings in *njomba no bi married*, dating a married man is like dating problems. Some would instead prefer to say 'marrying a girl from a very poor family is like marrying poverty,' that is to say *moneyintriguism* and *dragdownism*. But are they not here forgetting the wonders of love? That is, what is involved in the 'For better and for worse' vow? Or, is it just a scheming cliché used by some as the corrupting power of roses below shows? Whatever it is, the *ashawos* don't mince their words and go straight to declare that married men are not *bons payeurs* like the *kwankadas*. In short, to spare you of the meandering trouble of a *kilometric* story (in the manner of my French-speaking countrymen), the *ashawos*' reasoning boils down to saying 'birds of the same feather flock better together'. But, again, are these *ashawos* not also forgetting the Schemer versus Schemer Theory here? What silly question! Have the *Homonistaians* (homosexuals) not even already

---

[57] Just as "Chiefs in Africa have frequently tried to safeguard male control over women's productive and reproductive labour in their local communities, arguing that it was an essential part of African 'traditions'. Women who succeeded in escaping from patriarchal controls and migrated to towns had to endure social ostracism as 'prostitutes' for the rest of their days" (Konings, 1996: 331). *Ashawo* is what Dr. Konings means by 'prostitutes'.

disproved Sir Isaac Newton and other 'stupid' theorists of the 'Like Poles Repelling' nonsense?

I am sure there would be theories 'out there' already instructing us that we will soon be falling from the ground to the tree-tops; not to forget intentionally that Africans are already *tree-top habitaters* (see Fossungu, 2015a: chapter 6). But Vakunta's (2015) *African-denigraters* won't tell us anyway then that Africans first discovered that theory. Just as *Momanyism*'s immense contribution to the understanding of love, marriage and family would be considered by some of them with a mere wave of the hand because it is African-based and different from their 'normal' *lielisticalism*, as it is often said. As earlier mentioned, what is very remarkable is that our two outstanding personalities (Momany and Odilia) also never ceased cordially staying in touch, even being someone else's spouses. Was/is the love binding these characters just so strong or what? Everlasting love, as some people are bound to question? Why and how could they manage to do that? Why are they not husband and wife, for real? And a lot of many other queries in your mind, I know very well. Not as many are already thinking though, I can assure you. It seems to be as if true love always has the *Ritaian Crisebacology* or/and eye-opening *Annastasian Bolargumentalism* as its defining handmaiden(s) – see Fossungu, 2014.

In other words, I am trying to say that it appears that, when people love themselves for themselves (and not with any ulterior motives or intrigues – which you can encapsulate into *Asahchopinationism*, if you like and must certainly do), they are capable of separating things and dealing with these things in a manner that would not cause any harm to the one they love. *Lettingoolexism*! You just do not deliberately hurt those you truly love. That is pure love, as some would be pushed to say. *Mulovundism*, it becomes when mutual. If you must be reminded, it stands for Mutual Love and Understanding. Without the mutual, it is *Onsilovundism* and lots of complications for the 'one-side' lover. That is precisely what *Scholamanyism* stands for or captures. Is there a difference between love and lust, or are they equivalents? What about the distinction (if any) between *Momanijanism* and *Odilimanyism*? Maybe the question should focus more on the comparison of these similar Anglophones with *Momalizalism*? More sense in these issues is further made as we proceed, with Odilia in the driver seat, to find out what happened that they are not wife and husband.

Love Silencing What Happened on Earth?

On February 2, 2005 at 9.35 AM Odilia wrote back to Momany: "Hello Dr, Happy New Year. Thank God for the New Year and happy to know you people are fine. We are also in good health. You have been silent for so long. Bye for now and be blessed." You can probably see how this woman meets all her description given above, even from her use here of Dr rather than the 'Pierrot' that is known to be her favourite name for Momany. A lot of women would not even use their boyfriends' or husbands' titles at all. Henriette Flavie Bayiha, do I hear you well? On Thursday, February 3, 2006 at 12: 58 PM, Momany wrote, in response to 'Hi Odilia,' that "Let us just say that the silence is over. It's talking time now. Glad to learn you're as fine as I thought. Just take good care of yourself and family and keep the line of communication open. I just want to refresh my memory (so correct me if I am wrong) concerning your anniversary which I believe is on the 13th of this month? Extend greetings around."

If you do think that Momany actually responded to Odilia's concerns about his long silence here, then you are greatly mistaken. But that is not to say at all that the man evaded the question, as the Quick-Jumpers have often accused him of doing. Momany had so superbly taken care of the long-silence worry long before. That concern comes from both sides and is not new. For instance, the woman had written to 'Dear' Momany on February 15, 1996, making it known that, "With much pleasure I put before you these words. I wrote to you last year but no reply. Is it that you are too busy or you just decided not to write?" On the other side of the fence, on Thursday, March 10, 2016 at 3.49 PM Momany too had sent this reminder to 'My dear Odilia' "Just to find out how you're doing. Also to let you know I am itching to hear from you." Thus, as indicated, it is not a new issue. But what was the reaction from the 'accused'? This response is what aids in our enhanced comprehension of love.

Momany did address the matter of silence from Odilia in a 'loving understanding' missive that tells us more than enough about his own matchless understanding and practice of this LOVE Business. Could

LOVE really be the shorthand for *Let Over-reaction Vanish Evapouratingly* or, better still, *Looking at Others Vying Endlessly*? No one seems to know. But *Frantalkism* (or the science of love frank talk) had come into existence on Sunday, October 2, 2005 at 1:50 PM with Momany's "What on Earth Happened?" email to 'Hello Odilia,' theorizing that:

I believe everything is fine with you and family.

I don't just know why, after all these years and with the change in our marital statuses, my feelings for you still remain unchanged. I am sure that, if you genuinely look back, you will realize that, from the day I first met you in Yaoundé, I always respected and treated you as my wife-to-be. That is why, first, I was never in any hurry to do this and that with you and, second, I didn't (at the time) see why your elder sister who was also my very good friend should have been kept in the dark about our relationship (as you had suggested).

If I don't communicate with you as often as I would have liked, it is, first, because my feelings for you have not altered and I cannot write or talk to you without pouring them out (which at this time seems inappropriate). The second reason is the fact that I can't as yet figure out what else (apart from my not heeding to your suggestion mentioned above) I did wrong that today I am not yours and you are not mine. It is not going to change anything now but Odilia, please, be frank with me and tell me what happened and why, especially in early 1993 when we had both just returned home: you from Calabar, Nigeria and I from Alberta, Canada. Where did I go wrong and what did I do to deserve the poor treatment I got from you on the several trips that I made to Buea at the time?

Have a very nice day, take care, and let me hear from you, my dear woman.

Yes, indeed! Yes indeed! Again, I would say. I am really wondering if anyone not quite feeling it directly from the deep sacredness of his/her heart can communicate his/her feelings in words in this rare fashion? But then, this thesis leads to the other question of how one has to also explain away the other genre of lovers like Queenta? I think Momany's secret to the exquisite *letteristical* communication of deeply felt love could just be that he seems to be the synonym of *frantalkism*, whether in love or out of it. This appears to validate the well-publicized *Fossungupalogistic* idea that we must stay bold and true to ourselves all the time, if we must succeed in our enterprises in life; or the saying that only the truth is constant (see Fossungu: 2013c; 2014). You get this picture also from one of Momany's communications to his friends in Edmonton, Nancy particularly. I am here talking about the email he wrote (in reply to Nancy's "Nice Talking to You" of Tuesday, August 17, 2004 that has been noted in chapter 4) on Wednesday, August 18, 2004, theorizing to 'Dear Nancy' that:

Thank you very much for your continued prayers and concern. As I said during our talk, I can only be delayed but not stopped. I think that I have been able to get to where I currently am largely because I am almost incapable of hating any human being. I believe that hatred often consumes the hater more than it does to the hated. Rest assured that I will do my utmost best for my children, irrespective of how well or badly their mother(s) and I are faring.

Extend my greetings to every member of your family.

Notwithstanding the compelling dictates of *Chrichantism* "that two persons with almost the same personality traits would hardly be good matches in some of these matters" (Fossungu, 2014: 120), I would venture to beg to distinguish *Odilimanyism*. I do so because in her "Re: What on Earth Happened?" of October 20, 2005 at 11:30 AM, Odilia was writing back to 'Dear Peter' (one of the very few times she does not call Momany 'Pierrot'), stating that:

I do not really know what to say. There are certain things about me you did not know and so could not really understand. For one thing I was really scared of men especially when it came to having affairs and having sex. When I was in Yaoundé I was just nineteen and you would be surprised that I was still a virgin till about twenty or twenty-one. You never really did anything wrong to me but I was just shy. I cannot remember treating you shabbily; it may be I did not really understand what was happening around me.

Even if one may not be married to the people we really intended to, we should just try to be happy with who we are with. Every human being has a good and a bad side. We will always find certain good qualities in the person we have as partners. We should try to get the best out of life. It is very short. Each time I think of my mum who was very active and hardworking, I really see life differently. Let's try to be happy.

Remember I came back to Cameroon in 1994[?] and you visited me once in my office. I cannot really remember the year and you told me you were married. To me it was normal because one's life had to move on. I could not put your life in a standstill because of my naivety.

Pierrot, we are still very good friends. My son may one day get married to your daughter. Bye for now

That was really the Gospel according to *St-Odilickinology*, and *St-Janeckinology* seems to be a real synonym. Because you have also heard (and would still be hearing) Jane saying what looks like the same, same, same, same truth. Once more, would ladies like these have even engaged in gold-digging à la *Flavischolastical*? That is, like Henriette Flavie Bayiha (Photo #2) and Scholastica Achankeng Asahchop (Photo #1) have done with child support to both imprison Momany in Canada and ostracize the children? Surely not; but let us now dig some gold. I mean the rare and venerated kind of gold that lodges only in that other *mine* of an extraordinary human being. I am talking about knowledge acquisition. I guess that there is no censorship to digging for knowledge in the knowledge *mine*? The more so when it is that distinctive kind associated with just the inimitable? That is indeed the narrative of the *Uniquer*, if you will permit my calling Odilia this way, because I have found no better terminology in existing dictionaries to capture this rare phenomenon of a woman or lover. I begin to visualize why she is so dear to this rarity called Momany. Is it thus a rarity plus rarity equal rarity-plus affair here? Could Odilia's sound understanding in the domain be influenced by the fact that she, unlike Momany, is in a loving relationship with her spouse? Would her stance, in other words, be different perhaps if she too is on the same marital *dragdownist* plane as Momany? Is it just a character question? That is, her upbringing regarding what a perfect wife should be in an African marital or family setting?

The Triplex of Good Marital Life

In regard of some of these soul-searching questions, we could perhaps glean something helpful from Odilia's recent emails to Momany. I am alluding to, for instance, the one that she wrote on Friday, March 11, 2016 at 2:34 AM, congratulating Momany for being "a real African man" in having up to five children. The essential portion of the email runs thus: "Concerning your kids, I think I know of the first one not the others. Why did she decide to come back home? Hmm, you are a real African man with a good number of kids. Congratulations!!"[58] It is certain that Odilia was here obviously confusing the child (in paragraph 2 of Momany's Letter of May 7, 2006 in reply to Ngi-Nyam's) who "is named after my late father-in-law, Peter Ngunyi Asahchop (he passed away in February 2004)" with the child in the same letter's paragraphs 3 *et seq*:

I also have a twelve-year old daughter, Kelly… in Douala. Kelly, who has a different mother from Ngunyi and Nguajong, was obviously conceived (although unknown to me at the time) before I got married in December 1993. In December 1998 when I was already here, I learnt of her being my child from the mother (a widow) with whom I had a one-year relationship from when I returned from Alberta in November 1992. At that point of acquiring this knowledge, I could have unilaterally called off the marriage with Scholastica, especially as there were three years of separation already between us. But being a firm believer in sticking to my pledge of "For better or for worse," I thought my partner's contribution to the decision as to whether or not to continue with the marriage was necessary. I still did everything that was required to have her over here, and by April 1999 she arrived in Montreal. A month or so after, I sat her down as any right-thinking person who is so committed to the union would do and told her about the child. You and I, I explained to her, could choose who is to be our partner, but a child cannot decide who the parents would be. As things now stand, I continued, I have responsibilities toward this child; concluding that should my spouse find that the marriage could not go on because of this child, I will perfectly understand.

She had opted then to continue with the marriage even when terminating it at that time would have been less complicated as no other child(ren) were to be involved. It was so self-centred of her

---

[58] Talking about congratulations, after Momany notified her of the release of his new book, Jane, in "Re: My Book," told him on March 21, 2013 at 9.52 AM that "Dear Peter, On the road as I got this mail. Bravo! So proud. See you've been quite busy too. I'll make an order quickly. It is a must read. Call you this weekend and update you on latest events. Hugs to your wonderful family. Take care. Jane."

because, as soon as she became a permanent resident, she started behaving very funny towards me. She has since been harping on the issue of the child in Cameroon: taking all care to present it (to most people who don't have the full facts) as if I had this child after and during our marriage. She easily succeeds in painting me the way she likes because, for one thing, I don't often feel comfortable talking about my personal life to complete strangers.

I am not saying that I am an angel though. But I am not the kind of person who would say "It's okay" when in fact he or she means "It's not okay". I have tirelessly tried everything during the last four years to have things fixed to no avail. I think marriages do last and work the way yours has only because there is a determined effort from both sides to make it last and work. Otherwise, forget about it. And that's precisely what I have recently learnt to do. All that I, therefore, want now as we speak is to be able to move on with my life (with or without marriage), trying as best as I can to cushion the hard reality my three children are being put through.

Stay blessed both of you and, once more, felicitations!

Sincerely yours, signed. P. Ateh-Afac Fossungu.

Odilia's felicitations and observation quickly bring to mind the popular 'African Monogamy Story.' This African concept of family and marriage is also enlightened upon later in this chapter by using the communications from Liza and the most popular of the Royal Death Theorists, Chief Foletia (Photo #23). The vain *talkers* of African tradition like those we met in chapter 4 had better been told that a worrisome situation like the one illustrated in previous chapters would, for sure, never have arisen with Momany's other-half being our African-sensitive and unpretentious Odilia and Jane. Momany's *frantalkist* response (on Friday, March 11, 2016 at 8:49) to Odilia's heart-felt felicitations would also seem to be suggesting her being a perfect wife for the African setting of the marital/family institution. We thus hear him saying this to 'Dear Odilia':

Thank you so much for the compliment on my authentic Africanness. You are right; and I truly think I would certainly have gone further than that with you as my other-half. You would perfectly comprehend what I mean if you realize that the five [children] we are talking about are from three mothers! You begin to see why/how I can never stop missing you? The first you're talking of knowing is actually the second because the first never "decided to come back home," as Cameroon (Douala) is the only home Kelie has so far known. Quite a fascinating family story I have! It's all in most of the books I've written.

My dear, I only continue to steadfastly go on largely because of your sane advice to me (remember it?) that we must try to be happy 'cause life's too short.

Take care my darling and know that you're forever dear to me.

Many critics may want to point to Momany's bad marital home as the reason for the steadfast pull towards Odilia – the woman whose place the *moneyintriguists* swiftly took. The man was in a very deep mess, no doubt about it; and this suggested theory could be forceful if the pull was *onsilovundistic*. One-sided, that is. But, as it is clearly otherwise, such a thesis would not only also be *unsubstantiateingly* implying that Odilia too is/was in a bad marital home. It also cannot be easily sustained in view of the pre-2000 *Odilimanyist* monologues – the period that even the *Peterasachopist* ultimatum (to the Royal Fools in chapter 4) theorizes as the heyday of peace in the union. The best of the epoch's example (not to duplicate those already seen above) is Odilia's handwritten letter of October 25, 1996 in which Odilia stated:

Dear Pierrot: With much pleasure I put before you these words. I am sure you are really surprised by the long time of silence. I didn't do it deliberately but it is due to problems which I thought I would have solved before contacting you. Thank you for all the university forms you sent but I have not been able to raise any good sum of money to enable me proceed with the applications. The problems at my job side are still persisting and we have gone for countless months now without our pay packets. I am still interested in Canada. It is just that the means are not there. I do not know whether it is possible to do something in nursing because I hear that is what really pays over there.

Pierrot, how is your life in general? I hope you have adjusted to the style over there. As you already know, it is only a chosen few who actually enjoy Cameroon. I do petty business around to enable life move on. I hear most Americans are against the Lottery Visa and they would soon stop it. I do not yet know whether it is true but I will still send my passport picture and any other information when next I write.

How is your wife? Is she there with you? Any child yet? It appears I am asking so many questions. I hope I am not being nosy. You know one has to have children while one is still young and strong to take care of them. We should not wait for retirement before we start thinking of children. How is your sister in New York? I hope she is doing fine. I see your brother once in a while; they attend a meeting in our house.

I'll end here so far. Extend my greetings to all well-wishers. Hope to read from you soonest. Bye.

Three things have to be noted here: (1) silence (2) the nosing concern and (3) the interest in family. As to the first, in his letter of March 12, 1999, Solomon Tatah (Photo #10) wrote in the 2nd paragraph that "Power, where do I start and how do I continue? You know my silence was not because I was not thinking of you but rather I was distracted by too many worldly concerns. First, the job satisfaction is not there, and secondly, the meagre salary which cannot keep up with monetary financial obligations always disturbs our peace." Silence is thus not something that can be completely avoided at all times, even for a parrot. The important thing is to be frank about it when it occurs. Even Momany gets caught up in that, as you hear him telling his friend. I am referring to his 'Talk to You this Weekend' email that Momany sent to his friend, Solomon Enoma Tatah of Yaoundé, on Tuesday, October 18, 2005 at 6:33 PM:

Thanks a lot. I plan to call you during the coming weekend, beginning Friday evening. That is the only time we can chat as much as the calling card being used can permit. Actually I am working more than "too much" these days. I want to be debt-free as soon as possible so that I can start taking really good care of my three children and my damn self. Just imagine that you and entire family are only a stone-throw now from me [that is, in Boston, USA] and I cannot afford to even drive down there to welcome you all to North America! And all this is happening (and/or not happening) when I have spent more than a decade in this part of the world. Anyway, you know better than most others what went wrong. At the same time you, more than most others, know that it is not the first time that adversity has visited and attempted to derail me; and that I have always had to beat it and move on straight. This time, I guarantee you, I am not about to just beat it but also to put a final full-stop to its existence. I honestly think my boy, two girls and I do deserve better than this mess.

Extend my affection to the household.

Love Is Knowing and Knowing Is Love

Is this talk of completely *fullstopping* obstacles not breaking grounds like the homosexuals have done to the institution of marriage? Why must frontiers-expansion be left to the 'wayward' only? Is love not knowing and knowing love? This question leads us to the second point. We have just seen Odilia here asking a few questions about Momany's family (wife and children) and wondering if she was being nosy. It is only normal for someone who is in love to do so; it only fails the Love Test when it becomes scheming and intrigues, like Scholastica's. Which is very different from what Liza (like Odilia) also does in her email following. In her "Should I continue to Expect You in January" email (on January 10, 2007 at 3.08 AM) Liza had asked to know if she should continue waiting for Momany's arrival as scheduled; wanting to know if he still lives with his wife and children in Montreal; and how she didn't see herself not spending the night with him at home (not hotel room) were she to be in Montreal; concluding that she was still awaiting her greeting cards from him.[59] As said already, jealousy is an important part of the definition of love, only becoming reprehensible when malicious. For instance, "dis moi tout" is the caption of Liza's email of November 22, 2005 at 10.54 AM in which she wants to know everything: when the man last made love; whether or not he enjoyed it as he did with her; and how jealous she was of the woman in Montreal who was having what is properly hers.[60] How very far from the point she was!

---

[59] *Original text*: *"Dis moi Peter, seras-tu ici au Cameroun d'ici la fin de ce mois comme prévu???? Tu vis dans la même maison avec ton épouse et tes enfants? Par ailleurs si un jour je viens à Montréal, je dormirai chez toi, sur ton lit et avec toi. es-tu d'accord??? Pour l'instant, j'attends toujours ma carte de voeux. Bisous et à plus tard. Liza."*

[60] *Original text*: *"Chéri, Dis moi quand est-ce que tu as fait l'amour pour la dernière fois! Comment ça s'est passé? tu as éprouvé un réel plaisir? je suis subitement très jalouse de la femme qui te touche là bas à Montréal. Your wife, Liza."*

That takes us to the third point that has already been largely exhausted in previous chapters but on which Jane also has to now throw some light. Jane is one of Momany's Endless Loves and her love philosophy (*Janeckinology*) would be scattered all over the book. But here is something more about her that would aid understanding of just how everlasting in love she could be. In his "Remember Your Promise?" of October 23, 2009 the *Love-Poet* wrote to Jane, stating that "It seems you have never really come to understand what you mean to me. Because if you did or do, you would not say you're going to call and never call, you would not say you're going to send something to me and never send it; and you would not have stayed away from my send-off in 1991! I do hope you're really happy where you are and with what you have. I am not, but would be happy just to know you are happy. If my re-establishing contact with you is a problem, then I would rather put an end to this problem, if that makes you happy. Sorry my phone went off today while we were talking, the battery was low in charge. Take care, Jane, and bye now."

As it may already be evident from the discussion so far, no one who is not truly in love would bother this much to *frantalkistically* avoid hurting the object of their love. And it appears as if *Odilimanyism* and *Momanijanism* are synonyms that are only different in the sense that Momany never took away from Odilia what he took away from Jane. Thus, responding on the same day at 6.17 AM (in "Re: Remember Your Promise?"), Jane told "Dear Peter" that, "Unlike you seem to imagine, you really mean a lot to me and will always. I am just dashing in and out at the moment but this is just to reassure you I care. The girls are on a short break as from today so I'm trying to round up my shopping list before this afternoon. Promise, I'll send you some photos today. I still love you even when I'm not available. Cheers, Jane." Whoever said you can only love when you are *available* must certainly have gotten it all wrong, Gospel according to St. *Janeckinology*. And the promised "photos of myself and my daughters, Helena -7 and Sarah -4" immediately got to "Dear Peter" the next day (October 24, at 4.27 AM) with a notification that she was "Waiting for yours. Still waiting to hear all about you, your career, love/family, etc..."

That 3-point elaboration brings us squarely back to Odilia. It simply appears to me that this Buea-based lady does *Christickinologize* just like respectfully-bold Christine to such an extent that *Odilickinology* ought to necessarily emerge as an appropriate synonym for *Christickinology*. If for nothing else, you get the gist of what I am getting at from the second paragraph of Odilia's "Re: What on Earth Happened?" above. From it, the following can be quickly gathered. When one door is closed, many more are still open; and, therefore, do not keep on crying over spilt milk but rather make the best of out of what is available to you. (Nollywood would love to put it this way: When the desirable is unavailable, the available becomes the desirable!) Does it sound like the 'Bird in Hand' advice too? Is this counselling not as valid as Christine's 'Don't start living as husband and wife until you're husband and wife'? I don't want to consider it to be overemphasizing to point out that the description of Lady Odilia as 'unique' and 'Very highly intelligent and always willing to learn' and a real 'great joy just being around Momany's being' (Fossungu, 2014: 55) was superbly apposite. I take this view because, in all my variegated experience, I would say few are the ladies (and men too, of course) that would still be as loving and nice to their lovers (let alone spouses-to-be) that have been the first to break the news of being married to a third party to them, as Momany did to Odilia.

Odilia obviously got mixed up though (by the shock?) in the year she indicated for her return to Cameroon. Early 1994 is actually the year Momany broke the marriage news to her in her office, having married Scholastica at the tail end of the year before. Other than that (which is even taken good care of by her 'I cannot really remember the year'), she was very candid in her response and, certainly, *Fossungupalogy*-loving Momany was/is so moved by that. Hence, in his "Thanks A Lot for Your Frankness" of Thursday, October 20, 2005 at 6:35 PM, Momany stated to 'My dear Odilia':

Thank you so much for your email of today. Thanks especially for being this frank with someone who loved you, still loves you, and will forever love you. What you say about yourself when you were in Yaoundé and up to the age of 21 does not at all surprise me. It is true and I knew it from the first day. But it is still good to hear it from you and to know that I was not wrong in my knowledge. Odilia, dear, it is precisely because I knew most of these things about you in Yaoundé that I took it very easy with you. I was not just after messing around with you and taking off. As you have put it (and I think correctly), it could simply be that at the time you did not really understand what was happening around you.

Thank you, Odilia, for your second paragraph that is packed with very sapient suggestions. Very mature indeed! I think I am going to learn a lot from both it and its author. We have to try to get the best out of life and be happy, as you advise. I will certainly be very happy if, henceforth, I hear from you as often as you can make it possible.

LOVE

Wow! That seems to be all that comes out of me! This Momany of a man! He appears to be the sole possessor of the *virginometer*. Otherwise, I just cannot get to comprehend what he means by saying he knew from day one that Odilia was a virgin. And being so sure (and now being ticked correct) before he has even gone to bed with the said virgin? Does the mere fact of being *virgiluckistic* (luck in having virgins fallen for you) and *virgibrookistic* (act of deflowering of virgins) give someone the *virginometer*? Like *Kontchoumeter* that is a scientific device for measuring lies (see Fossungu, 2013a: 71), *virginometer* is also a scientific apparatus for detecting virginity. If he, in effect, has it, could Momany's *virginometric* gift be tied somehow to the unusual ADVB or *Annastasian Double-Virgin Blessing* (Fossungu, 2014: 17)? And how could *Odilimanyism* generally be properly explained off?

The *Janeckinology* of Love and the Puzzles of Flowers

This part of the chapter problematizes this thing called love by attempting to answer the questions posed on the *virginometer* and the general explanation of *odilimanyism* with the Deflowering Theory. If Momany could so correctly foresee a lot of things plaguing Cameroon today long ago (see Fossungu, 2016b), would the surprise about his correctly detecting a virgin on first sight not itself be surprising: the more especially so for a famous *virgiluckist*? And could the use of the 'deflowerist' thesis to explain *Odilimanyism* also be *lielistical* in a way? For an appetizing start, I would want you to know, first, that, interestingly, *Odilimanyism* and *Momalizalism* have a curious connection. And this does not just relate to their apparent *scopical* differences but also touches on how Momany was able to be miraculously reconnected with Liza, the miracle link being the sister of Odilia, whose virginity was also miraculously detected by the Professor of Love. Let's tackle the general explanation of the *–isms* (*Odilimanyism, Momanijanism* & *Momalizalism*) to attempt a response to the worries.

In attempting responses to the hard *Odilimanyist* question, some critics would again postulate that deflowering a woman gives the man, or *deflowerer* (or, better still, *virgibrookist*), some long-lasting powers over said woman that endure even within her marital home. The theory would seem to gather a lot of force from *Momalizalism*. *Momalizalism* is especially useful to the theory under discussion, explaining in a way perhaps why Liza's husband "too would *moutonly* go straight on and heartlessly terminate his wife's four-to-five-month pregnancy (his very own child): just on hearing that Momany was briefly in Cameroon" (Fossungu, 2014: 87). It was clearly a callous act on the husband's part. But complete the exemplification of the *deflowerist* thesis to better judge the man, if you even want to assume God's role.

"Un Coucou" is the title of Liza's email of November 22, 2006 to Momany. It was written a day after the man who took her virginity had announced to her that he would be coming to Cameroon in early 2007 to assume duties at the University of Douala:

My First Love, I am really disturbed and have not stopped thinking about you since we talked yesterday. Promise me, please, that during your stay here in Cameroon we shall devote a whole weekend to ourselves in Kumba where we will relive our 20 years of love in two days. I am very much looking forward to this day and I am already longing to cuddle you even as I write this mail. I thought you were going to call again today so that I could listen to your sweet voice and familiar laughter that always enthral me. I just don't understand why after all these years the love I have for you has never died. Of course, you know that you are the one who deflowered me and I will never forget that day it happened and the question you posed to me. Do call me tomorrow please. Know that you have awakened the love-demon that has been asleep in me since 1983. I love you very much. Liza[61]

---

[61] Here is the original version:

The Virgin-Lock of Pandalogy

That so far could be what may be propping up the so-called *deflowerist* narrative, irrespective of whether or not the said *reliving* in Kumba took place. One of the staunchest advocates of this *deflowerist* theory is a Zairian that Momany knows in MYR Inc. Momany's friend, Jean-Pierre Panda, is about Momany's age but still single. We ought to be clear about the fact that it is not that Panda doesn't love women and marriage. Far from target indeed! Because he would easily be described by Cameroonians as a 'woman wrapper'; it is just that he has not yet accomplished the Herculean task he has set for himself. That of finding a virgin of his own to marry since, to him, marrying otherwise is a sure passport to heartbreak in marriage. Marrying a non-virgin (or someone else's virgin, as Panda loves to put it) is equal to giving the lady's *virgibrookist* a *carte-blanche* to your "food that is not to be shared" under any circumstances. It amazes me how most people often limit their concept of *hardliner* to other fields like political politics, and I justly begin tremendously wondering where they would place marital *Pandalogy*. Extremism! Some are already saying.

That is not the only awkward side of *Pandalogy* because its author is well known in the MYR camp not to breakfast or take along lunch to the terrain; eating just supper everyday! Don't venture to have Panda explain to you why and how he survives the tedious job with

---

My Love,

Depuis hier je pense sans cesse à toi. Tu m'as vraiment trop troublée. Please, promise to me that when you will arrive here in Cameroon, we will enjoy one weekend in kumba. Nous allons nous parler, nous toucher, se regarder dans les yeux, causer pendant des heures. Bref, nous allons revivre nos 20 ans d'amour en 2 jours. En ce moment précis que je t'écris, j'ai fortement envie de t'embrasser. Je croyais que tu allais m'appeler aujourd'hui, j'en ai besoin, je souhaite entendre ta belle voix qui me fait toujours frissoner, ton rire qui me fait palpiter.

Je ne comprends pas pourquoi après tant d'année je pense toujours à toi, à mon amour. Sais tu que tu étais mon 1er homme? Lorsque nous avons fais l'amour pour la première fois, ton drap était tâcheté de sang et tu m'as poser la question: "éhéééééééé tu étais vierge?....."

Stp appelle moi demain. Tu as reveillé le "démon" qui dort en moi depuis 1983.
Je t'aime bien
Je t'embrasse tendrement
Liza

such a meal plan; but do so, if you want to be baffled further with his brand of God-relations-wise philosophy. I am not venturing that far, limiting myself instead to the topic at hand. Momany actually drove with Panda from Dolbeau-Mistassini to Senneterre in August 2015. It is a journey of about five hours. During the entire trip, the virgin palaver was the topic of contention. Panda would just not want anything to do with marriage to a woman he is not the deflowerer of. Momany's suggestion was that it could one day lead to Panda's doom. Because, as he elucidated, a virgin of Panda's in his home would surely want to sexually adventure a bit and could then realize what she had been missing and then go permanently outside-sex-crazy. That is, by realizing the foolishness in 'eating only garri and *okro* soup' when more tasteful 'rice and beans' (which Sasse boys call 'Match'), etc., were also 'out there'! In a scenario like this, Momany concluded, "your virgin would become worse at prostituting than the non-virgin that might have entered your home, having already tasted all the food types 'out there'."

Panda now saw the dangers though but thought he had a checking device to it: the virgin must only be from 'within his family circles'. Momany then drew Panda's attention to his (Momany's) own rubbish marriage which is characteristically 'within the house' (as also seen in Violet being cousin to both of them). The Zairian was evidently thrown into confusion. To aid him out of the apparent irreversible move toward 'no marriage,' Momany dutifully explained to Panda how success in marriage is largely a question of being lucky to find someone who is just as dedicated to the union as you are. You don't have to ask for too much from the other's qualities because, like Odilia has said above, whoever you take as a partner must have both good and bad sides of them. That some people have actually married women that they first met as prostitutes but are having happier marital homes and lives than others who married their first loves that they *virgibrooked*. (Do the stupid Fossungus now see what they chased away from Nwangong?) I have not yet seen Panda (at moment of writing) to be able to know if his Special *Virgisearching* Mission to Zaire after 'Saison 2015' did accord him his virgin and wife-to-be that would dutifully remain his "unshared food". All that notwithstanding, perhaps (just perhaps, I say) Liza's case could support the *deflowerist* thesis, quite apart from the entire contents of what has already been set out above.

Rethinking the Marriage, Happiness and Sex Nexus

If the 'rice-and-beans discovery' logic above has not yet been sufficiently sucked in, then a bit of *Momalizalism* and *Janeckinology* could further help by answering the question: Is there a problem in not forgetting an *ex-love* while in marriage? Not any at all that Jane knows within her *Janeckinology*. In his "Happy Christmas & New Year 2010" email of December 21, 2009 Momany wrote to Jane, stating: "Jane, How are you and the girls doing? Just to wish you the best in the coming year. I just have the feeling that 2010 will be the magic year you've been dreaming of. I don't know why I feel so but that is how I feel. I LOVE YOU, JANE. I can't say why I still love you after all these years but I know that is how I feel for you, and just can't understand why you and I got to where we are today. PAF" The "problem" I could find with this Momany could be firmly linked to *dooractionism*. Or is it not? I am talking about one of the 'A's in the AAD Theory (see Fossungu, 2014: chapter 1 & 120-123). Whatever the good or bad with the troublesome 'A,' that may not be unique to just Momany because you could see that also in Jane's reply which came in on December 21, 2009 at 4.24 AM, stating with a lot of love wisdom and precision: "My Dear Peter, Merry Christmas and an excellent 2010 to you and your family! I just have the same feeling about you and I pray the feeling stays the same throughout. I have always loved you even so far away and it's so real and it feels so good. It took me a while to come to terms with this situation but I have come to realize that just loving you is what matters. I love you sincerely Peter and maybe it was meant to be so, even though we've married and had kids. Big Hugs. Yours Jane."

Whoever began condemning single-sex academic institutions for not being suitable for bringing up students who are savvy enough in 'The Business of the Two Sexes'? Oh the wonders of love! But *Momanijanization* is not yet done with the *faux-love* theorists. Jane's "HAPPY NEW YEAR 2016" email of January 1, 2016 at 3.12 PM did unmistakably tell Momany that "I will always love you Peter. So [I am] wishing lots of love and happiness as well as good health and prosperity for you and your family. Kisses and Hugs!!!" It is evident but it is good to still remind those carelessly talking adultery and the like that the duo talking here are people not married to each other. In "RE: HAPPY NEW YEAR 2016" on January 6, 2016 Momany answered back, indicating: "My Dear Jane: I don't know what to say now that you've already stolen the words (I will always love you) from my mouth. Thanks for everything, but most especially for thinking of me on that special day. I am currently in Cameroon and had even called Bathé to get your parents phone contact, to no avail. The [phone] number I am using here is XXXX-XXXXX. Jane, I will always love you. PAF." The *Janeckinology* of Love would fill volumes of its own but let's leave it at this point because someone else's hand is up.

Momany now comes in to prop up both Sakerites' *Janeckinology* and *Odilickinology* (remember them as being behind *Janodilism*?). They both seem to have matured up in the domain so much that Momany can't help trying to be able to become Hercules and, perhaps, turn back the heavy 'no-back-going' hands of the clock. But he is not regretting though, since he might not have learned as much as he has without the slumps. Learning from failure, the best learning, you do remember? In other words, who would have been *Momanynizing* to you here and now? By the way, as Momany poignantly questions the 'quick-jumping' 'adultery-thinkers,' does happiness in life even depend solely on being married? And does it also axle exclusively on sex? Don't forget that we are here dealing with a man to whom 'a woman is first and foremost a teacher' (Fossungu, 2014: 3). And don't some successful marriages actually derive their strength from extra-marital love (don't necessarily confuse it with love-making or sexual) relationships? This thesis may even seem repulsive until you peruse Panda's virginity demands closely again. In other words, one could be *Eboalontinly* looking at the issue. Cameroon's singer and poet, Eboa Lotin, theorizes in a song of his that, materialism has so spoiled the world that, all what the man or husband should be worrying *only* about these days is the issue of conveniently having the wife's *fecundity* period strictly reserved for him in order that he does not father children that are not his. Period! This artist, like many others including Jane and Odilia, perfectly grasp the 'Variety is the spice of Life' theory or maxim.

On their own part, what should the wives be wary of? Many of them know exactly what it is when they openly furnish their 'hussy' with condoms: because the 'Tromper, Tromper' song of another Cameroonian singer called Mathematik (de Petit-Pays) is no longer a secretive affair, Musicians Papillion and Prince Ndedy Eyango attesting strongly too. As one social critic has then put it, "All these instances cannot fail to create or invent puzzling puzzles for the traditional institutions of marriage and religion" thus cleanly turning the 'virginistic' *Pandalogists* into one of those groups that "want to eat their cake and have it at the same time; [such as] the feminists wanting to have their exclusive world that one may venture to call *Feminista* while still living in *Masculinista*; and the homosexuals theirs of *Homonista* while still inhabiting *Heteronista*" (Fossungu, 2015b: 123). Perhaps, it was in clear and genuine recognition of the (African) man's high (superior, as some would prefer) sexual drives that polygamy became the norm in our conception of marriage? Is polygamy even uniquely African? Was it not functioning perfectly (in societies practising it) without all the upheavals of today (that musician Prince Aimé sings about); with the women (wives) perfectly groomed in the lovable *Janeckinological-Odilickinological* instruction we just got a while ago? 'I love my husband very much, and if having many of us is what ensures his happiness, then so be it.'

That understanding is supported by *Momalizalism* when Liza happily calls herself "Mme FOSSUNGU 2" (second wife). You get this willingness to be happily married as a second wife in their frantic attempts "to just talk to each other". Jane and Odilia (the Sakerites and Anglophones) may look like Momany's endless loves but the *Momalizalist* (Liza-Momany) exchanges would appear to be where the talk of endless love could get its spring, and especially from *E-Carding Endless Love*. To make enough sense of the *Momalizalist* communications, it must be noted right away that I have actually been referring to only Liza's DIRECT emails since I just cannot be accurate in counting the numerous e-cards sent by 123Greetings.com on her request (which always bear a title). You get this sense of multitude from Momany's "Thanks for Your Endless Love" communication of Wednesday, October 5, 2005 at 5.21 PM, with him stating to Liza that:

Any other person would, by now, have completely given up on me. Not You. Not You at all. For that, I say thank you so much, my Endless Love.

I know that you last sent me two e-cards whose contents I have not been able to read: since I only got back to my emails when the one month period for keeping these e-cards had long elapsed. I just want to cut a very long story short here by telling you that I am now internet-ready to be communicating with you on a daily basis. I know we both need this for the love we share is simply endless.

Take care, my Love.

Yes, they are endless indeed. But a few examples from the 2005 year could be mentioned in passing, such as: Missing you from Liza of May 24, 2005 at 5.07 AM; Hello from Liza of June 10, 2005 at 6.43 AM; Liza sent you a Yahoo! Greeting of January 17, 2005 at 2.40 AM; Thinking of you from Liza of June 24, 2005 at 11.28 AM; A warm wish from Liza of October 20, 2005 at 5.48 AM; Liza sent you a Yahoo! Greeting of January 17, 2005 at 3.16 AM; and A Special Message from Liza of December 29, 2005 at 4.30 AM. As I have said, the list is inexhaustible; making sense perhaps why, in his "Re: A Warm Wish from Liza" Momany wrote this to Liza in October 2005: "My Everlasting Love, Thanks a million. You're a one-in-a-million kind of lover. I just love the way you love me with all my faults. LOVE" Lover-boy indeed! What would his Odilia be thinking right now? Momany may actually be in safe hands with Odilia here. She appears to comprehend the love dynamics better than the Rebellious Girl called Liza as we see in the rest of this book, and especially with Odilia's beautiful advice on happiness. That is, when she advises that we should try to be happy even if we weren't married to those we would really have loved having as spouses. Isn't that also in line with the 'many doors to happiness' thesis? So, if continued social contact with his *ex-lovers* for learning and growth purposes is what makes Momany happy, why must he be deprived of that simply because said persons are married? Thank you *Odilickinology*! That is what I can hear Momany saying. Is there a problem then? Jane's *Janeckinology* has also already said NO to that.

Coming squarely to the second-wife acceptance and communication questions, I am here specifically talking about the

November 22, 2006 email from Momany titled "I Actually Called You Today" which stated to "My Everlasting Love" that:

I actually called you today several times. At 9 o'clock Cameroon time, I called your cell phone and it rang for so long but no one answered. I suspected that maybe you were still at home and then waited until I got to work and called again at 2 pm Cameroon time. Again it rang for a while and no answer. I could not work today and returned home because all I wanted was to talk to you. At home, I have been trying to get you on the line to no avail. I don't know what is wrong with your phone because I have had to verify the numbers which I have in my head to be 237 XXX XXXX and it is the same as you indicated in your email. I will be home all day tomorrow, so that if you don't hear from me by 3 o'clock then call me at home so that we can sort out what the problem is.

I like the photo and I can't wait to be in Kumba with you as you suggest. I am really wondering if I would thereafter be able to return to Canada without you.[62]

Liza's response ("RE: I Actually Called You Today") was in next day (November 23, 2006 at 2.39 AM) and she explained that the number indicated as hers that was called was erroneous, pleading for him to call again using the corrected number as she will try to stay a little longer in the office just to receive the call since she too had unsuccessfully tried calling the day before. That she was itching to hear from him because she has truly been in love-making mood since reading his email, ending with hopes of hearing from him soonest;

---

[62] In "What's the Matter with your phone?" of Friday, September 30, 2005 at 11.54 Momany wrote to "My dear Queenta" that,

> It is rather unfortunate that we have not been able to get through to each other for so long. I have tried countless times to contact you by phone to no avail. On the other hand, you sent an email in July which I only saw a few days ago because I have had no access to the internet for quite some time now. When I finally repaired my computer, I read your email at home here but only to discover that my replies could not go through. The other day I typed just a line to you and was surprised that the email went through. I then tried several times to send a lengthy mail explaining the situation to you but the computer refused as usual. I am able to write this mail now simply because I have just acquired a new computer today.
>
> I am itching to hear from you soon.
> LOVE

and most significantly signing as Momany's second wife.⁶³ Momany speedily wrote to Liza, explaining that:

I made a mistake in typing 3XX instead of 7XX but it is 7XX that I have been calling. This is the complete number as I dial it from here: 011 (237) 7XX-XXXX. I have just called it again and again since I got your message and it rings as usual but no answer. Are you sure your phone is not turned onto "Silent"? Check to see if your ringer is turned OFF. I really want to talk to you now. I have almost called your friend Claudine at 011 (237) XXX-XXXX in order to get to you but changed my mind at the last minute. Check your phone well and call me so that I can call you back right away, please.

Liza must surely have been completely rendered "a craze woman" by now when she herself made that known. In her "Please" email of November 23, 2006 at 10.12 AM Liza told Momany to stop making her go crazy by not calling her as expected so that she can just hear his voice, a thing she so badly wanted that she had even called him only to be told that his cellular number was then not available;⁶⁴ and urgently requesting, six minutes later, for them to use Yahoo Messenger to talk since these uncooperative phones had already clearly driven 'Mme FOSSUNGU 2' nuts.⁶⁵ That is the power of LOVE! Do add PURE to it, please. That would be to distinguish it clearly from the pretentions of today passing for love. Don't confuse me for an advocate of polygamy. But if people do so to

---

⁶³ "Mon Cher, Je constate qu'il y a une erreur sur mon numéro de téléphone c'est le 237 7XX XXXX (not 3XX but 7XX)) so please try again today. J'attends impatiemment ton appel. J'ai aussi essayé de te joindre hier en vain. Je veux d'entendre rire dans mes oreilles. Sais tu que depuis Mardi que je lis tes mails j'ai envie que nous fassions l'amour???? Je t'embrasse fort et au plaisir de t'entendre. Mme FOSSUNGU 2."

⁶⁴ *Origanal text*: "Peter, Ne me rends pas folle s'il te plaît. Depuis ce matin je marche partout avec le téléphone dans l'attente de ton appel. Fais le 00 237 XXX XX XX (cell) ou mon bureau 00 237 XXX XX XX. Ton portable aussi me dit "you are unavailable," le téléphone de la maison sonne et tu ne prends pas. Je ne dors pas depuis mardi à cause de toi, tu me trouble le coeur."

⁶⁵ In "as-tu une adresse messenger?" of November 23, 2006 at 10.18 AM she wrote: *"Peter, As-tu une adresse "messenger"? Really, I don't know what is wrong. I think my phone wants me to be crazy. I will still be in the office in the next 30mn, waiting for your call. Please try my office number. Your crazy Eli."* Also, in "J'ai pas de micro" of November 29, 2006 at 9.34 AM Liza had written: *"Peter, s'il te plaît connecte toi sur yahoo messenger pour que nous dialoguons. Je vois que tu m'appelles à partir de ton ordinateur mais Je n'ai pas de casque et micro pour te parler. Liza."*

monogamy, what is even there to stop anyone from doing same to any other marriage genre? As noted above, a woman who truly loves a man (as our foremothers did before the commercialization of love invaded) would not care about being whatever number of the man's wives: so long as that makes for their happiness. Why do you think our *14-wiver* in 'The African Monogamy Story' did not have even one-thousandth of the issues 'in Uncle Richard's home, turning this fine gentleman into a heavy drinker and what have you' (Fosungu, 2013c: 157)? Simple enough, you already have been told. Synchronization; Non-Commercialization of Love; and 'No civilizing with *Uncivilization*'; that is it! If Liza's love stood/stands clear of these vices (pure), why is she not Momany's 'legal wife' today? Good question that will be addressed later (if space permits, elaborately too) and also as we examine the introduced monogamy.

Love, Love, Love or Just Thinking of Your Sex?

In order to attain the *lielistical* purposes found in 'The African Monogamy Story,' another non-synchronizing version of love and marriage was forced upon the solidly harmonious African structure. What else would anyone then expect other than the 'marriage-love-sex' confusion of nowadays? Very faulty and devilish propositions that so-called churches are utilized to embellish! Africans are straightforward people to call it in the open what it is, polygamy; while the hypocrites practice the same thing (or even something worse) but fool the women by giving them assorted names like 'mistress,' 'common-law,' 'legal'. And yet they jump to camouflage all that with this other untenable talk of 'fornication' and 'adultery'. Who is actually adulterating who or what?

Imagine what pure love can do! Lust and Love could never be synonyms except we are to consider just the 'L' as defining the concept. In that case then there will be no other concept with the L-beginning but Love. What a pleasant world it would then be! Why didn't God just think of that before getting tired on the seventh day? Could all the other 'L's have just slipped off while God was sleeping/resting (contrary to Africans' understanding[66])? That could not be the case, following the Gospel according to St-*Janeckinology*. In her "JUST THINKING OF YOU" email of March 12, 2015, Jane wrote to Momany that "Sitting here, and sending out a mail to a customer and just like a flash I saw your face on my screen! Warm thoughts filled my mind and I just want you to receive this mail with lots of love and good feelings. I hope you are doing fine today. Will always love you Peter. Take care and have a very, very nice day. Hugs and kisses. From your Jane." Now, come to imagine just how productive Jane must have been for the rest of the day with those warm thoughts lightening her whole being. Not only her company but also the entire French economy profited. That is the Power of Love. Hasn't it been said endless times that love can change anything, everything? Can we not also take that demonstration home? Can you imagine the HELL Liza's husband must have been subjected to at home during the evenings of those two days of the 'Phone-Talking-Problems' just talked about above?

Furthermore, even coming squarely to the sex that most of us like to think of when the word 'love' (whose definition itself does not leave out sex), how would Liza, for instance, have been able to sexually satisfy her husband (by not becoming that nameless Cameroonian lady artist singing "Il Faut Liberer") without her fantasizing with her first love, Momany? On March 9, 2004 at 12.04 PM, Liza sent this no-subject message to Momany: "I woke up this

---

[66] In the course of giving Chief Forbehndia's biography at his funeral on October 19, 2002, Chief Foletia highlighted the fact that God does not sleep, contrary to the flawed European notion that God got tired to have even rested on the seventh day. For his theory, Chief Foletia *expibasketized* it with the fact that "Bernard Mbancho came all the way from South Africa, sent by his employer for work purposes; but he got to Cameron and (without even beginning work) was the last one his father talked to; and, therefore, the one who put his father's corpse in the mortuary! *Ndem atelliy mbooh*!" The crowd agreed with him that God does not sleep. Or, does only the 'European' God sleep while they are committing all the atrocities around the world that Europe is known for? Also going on to talk about all the many things they had opened Chief Forbehndia's 'Book of Things to Do' and found, Chief Foletia rhetorically asked: "Is it still Chief Forbehndia who is going to do all those things?" It was then in answer to his own question that Chief Foletia brought forth his well-know *Uglah-Uglah-Uglah* (or Procrastination) Death Theory seen in chapter 2, in connection with 'the 2007 Cameroonian deaths' mentioned there.

morning of March 9th at 5.30 AM and you immediately filled my thoughts as I visualized you sitting before me in my office and gently fondling and practically undressing me. Being so charged up, you unzipped your trousers and brought out your penis and I turned and leaned on the table and.... (all this imaginary love-making with you did greatly put me in the right mood and at 6.00 AM I turned towards my husband who did not understand what was going on but we made love all the same). Now I doubt if I made love to you or to my husband? Even at this moment that I am writing to you I am still in the mood and ready to gleefully feel you making love to me."[67]

While I leave it up to you to best answer Liza's graphical question (with more light from her other no-subject email of January 24, 2005 at 6.03[68]), I cannot fail to see (1) the validity of the question in the title of this chapter and (2) the staggering analogy in its 'Momany and my husband' with 'the UNIYAO and UNIBU'. That UNIYAO-UNIBU mess having been examined elsewhere (see Fossungu, 2016a), let us get the other side of the *Momalizalist* coin that would appear to also greatly strengthen the *Pandalogist* marital extremism. In his "Re: Love, Love, Love" email of Monday, January 17, 2005 at 8.08 PM Momany wrote to Liza, stating that:

It is now exactly 2 AM (Cameroon time) and I know, although you're physically there with someone else, you're only with me. I just can't wait to also have you physically with me.

Thanks a lot for still finding the time to scribble the few words in spite of your busy day. I don't think a day can now go by without us communicating, even if it means just reminding ourselves of the

---

[67] *Original text*: *Je me suis reveillée ce matin du 03/09 à 5h30. Immédiatement mes pensées se sont tournées vers toi. Je t'ai revu dans mon bureau, assis face à moi. Tu as passé la main dans mes cuisses, puis à travers mon slip, tirant mes poils. Etant très excité, tu as sorti ta verge par la fermeture de ton pantalon. Je me suis retournée et …(toute cette imagination m'as alors excitée physiquement dans mon lit, je me suis retournée vers mon époux à 6h00, il ne comprenait rien du tout, mais nous avons fait l'amour). Je me demande avec qui j'ai fais l'amour finalement? Peter ou… [husband's surname]? En ce moment où je t'écris, je suis encore excite.*

[68] In which Liza also wrote:
> *Bonjour Chéri! J'ai rêvé de toi dans la nuit de samedi à dimanche. Tu m'as prise dans tes bras en disant "viens darling" et tu m'as serrée très fort contre toi. Tu étais très mignon!!!!!!!!!!!!! Bref comment vas-tu? et ton boulot? Bien de chose à toi*
> *Bisousssssssssssssssssssssssssssssssssssssssssssssssssss*
> *Love*

endless love that we have for each other. Whatever you do with yourself, don't you ever forget to preserve the best of yourself for just me. LOVE.

(Did you ever receive the photo I sent through the post office?)

The Corrupting Power of Roses: Rosy Love or All-Weather Love?

Asking for pardon is a natural thing to do when one has wronged another or made a mistake. This is more so when those we care for are concerned. Thus, we hear Solomon in the first two paragraphs of his letter of February 25, 1997 pleading: "Dear Peter: Please forgive me for the long silence. It is unlike me. In fact, I have been very busy in the past one month. I was trying to move to a cheaper accommodation that can enable me save more. This, I did two weeks ago and you can find my new details above [the address being in The Hague, Netherlands]. Power, the programme is very charged. Besides term papers, we have a small dissertation to submit in June. So I am really back to school and it is not easy for me to adapt. However, I'm doing my best. What about your own academic situation?"[69]

---

[69] On Wednesday, February 17, 2016 at 7:46 PM, Momany also wrote to "My Dear Patricia," indicating that,

> I am really sorry for notifying you this late of my safe return here. I am sure the family is doing well at this time, and that your doctoral programme is nearing its end. Let me also use this medium to thank you so much for the warm welcome Kelie and I had in Buea. She, in particular, just cannot stop talking about you; and that only goes to add to my regrets that I never acted as fast as I ought to have. I had been thinking of coming back to Buea so I could get to meet Randy and Wilma (not sure I got the spelling right). But on my return to Douala a lot of burdens unexpectedly leaped onto my plate. Even until the day of my return trip my sister in Ekona (who wasn't home when we arrived there) was hoping to see me, to no avail. Cameroon is such a tough place to visit for more than a month.
>
> Did your husband lay hands on any of my books he was keen on perusing? He is such an interesting personality to be around. I think I would like to *surprise* him with one or two copies of the books when I have recovered a bit from my current financial debacle. Just let me have his full contact info the next time you write.
>
> Take care. PAF.

Talking of rosy love and all-weather love, on October 21, 1998, for instance, Cameroon's Scholastica wrote this letter that shows how to ask for forgiveness when in error, totally different from Canada's Scholastica:

Hello Dear! How are you at the present moment? Hope things are a bit okay and there are hopes of fortune. Dear I keep imagining when we shall meet each other and when things will be fine.

Dear, I talked with you this morning and realized that you were not happy with me at all. Even to laugh was more than you. I didn't call you earlier because I wanted to have something serious to tell you. Please, I am sorry. I didn't mean to hurt you. Next time I shall call immediately and let you know what is happening.

I don't just know what to tell you since we talked this afternoon and discussed many things.

Have you got the letter I sent through Romanus? It was carrying a lot of information. The last letter which was sent back to me is there.

Power, accept greetings from Francis, Dominic, Bridget and my parents. Stephen is now in Yaounde, he was asking about your program and I told him that you have not yet finished. That is the question everybody keeps asking. I mean those who know you.

What of the Whistance-Smith family? Hope they are all fine

But why is it that no such apology would come forth while in Canada? Why the silence on this issue in Canada? On this issue of aching silence, both Odilia and Liza are also on the same plane. On Valentine Day 2007 Momany had written: "My dear Elizabeth, What on earth is going on with you? I do not understand the sudden silence. Whatever the case may be, this Valentine 2007 could not slip away without a word or two from me to you. I LOVE YOU." In 'Re: Happy Valentine' of February 15, 2007 at 4.10 AM Liza wrote back, stating: "My dear, Thanks for the kind words. Really I am not steady in my mind these days due to my late junior brother's memorial ceremonies in Kumba this week-end. Do excuse me for the silence. I am going to travel tomorrow (Friday) early morning. Have a nice time. LOVE" The constant keeping-in-touch issue got to a climax in the 2006-2007 periods as you have seen in the few exchanges above.

Liza will again help us to continue watering the rosy issue as we take Momany's roses-filled email of Tuesday, August 3, 2004 at 8:21 PM in which he wrote:

🌹Liza!🌹

Please, can you not excuse me? You may think I am a soul-less, heartless creature but that will be a big mistake. Otherwise, I will not be aching the way I have been doing for the past month or so. Believe me if you still have any feeling of love for me. If you do not, then you are entitled to treat me as a rascal. But I know deep down in me that I am not one.

Take care. Your crazy Fiancé 🌹

The Corrupting Power of Roses! I had never understood its significance; always believing in natural things. But artificiality seems to have taken over the world with commoditization of everything, not leaving out love. Who ever said (in the Garden of Eden) that you must appear on your first date (in particular) with beautiful flowers to win your date's love? In that case, are you winning over love of you or that of the flowers? Doesn't it tell you that as soon as the flower dies off it does so with what was anchored on it? Yes, North America! I now see why nothing real appears to exist here. And why flower-shops are a very lucrative business here. Don't think though that our dear Africa is still immune to these Westernized or *UDSized* things. The new term here is from the Upside-Down System whose principal purpose is to *infinitize* Longue Longue's *Ayo Africa*. Some of our people (the larger majority of the majority) have taken to these odd ways to such an extent that no amount of *Afrikentication* effort would seem to be enough to turn them around.

You obviously get the picture (from Momany's note in question) that he had been asking for pardon from Liza for quite a while, all in vain. See what the flowers did now. When Liza wrote back, she was asking when their marriage would be taking place, submitting that she had decided never to be thinking about Momany but that his email to her that was embroidered with beautiful roses immediately awakened the ever-present love demon in her: making her wonder what this thing called LOVE is all about.[70] Let's coat that up with Scholastica's January 7, 1997 letter (in chapter 4) whose first paragraph talks of 'the symbolic red roses' which 'are the things which occupy me here when I am feeling lonely' before continuing with the virgin girl. Quite aware of the fact that Momany is her deflowerer (as Liza herself has made known above), could Liza's situation thus validate the *deflowerist* thesis?

Whatever you give as response to *floweristic deflowererism*, the theory clearly does not even come near to explaining the case of Odilia. We have heard both Odilia and Momany making it clear that no sex took place between them which is even why we are wondering why the man knew she was a virgin. He is, consequently, not her deflowerer. Yet, it would be difficult, absent their honest communications exposed here, to believe that fact. Nothing else, one is inclined to think, would appear to best explicate *Odilimanyism* than pure love – call it *Ritannastasianism*, if you are a fire-brand lover of love-science terminologies. Anything else would make little or no sense; and, perhaps, only unnecessarily credit the loveless comportment of the woman who gratuitously presented herself to Odilia in the latter's office! You have already seen this loveless *moneyintriguist* pretending comportment of Scholastica as we were *Barthelizing* endless love and academics in chapter 2.

It is also important to see what differentiates Liza from Odilia. This query is important and requires the making of some sense of *Momalizalism (*or the Elizabeth-Momany relationship) which differs from *Odilimanyism* in some important respects. Making sense of range differences cannot be meaningful without first briefly making sense of the one in Momany's matrimonial home because it greatly impacted on the *Odilimanyist* and *Momalizalist* scope difference too. The matrimonial issue will, at this point, need no further extensive embellishment that would not be unnecessarily superfluous, except to simply stress that it shaped and restricted outside endless love. You get the picture of what I am saying from Momany's response to Liza's

---

[70] "*My crazy fiancé, A quand le mariage? J'étais décidée à ne plus te faire signe de vie mais lorsque j'ai lu cette lettre entourée de fleurs, le démon qui circule dans mes veines s'est une fois de plus reveillé, Ah ! c'est quoi l'amour? Tu peux être rassuré: I still have a bit of feeling of love for you OK? Je t'embrasse très fort et espère te lire le plus tôt possible. P/S: comment est-ce que tu as procédé pour mettre ces fleurs?*"

email of January 12, 2007 at 3.59.[71] Momany's reply advised simply that: "Thank you so much, dear. I am always thinking of you. It is just that I am now going through a very difficult moment, family-wise. Please, just keep on keeping in touch even if I am not regular with my mails to you. Do send me many more of your photos by post. I love looking at them especially when I cannot see you in person. Thank you enormously once more. LOVE." As you can see, the loveless situation inside was greatly disrupting the available endless love outside. Did I just hear someone questioning 'everlasting'?

Momalizalism would not seem to sound well unless properly defined. That circumscription necessitates understanding of what could be the invisible hand behind its apparent loveful-loveless endlessness. What has been said above about Momany's 'inside house' condition does not quite explain it because *Odilimanyism* contradicts it. He clearly was not out of that 'inside house' drag-down-plane to be able to be different with Odilia. And the issue cannot just be lodged in their *Francophoneness* and *Anglophoneness*, of

---

[71] In this email which she titled 'Hey,' Liza (don't forget she is Francophone) wrote:

> Darling, I think you don't really understand what I feel, I mean what love is. If I didn't ask you to confirm your coming here in Cameroun, I should have continued making my programme with you. For example, I have already arranged a lovers' week-end in Kumba with Peter on the 3rd of February, I was going to plait "rata" on, my hair tomorrow, I have started a sports schedule so that you will find me more sweet! You! Peter......
> Starting loving you again is a great trouble for me.
> I know you are a very bad buy (for everything that concerns me), you [have] always turned a deaf ear to my demands. But let me shout out that my mother and I have a memorial ceremony for my late junior brother in Kumba on the 18/02/2007. What I am asking from you is a symbolic and sympathetic gesture just as offering me some bottle of "TOP" if you like.
> My Darling, I will be very happy if I can hear from you today from 9 AM to 9 PM Camaroon time. Demain j'ai des courses à faire, je ne sais pas exactement à quelle heure je vais quitter la maison. Si tu veux, je te bipe demain afin que tu m'appelles.
> Je veux d'entendre rire dans mes oreilles. [I would be very busy tomorrow and don't know exactly when I will leave the house; but I will try to signal you when I am out for you to then call me because I really want to hear your laughter].
> Have a nice day. Eli

course. That both Liza and Odilia are Momany's endless loves, there is hardly any doubt. That Liza's love is so deep too, no doubt is cast there also. So, what the hell makes the difference? Why the questions, you are wondering? Liza's *restrainlessness* is awfully not lacking in *restrainlessness*; and I wonder if that does not exceed the borders of love to become something else: taking into consideration that you wouldn't do anything to detrimentally hurt those you love. In other words, is love so blind to realities? Since understanding the difference is enhanced by an understanding of the similarities, I have already highlighted some of the remarkable similar features. What then could be the *Momalizalism* Hercules – the student-teacher communication breakdown, *scholaparentism* (or parental callousness), or the virgin ground?

Explaining the 'Loveful-Loveless' Nature of Momalizalism's Questions and Desires

What could explain the vagaries of *Momalizalism*? Good Questions! It is such a long story (for another book) that has been aptly shortened by the frank talk between the two of them; also validating the love theories so far advanced. Their individual letters on the issue would surely educate a lot of people, especially parents and other educators and other researchers. That long story of understanding all started with Liza's popular No-Subject email of March 10, 2004 at 3.10 AM in which she talked of the reminiscences her trip to Manjo brought back to her: "Hi Darling! I was in Manjo last week-end and I saw the house [in which] we made love the first time (in Quartier 4). What a foolish lady! All the best!" Momany was not amused by her calling herself a foolish lady for having followed her heart and saw the need to Love-Lecture his lover who also frankly admitted that she had never gotten anything of the sort from anywhere or anyone. That is, that she could not afford to do anything at the moment, even including her most popular thing to do – calling to listen to his adorable voice – because "*Pour le moment, je digère d'abord ta si merveilleuse lettre. Cette fois-ci tu as vraiment écrit comme un grand-frère à sa petite soeur. Bisou!*"[72] Here then is what Momany who was at the apex of loveless marital woes brought forth (in March 2004) that has become a classic in the School of Love and Understanding or *Scholovundism*. Titled "You're Not Foolish in Hearing and Heeding to Your Heart's Message," it protractedly *Momanynized* as follows:

Hello Elizabeth, I have told you time and time again that one is not foolish simply because one listens to one's heart. Only those who don't do so are foolish. Know that you are not foolish simply because you love me so much. Perhaps I am the one that is foolish in not having realized long ago just how much I mean to you and to try to fearlessly reciprocate your love in equal measure. TODAY I DEEPLY REGRET THAT I DIDN'T GET TO THIS REALIZATION IN TIME ENOUGH. But that does not mean at all that I regret the good time we had (and may still have) together. If you want to spend the rest of your life regretting rather than try to catch up with what we should have had forever (if we both knew then what we know now), then go ahead and do so alone. As for me, I wouldn't let regrets take over my life. You could better understand me in this if you know what had happened to me, love-wise, just before my arrival in Manjo in September 1983.

In July 1983, I had forever lost a very special lady in my life – a wife-to-be. Not through the fault of either of us: the parents forcefully married her to another man. We were both helpless, I had left high school in 1981 and did not have a job and she had just been pulled out of school in form five! The devastation was too much. But I have learned at a very young age to be strong in the face of adversity. That is why nobody in Manjo, including you, could have realized that I was carrying a torn heart in me. I am sure that contributed a lot to blinding me in not seeing then just how much love you had on the table. And that you could be the perfect replacement sent from above. To the blind me at that time, the question of marriage was almost completely out of the equation. And, as you can see, it took

---

[72] On January 22, 2004 at 12.26 AM, Liza wrote in this No-subject email from which I am quoting: *"Chéri, Tu comprends pourquoi je ne cesse de poser des tas de questions sur ton attitude. Ce numéro de téléphone dont tu demandes, je te l'ai déjà communiqué dans l'un de mes e-mail. Tu sais, j'aimais bien t'entendre rire (et j'aurais souhaité l'entendre encore de temps en temps). Pour le moment je digère d'abord ta si merveilleuse lettre. Cette fois-ci tu as vraiment écrit comme un grand-frère à sa petite soeur. Bisou! Ta fiancée (rires) Liz."*

almost ten years for me to come around on this marriage issue, fatally though.

Today I can tell you this. True love knows no barriers. True lovers will continue to love each other irrespective of whether they are spouse to each other or spouses to third-parties. Otherwise, why have we been (and are still) having this discussion? And why has the "lost lady of 1983" never stopped attempting to stay in contact with me since then? I was kind of "lost" between Cameroon and Canada but you tracked me down through the Buea Lady. That is real love. Since then my timid love for you has just kept growing bolder and bolder until today I can't help regretting that it didn't do so even during your days at INTEG and mine at UNIYAO. I WAS REALLY DEVASTATED WHEN IN ONE OF YOUR MOST RECENT MAILS TO ME YOU STATED THAT I HAVE NEVER ACTUALLY LOVED YOU ANYWAY. I cannot blame you very much for holding that opinion now since you are unaware of the splendid heart transformation that has so far taken place. I will have to wait and only ask you to repeat yourself after I must have been with you in person.

I am so sorry regarding the recent death. I know the November ceremony in memory of your dad (biological) must have let you to the conclusion you reached in your mail that has just been discussed above. You told me a long time before and that you needed aid. I promised some. But from August last year to about January this year I have had to live in a kind of hell. Lots of deaths happened in my large family back there. And since my last visit there two years ago I am now a big 'notable' in the village. I am sure you must have had some of your emails returned within that period because I was no longer able to afford internet services and my email expired after a number of months of dormancy. I lost every mail and other materials that were in my mailbox. As soon as I reactivated my new Yahoo email address, and without having written to anyone at all, I got a mail (postcard) the next few hours. IT WAS FROM NO OTHER THAN YOU. Can you now see why I wrote the reply to that mail of yours the way it was written? I was still preparing to write to you and excuse myself and explaining what had actually happened and provoked the silence. But your card in response simply shut me out. I had decided (hard as that may be) that I will just do as you ordered and let you love me alone, if that is indeed your desire. But when I heard of the loss of your daddy in Manjo, I could not stay indifferent especially as I also lost my daddy-in-law last month. Only his daughter (my wife) could be there in Cameroon for the burial. She only came back two days ago. And my mother's health condition is said to be very critical now. That's how things have just kept getting harder and harder for me financially.

All the best to you, Elizabeth.

So Chief Foletia was right in his death theory? That is, that death could resolve existing love/marriage problems? Of course, that could happen only with the willingness on both sides to make it happen; which is characteristic of real love relationships. On March 29, 2004 at 4.13 AM Liza wrote in her "Re: You're Not Foolish in Hearing and Heeding to Your Heart's Message" and admitted that the lengthy and formidable School of Love and Understanding (*Scholovundism*) lecture had greatly helped her to actually know and understand a lot of things in regard of Momany and life generally.[73] But she later went on to pose questions of hers, regarding the timing of the revelation. I cannot here go into all those questions, essentially making it clear that, if Liza understood anything at all regarding the Manjo years until the moment of the letter above, she appears not to be able to ever understand a lot more. For instance, Liza cannot understand why Momany, who she so wonderfully helped, financially, in 2007 to reschedule his return to Canada (after the tragedy you have just read in chapter 2), could not on his part help her in partially sponsoring her 16-year son "*qui vient d'avoir son Bacalaureat D*" to study "*Gestion ou Banque finance ou Management ou télécommnication*" in Montreal, Canada (Liza's No-Subject email of June 9, 2007 at 4.36AM).

The loan of 200,000 FCFA she made to Momany then was repaid with a 10,000 FCFA on top of it as a 'Thank You' appreciation. Thus the Western Union MTCN #888-595-8664 of 210,000 FCFA was sent to her on March 22, 2007 (agency #0620, operator 301) being CAD $536.48. Liza openly confessed that she "was panic-stricken with joyful surprise" (to use some *Maylatelization* expressions here) because she wasn't actually expecting that Momany would even repay

---

[73] "*Hi, C'est lundi matin. je suis au bureau et je commence ma journée par relire ce mail. Sa teneur est formidable et elle me permet de comprendre beaucoup de choses sur toi et dans la vie en société. Je t'embrasse et espère de lire bientôt.*"

the money, let alone over pay it! But that would only go to add to the questioning relating to whether one can really love someone without actually understanding them exactly. If Momany can repay a loan to a wife who is so completely dependent on him while loaning him money to go for the burial of his dad (and her so-called father-in-law), without whom the wife would be nothing today, then it would simply be *wordless* (since no appropriate word exist to capture that) for him to do otherwise to a 'mere' lover who so kindly took him out of a very trying situation with a hefty loan. Paying off the loan does not mean that he had so much money to throw around as many would think. It is quite a lengthy affair that can just be shortened by saying that Liza (like Richard Fossungu and Chief Forbehndia, to name just these two) cannot see any other explanation other than that Momany is only being wicked in their own regards. In short, all these cases and more that cannot be sufficiently (and have not been) catalogued here, just keep increasing the number of the victims of *moneyintriguism* and *dragdownism*.

Conclusion

Ritannastasianism + Crisebacology = Mulovundism?

It appears so far that Odilia/Jane and Momany are still very much in love with each other. But it also seems that they are not letting their love get in the way of their marital life. Neither are they, it also seems, letting their marital life get in the way of their love. How they go about doing all of these things is rather hard to explain without 'the theory of love and understanding' as embedded in *Africa's Anthropological Dictionary on Love and Understanding*; namely, that you cannot truly love someone without understanding him/her, and that true love is not just about sexual intercourse. That is indeed what could be termed the sure result of combining *Crisebacology* and *Ritannastasianism*. You can then polish it up with the concept of *lettingoolexism*, which seems to be synonymous to *crisebacology* – the science of appropriately balancing matters of the heart with other issues, especially academics. You could divine all this in a most recent exchange between Momany and the two former Saker Baptist College ladies. But let's leave Jane aside here, for being *physically inaccessible*.

Momany went to Cameroon in mid-December 2015 and returned to Canada in late January 2016 without seeing Odilia with whom he actually talked once on the phone while in Douala. It was not (and could never have been[74]) a deliberate neglect but he felt so bad about it, as duly expressed in his email titled "What Is Wrong with Me?" Penned on Saturday, March 5, 2016 at 1.38 PM, it told 'My Dear Odilia' that:

---

[74] A thesis that could evidently be fortified by his earlier message of July 2014 that indicated to "My dear Odilia" that:

> I love you more than words alone can ever express. I just still cannot bring myself to believe that some other name, and not Fossungu, now appears after Odilia. The good Lord who knows everything is certainly going to guide and protect us in all our undertakings. Odilia, I am itching to set my eyes on you.
>
> Do take good care of yourself so that your family can be well cared for.

If I tell you that I am not doubly ashamed that I came over to Cameroon and left without seeing YOU, then know that I am no longer the authentic and straight-talking Pierrot that you know. Odilia, my feelings for you have never changed, and will never do so. I just hope that you will be able to understand that I had all the desire and plans to meet with YOU particularly, and that it was truly not intentional on my part that this did not happen. I cannot really begin to explain things here, reserving them for when we will meet, most probably before the end of this year. In the meantime, I am pleading for your comprehension. It takes only a man with a clean, open and loving heart to do what I am now doing. Frankly, I have been aching a lot in your regard since my unceremonious return here.

Take care, my dear.

Very unlike many others in her shoes that would have created more than the Pandemonium in John Milton's *Paradise Lost* (Milton; 1993),[75] Odilia remained true to herself and *crisebacologically* handled

---

[75] Just hear Liza's response to this email message to understand the point. Momany told her, "Elizabeth, I am back in Montreal. Unfortunately I left Cameroon without being able to communicate with you. Lots of things kept me down and the only time I could call you was when I am not supposed to call you (after 5 p.m.). Hope you are doing fine with health and work. I could not come here with my mother as I thought I would. Talk to you later, my dear. Peter." To this message, Liza then wrote in a "Re:" (no-title) email of July 5, 2004 at 4.04 AM that "So you are back to Montreal? Then OK!," following that up with her "quel mépris?" email of July 08, 2004 at 4.15 AM that is just kind of hard to translate as it is also hard to understand:

Peter FOSSUNGU!
qu'est-ce que tu veux que je te dise?
- que j'étais en train de chercher un endroit où nous mangerons du poisson?
- que nous avons parlé seulement du passé et que nous devrions parler de notre vie actuelle et future et aussi d'autres belles choses?
- que tu disais dans tes courriers "lorsque je serai à Douala ......" mais rien ne s'est passé lorsque tu as été à Douala
- que tu aurais pu venir à Douala un jour avant ton départ, ne serait-ce que pour me dire aurevoir!
- que tu aurais me laisser quelques billets de banque du Canada puisque ta maman est restée au Cameroun. Je me considère toujours comme ta fiancée (rires)
- que j'ai réalisé qu'après 18 ans et malgré tout mon coeur a battu lorsque tu étais dans mon bureau!
- que tu m'as fais honte et m'as obligé à mentir devant ma collègue qui ne cesse de me demander si je n'avais pas de tes nouvelles
- qu'enfin je suis fatiguée, vraiment fatiguée voire épuisée de courir après toi.

the situation with this email of March 5, 2016 at 1.14 PM that told the man this: "Doctor, nothing is wrong with you; maybe your instincts made you not to look for me. I was [also] unceremoniously called up in Nigeria for my defence. I read [for] a Master's in Library and Information Science in the University of Calabar and defended in January. So I am a full flesh [full-scale?] Librarian now. How is your daughter? I hope she is OK and forging ahead with her studies. I am OK with the kids also. Stay blessed." To this very exceptional understanding and precious news of hers, Momany told "Dear Odilia" the following on Saturday, March 5, 2016 at 3.10 PM:

My congratulations, first of all! Great news! Thanks also for the prompt response.

You are such an intelligent lady. I have always known this but you're now more than consolidating this knowledge and making me feel really privileged to have ever known and fallen so deeply for you. You also seem to be confirming this other side of me that a lot people have talked about - my instincts. But I frankly don't think my instincts actually had any DIRECT bearing on stopping my coming after you before my return here. As I said earlier, that will be talked about when we meet, during which time too we will also celebrate your most recent accomplishment. Once more, felicitations; and I am looking forward to more and more of such achievements. YOU can accomplish anything you want to do.

Odilia, I love everything about you but one thing that stands out very tall with you is your FRANKNESS. It just makes me feel so at home with you, no matter what temperature or adverse conditions. I hope it is not asking too much saying you should not go for more than two days without communicating with me?

My daughter in Douala must be the one you're referring to, I am sure. She's okay and academically forging ahead as you rightly suggest; her main problem being the unwarranted separation from her daddy. How many are your kids now?

Thanks a lot for understanding. Bye now.

Sans commentaire! No further comments, if you will. But if you think this measured or *crisebacological* comportment is a general rule with all of Momany's *(ex-)lovers*, then you would have grossly missed grasping the wisdom in Momany's grandfather's theory that "every individual must have something that sets them apart from the rest of us" (Fossungu, 2013c: 4); a thesis that is somewhat sustained or buttressed by not only *Momalizalism*. *Momanyism* itself props it and this relates to the wonders of love. For instance, many must be wondering why Momany should be having more than one lover, contrary to an earlier theorization on the AAD cutting off effect (see Fossungu, 2014: chapter 1)? To that, the response is that, it is good you brought up the AAD because it is precisely one of those 'A's that explains Momany's everlasting love with the 'excessively fearful of senior siblings/acquaintances' (the *Janodilists* and *Annaspectists*) and many others because *Dooractionism* has never taken place (see Fossungu, 2014: 120-123) to completely shut them out (like it did to Joan and Adela), notwithstanding their not being his spouse(s). The testimony of the non-operation of *dooractionism* could be found, for instance, in the fact that Jane was earnestly invited to the send-off party at which the Grand announcement and formal request for her hand in marriage was to be made *à la Benrad-Mbancho* (as seen at the beginning of chapter 4); and in the fact that Momany made the numerous trips from Douala to Buea in 1993 in regard of Odilia.

The Anna and Liza cases are a little bit complicated, being those of forced marriages that were carried out by parents and siblings who knew very well where the child/sibling's heart actually belonged; a comportment that pushed Liza to become an unthinking pregnancy user (like Bernard has just been telling you in chapter 4) in order to by-pass the parents' stance. That would inevitably call for the following general advice. To discipline a child is not synonymous to creating unnecessary fear in that child. At a certain age, a child becomes mature enough to know what he/she wants in life to be happy and successful. Most children know this but fail to stand up for the things that are required for attaining their goals, most probably because of the fear that is often wrongly equated with respect: *Janodilists* and *Annaspectists*. Respect goes both ways and encourages mutual and meaningful dialogue, the presence and availability of which would certainly have averted the calamities that befell the many children mentioned in this book, including Momany himself, of course.

As you have amply seen, a lot of non-family members have been very successful in attaining their goals through just having the little push that Momany has been able to provide them; whereas his own family members who have had even more than just a little push from him, have woefully failed to succeed. That has only made things very difficult for Momany, quite apart from the *dragdownist* household situation he finds himself in. This being because even those Nwangong Royal Family members with whom Momany could have worked to very easily achieve the uplifting objectives, have themselves heavily engaged in bizarrely sabotaging most of his farsighted and progressive agenda. Brief, it is not farfetched to just say that Momany has been waging a war on several fronts and, as anyone must know, victory in such circumstances is, to cite Solomon Enoma Tatah who wrote it in his letter of February 2, 1998 to Momany, is "more difficult than putting an elephant through the eye of a needle."

And talking of his calamity (quite apart from the analysis on the *Long-Distancing of the Wonders of the Scholastica Question* that should be read in here again) certainly leads to the questioning of whether love and four-eyesism are incompatible? That is, specifically, whether in going ahead to marry in the family of very clear *Moneyintriguing Dragdowners*, was Momany not properly making use of his celebrated science of Four-Eyesism? This query, too, like the other one above, is easy to answer and it is the same Four-Eyesism that provides the response. To begin with, a real lover is not a schemer for, as theorized elsewhere, reading too much into the actions and words of the other transforms you from a lover into a real schemer. "Does this quite look like the 'my way or no way' lady? Was I too blind not to read the writing on the wall? But would you really be in love if you read too much into every act or word of the other? Wouldn't that have transformed you into a real schemer rather than lover? A real lover, I think, would fight to keep his/her loved one, whether or not the need for competition is clear" (Fossungu, 2015b: 20).

Furthermore, Four-Eyesism is linked to Momany's objectives if you bear in mind that the amelioration of living conditions for the "greatest number of persons possible" net does not distinguish the people to be captured by it. *Moneyintriguists* or not, family members or not, his birth children or not, friends or foes, the important thing is that life is made more convenient for the greatest number of people possible. Those who are *dragdowning* Momany are NOT dragging MOMANY down because Momany can never be dragged down. It is rather the vast number of persons that could be augmenting the objectives-list that are being prevented from having the amelioration in their lives and situations that they so badly need. A very simple case (for those who are four-eyesismistic enough) is how what was involved in the Chief Forbehndia (Photo #19) case in 2001 could be directly traced back to the Bombshell in Yoke in 1981 against Chief Forbehndia's "able" son (see Fossungu, 2013c: chapter 3). Continue figuring that out the way you may with imagining what things would have been with Anna Ngomateka Bilong (Photo #34) being Momany's wife since the early 1980s but for that bombshell on Momany's academic progress (from Chief Forbehndia) which directly led to the flop with Anna, while I move on to tell you what Momany simply wants. What else other than the realization of those goals does Momany, *as a person on his own*, need to achieve (academically and socially, for instance) that is yet to be done? Again, let me end by emphasizing on the need to always look at the larger picture of things and echoing Cameroonian musician John Minang that you should always be kind to those you meet on your way up because you may likely meet them on your way down.

References

Ayah, Paul Abine (2013) "In Cameroun One Man is Worth 20 Million Persons" @ http://bamendaonline.net/blog/in-cameroun-one-man-is-worth-20-million-persons/ (June 17).

Boh, Herbert (2014) "A Tribute to Lapiro de Mbanga Cameroon's Best Political Activist – Ever" @ http://www.postnewsline.com/2014/03/a-tribute-to-lapiro-de-mbanga-cameroons-best-political-activist-ever.html

Fossungu, Peter Ateh-Afac (2016a) "Making Sense of Cameroon's Incomprehensible Certificates Story" @ http://bamendaonline.net/blog/making-sense-of-cameroons-incomprehensible-certificates-story/

_____ (2016b) "Afrikenticating and Revisiting the Anglophone Lawyers' Imbroglio in Cameroon" @ http://cameroonjournal.com/national-news/opinion-afrikenticating-and-revisiting-the-anglophone-lawyers-imbroglio-in-cameroon/; also @ http://worldnews.usa.extra.hu/latest/30249_opinion-afrikenticating-and-revisiting-the-anglophone-lawyers-imbroglio-in-cameroon

_____ (2016c) "Freedom is Free: Liberating Cameroonians (Africans) with the Trilogy of Good Governance – Multiculturalism, Federalism, and Fossungupalogy" available @ http://bamendaonline.net/blog/freedom-is-free-liberating-cameroonians-africans-with-the-trilogy-of-good-governance-multiculturalism-federalism-and-fossungupalogy/ (May 6)

_____ (2015a) *The HISOFE Dictionary of Midnight Politics: Expibasketical Theories on Afrikentication and African Unity* (Bamenda: Langaa RPCIG).

_____ (2015b) *Africans and Negative Competition in Canadian Factories: Revamping Canada's Immigration, Employment and Welfare Policies?* (Bamenda: Langaa RPCIG).

_____ (2015c) *Family Politics and Deception in Northern North America and West-Central Africa: Litigating God's Marriage Intention?* (Bamenda: Langaa RPCIG).

_____ (2015d) *Canadian Institutions and Children's Best Interests: Henriflavipeterism as the Quebec 'Money-Only' Sole Custody Case Meant for the Hall of Shame?* (Bamenda: Langaa RPCIG).

_____ (2015e) "African Democracy vis-à-vis Western Democracy: Afrikenticating, Follyfying, Expibasketizing, and Reversing the 'African Democracy' Debate," in Munyaradzi Mawere and Tendai Rinos Mwanaka (eds.) *Democracy, Good Governance and Development in Africa* (Bamenda: Langaa RPCIG), 71-124.

_____ (2014) *Africa's Anthropological Dictionary on Love and Understanding: Marriage and the Tensions of Belonging in Cameroon* (Bamenda: Langaa RPCIG).

_____ (2013a) *Understanding Confusion in Africa: The Politics of Multiculturalism and Nation-building in Cameroon* (Bamenda: Langaa RPCIG).

_____ (2013b) *Democracy and Human Rights in Africa: The Politics of Collective Participation and Governance in Cameroon* (Bamenda: Langaa RPCIG).

_____ (2013c) *Africans in Canada: Blending Canadian and African Lifestyles?* (Bamenda: Langaa RPCIG).

_____ (1998) "Intellectuals in Politics: Essential Education from the Villages?" *The Herald* N° 604 (6-7 May), 10.

Fozo, Abongwa (2015a) "Is Cameroon Ready for a Bicameral System?" @ http://bamendaonline.net/blog/is-cameroon-ready-for-a-bicameral-system/

_____ (2015b) "Biya's Fake Homage to Fallen Soldiers: The Embarrassment of a Nation" @ http://bamendaonline.net/blog/biyas-fake-homage-to-fallen-soldiers-the-embarrassment-of-a-nation/

Hawker, Sara and Maurice Waite (eds.), (2007) *Oxford Paperback Dictionary & Thesaurus* (Oxford: Oxford University Press).

Konings, Piet (1996) "Chieftaincy, Labour Control and Capitalist Development in Cameroon" *Journal of Legal Pluralism* 37-38: 329-346.

Milton, John (1993) *Paradise Lost* (New York: W.W. Norton & Company).

Nyamnjoh, Francis B., Walter Gram and Piet Konings (eds.) (2012) *University Crisis and Student Protest in Africa: The 2005-2006 University Students' Strike in Cameroon* (Bamenda: Langaa RPCIG).

Vakunta, Peter Wuteh (2015) "Aporia: The Manichaen Stigmatization of Africa" @ http://www.postnewsline.com/emmanuel-konde/

_____ (2014) *The Life and Times of a Cameroonian Icon: Tribute to Lapiro De Mbanga Ngata Man* (Bamenda: Langaa RPCIG).

Appendix of Photos

Photo #1: Momany & Scholastica Achankeng Asahchop (1994)

Photo #2: Momany & Henriette Flavie Bayiha (2009)

Photo #3: Ngunyi Ateh-Afac Fossungu, Momany and Nguajong Forbehndia Fossungu in Windsor in October 2013

Photo #4: Kelie Tsopzem Fossungu and Momany in Limbe in January 2016

Peter Ateh-Afac Fossungu, Jr., Momany, and Peter Peteraf Karlemon-Ethan Tale'eh Fossungu in May 2014

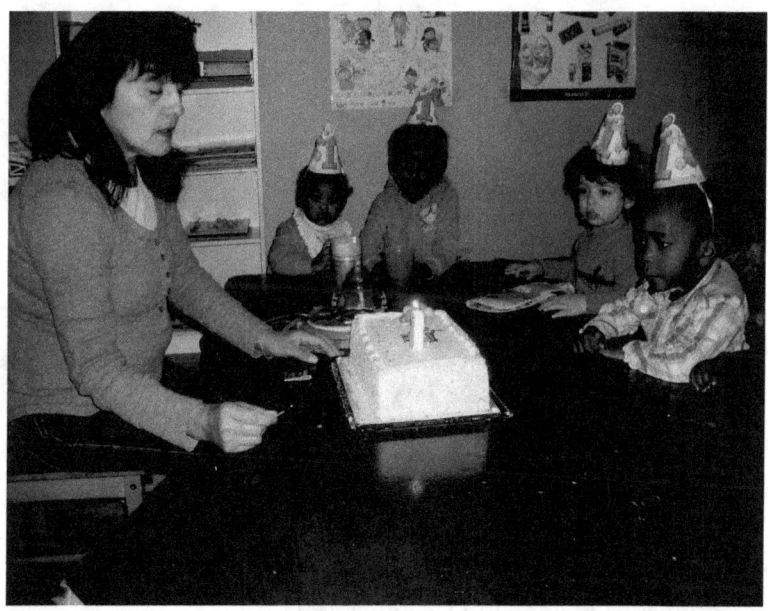

Photo #6: Filomena Pina Gonzales at Daycare with children (it's Peter's birthday)

Photo #7a: Peter & Elizabeth Asahchop drinking marriage ceremonial palm wine, as their daughter, Scholastica (left), joyfully looks on.

Photo #7b: Scholastica Achankeng Asahchop & Momany taking the marriage vow 'for better and for worse' as they drink the ceremonial palm wine in December 1993

Photo #8: Momany and Bernard Mbancho Fosungu in January 1993 in Yaounde

Photo #9: Stephen Z. Fomeche in 1998 (making a speech at Scholastica's UB graduation party)

Photo #10: Solomon Enoma Tatah

Photo #11: The two POWERs (Solo & Momany) at their initial meeting in October 1984 in Yaoundé

Photo #12 Momany & Paul Takha Ayah at Paul's residence in Montréal

Photo #13: Violet Maylatey Fonenge in Nwangong Fondom

Photo #14: Chief Fonenge (aka Vincent Temenu Fossungu) at his residence in Nwametaw

Julie Fonenge making speech during the Scholastica-Momany marriage in Nwangong

Photo #16: Elizabeth Asahchop & Momany in October 2002 in Fontem

Photo #17: Quinta Asaah in Montreal, Canada

Photo #18: Momany and Marie-Claire Efuelancha Fossungu in 1989 in Yaoundé

Photo #19: Chief Forbehndia, aka Emmanuel Nguajong Fosungu (1931-2002)

Photo #20: Momany and Edith-Rosa Khumbah in 1994 at the University of Buea

Photo #21: Eugene Lekeawung Asahchop and Scholastica during sister's graduation at University of Buea in 1998

Photo #22: Peter Ngunyi Asahchop & Momany in October 2002 in Fontem

Photo #23: Chief Foletia, aka Vincent Aghendia Sixtus Fossungu

Photo #24: Elias Akendung, Margaret Akendung (his wife) and Momany in 1990 in Douala

Photo #25: Mafor Odette Ateafac, Momany, and Kelie Tsopzem Fossungu in December 2015

Photo #26: Lucia Zinzi in December 2015

Photo #27: Regina Akiefac Fossungu (1931-2014)

Photo #28: Momany and Queenta Ngum Afanwi in Bafut in January 2007

Photo #29: Queenta Ngum Afanwi and Regina Akiefac Fossungu (Momany's Mum) in Nwangong in July 2004

Photo #30: Barthelemy Dongmo Jiomeneck

Photo #31: Dieudonné Asongu Fossungu and Momany

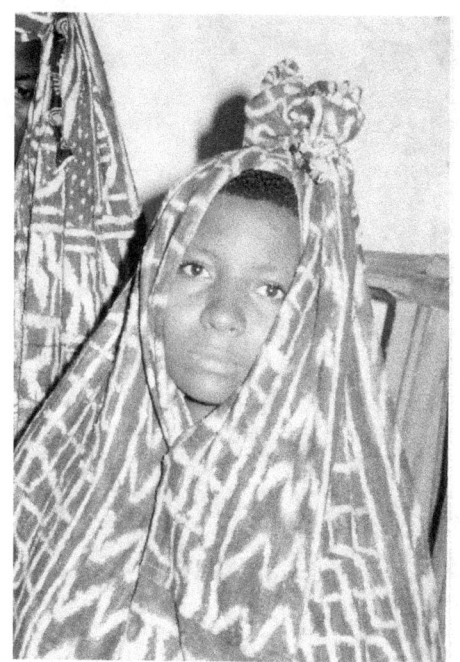

Photo #32: Justine Mamefat Fosungu on day of her coronation as Mafor Forbehndia - October 19, 2002

Photo #33: The Whistance-Smiths (L-R): Greg, Tim, Andrew, Emily, and Nancy.

Photo #34: Anna Ngomateka Bilong

Photo #35: Anthony Mbabe Bilong

Photo #36: Richard Ngufor Fossungu in June 2004

Photo #37: Ngi-Nyam and Wife at their Marriage Golden Jubilee event

Photo #38: "Tossing" at Momany's 1st Oversea-Going Send-Off Party in Yaoundé in 1991

Photo #38a: Africans just enjoying their thing: Dancing

Photo #38b: Africans just enjoying their thing: Dancing

Photo #38c: Africans just doing their thing: Dancing

Photo #39a: Kinsmen & acquaintances at Scholastica's graduation

Photo #39b: Kinsmen & acquaintances at Scholastica's graduation

Photo #39c: Kinsmen & acquaintances at Scholastica's graduation

Photo #39d: Kinsmen & acquaintances at Scholastica's graduation

Photo #40: Georges and Christine Neba, and the Best-Man, Momany, at their Wedding in Montreal in 2007

Photo #41: HRM Fon David Foncha Fossungu of Nwangong and Momany in November 2002

Photo #42: Patricia Temeching-Etukeni and Momany at her Buea residence in January 2016

Photo #43: Nkemanang Calestus Fossungu, Bridget Manifuet Fossungu (his wife), & Momany in January 2016

Photo #44: Nancy Whistance-Smith (carrying Tim) & Momany at his LL.M. graduation ceremony in November 1992 in Alberta

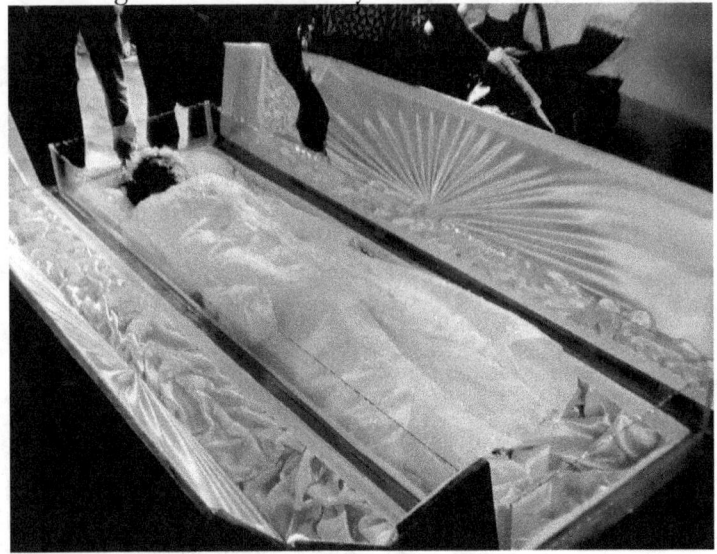

Photo #45a: Sample of Regina Akiefac Fossungu's corpse removal from mortuary on July 17, 2014

Photo #45b: Sample of Regina Akiefac Fossungu's corpse removal from mortuary on July 17, 2014

Photo #45c: Sample of Regina Akiefac Fossungu's corpse removal from mortuary on July 17, 2014

Photo #46a: Maurine Nkengafac Fossungu and Annastasia Chamo Fosungu in October 2002

Phtoto 46b: Kelie, Momany, and Quinta Lonche Fossungu in Limbe in January 2016

Photo #46c: Scholastica Nkengafac Fossungu

Photo46d: Beatrice Nguika Fossungu (carrying her daughter, Minette) in the 80s

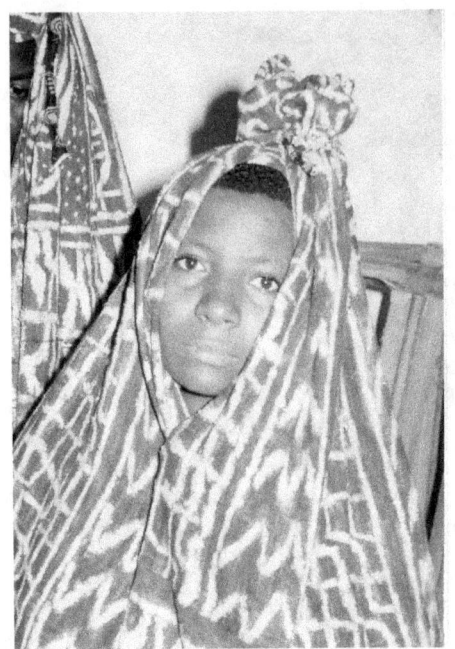

Photo 46e: Justine Mamefat Fosungu on day of being crowned as Mafor Forbehndia

Photo #47: Commandant Michel Njumo (with microphone) and wife, Marie Njumo (on his left)

Photo #48: Therese Nkengafac Fosungu and Momany in the 80s

Photo #49: Momany and Tangwa Solomon during the burial and funeral of Chief Forbehndia in October 2002

Photo #50: Scholastica (standing) and Madam Catherine Fossungu in 1995 in Yoke, Muyuka

Photo #51: Josephine Forzi Fossungu and her grandchildren in Yoke in 2002

Photo #52: Momany and Nkwetta Nkemtale'eh Vincent in May 2014 in Nwangong

Photo #53: Mafor Nkemtale'eh Esther and Momany in May 2014 in Ekona

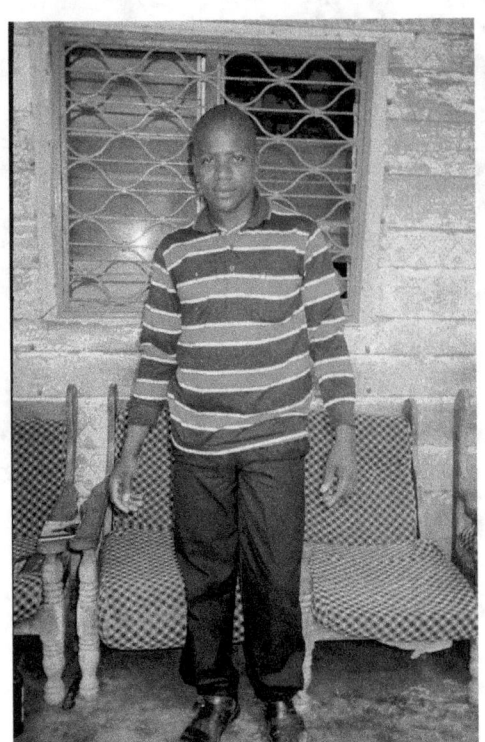

Photo #54: Mitterand Tale'eh Fossungu in July 2014 in Douala

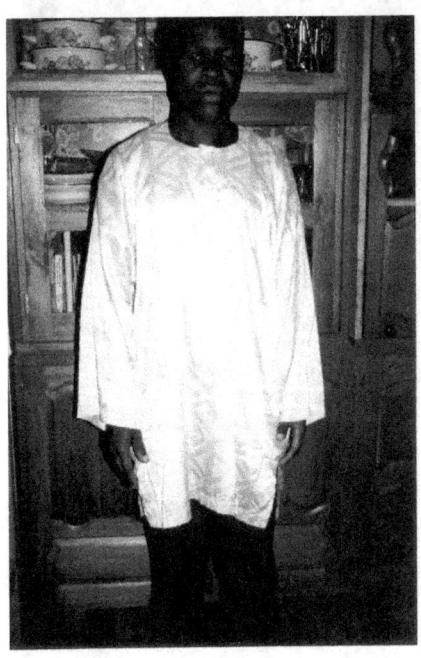

Photo #55: Chief Fonjenachop (aka Paul Njukang Morfaw)

Photo #56: Scholastica Achankeng Asahchop & Regina Akiefac Fossungu (Momany's mother) in December 1995 in Fontem

Photo #57: HRM Fon Nicasius Nguazong Fossungu of Nwangong

Photo #58: Momany & Asah William Ndem in May 2014 in Ekona

Photo #59: Momany, Lysly Ako Ayah, and Donatus Ayuk Ako-Arrey in Montreal